STAND FAST.

THE HISTORY OF CLAN GRA

Copyright: Celtus.

Special thanks to Rod Grant, Headmaster of Clifton Hall School, near Edinburgh. Without his help and direction I would never have produced this and other Histories of the Scottish Clans.

THE TRUE BLOOD PRINCE OF THE CELTIC NATION.

CONTENTS PAGE

MAPS AND DIAGRAMS

INTRODUCTION

In ancient Scotland the word 'Clan' or 'Clana' simply means children. These children are the descendants of the actual or mythical ancestor from whom the community claim descent. The Chief of the Clan formed the centre and sacred embellishment of the race. He was the supreme individual who gave the Clan its identity and coherence and it was through his actions that the destiny of the clan was decided.

The essence of Clanship is 'belonging' and the history of the Clan gives the individual a sense of where he comes from and how his ancestors helped to shape Scotland and Scottish Society. Some modern-day critics claim that the Clan is a meaningless institution today as each individual, tracing back all their ancestors, must have hundreds of surnames and belong to many clans. In part this is true, hardly is there a Scot today (and a lot of Australians, New Zealanders, Canadians and Americans) who cannot, in some line of ancestry, connect themselves with the ancient line royal line of Fergus Mor McEarc, the first King of Scots, or Robert the Bruce, the most famous King. In addition, sceptics say that the Clan, and more particularly the Clan Chief, is today a meaningless term with no real relevance in modern society. Again, this is also partly true, the majority of Chiefs gave away any right to Clan leadership after the 1745 Jacobite rebellion, when they sold their Clan lands and promoted the Clearances which had such a devastating effect on their people.

Notwithstanding this, however, everyone has a surname which is so much a part of them. They carry it about with them and use it on a daily basis all their lives, and usually with quite a bit of attachment. It is part of their character and personality in the eyes of others and is therefore very important. The history of the name links each individual with the past. Unfortunately, for the most part, history only identifies the Chiefs and their immediate family members. But then again the Chief's story is important to each individual as their own ancestors, however lowly, would have been affected by his actions.

This is the history of one of Scotland's oldest and most successful clans: Clan Grant. And What a Clan!. Undoubtedly Clan Grant became one of the most successful and resilient Scottish Clans. From humble beginnings they became, arguably, the predominant clan in the eastern central highlands. This was due to a combination of both the sword and the pen, something very few other clans achieved. They also attached themselves early on to the Scottish Monarchy, particularly the Stuart dynasty. This was in direct contrast to other great clans, such as the Camerons and the MacDonalds, who spent much of their time and energy fighting against domination from Edinburgh.

The heartland of the clan originated in the lands around Inverness. They were early on given the lands of Stratherrick on the southern shore of Loch Ness. Eventually, however, they took over almost the whole of Strathspey to the south of this area and gave up their interests in Stratherrick. This part of Scotland is now the most important area for whisky distilling. Later on they acquired the lands of Urquhart and Glenmoriston on the north side of Loch Ness. As a very successful clan they continued to expand their territory around the towns of Elgin and Forres along the southern shore of the Moray Firth.

Map 1. MAIN LANDS OF CLAN GRANT.

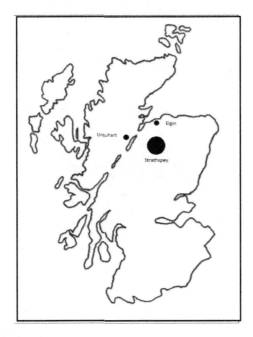

The success of Clan Grant was also in its ability to fuse the best and most important elements of Gaelic culture with the legal system of Lowland Scotland. Unlike many of their rival clans they came to the easy realisation that to be influential in the affairs of the nation they had to look beyond their own glens and hills with a broad view which reflected the political position within the wider Highlands and the Central Government of Scotland.

The Clan Crest Badge "is the Chief's crest of a burning mountain….- This signifies the bonfire lit on Craiglelachie at Aviemore, and another some miles east of the former. This crest is surrounded by a buckled belt carrying the motto and war cry 'Stand Fast Craigelachie'."(1) By tradition Craigellachie was an important place for Clan Grant, being used as a vantage point and as the site for signal fires to gather the clan. It lies to the west of the village of Aviemore in Strathspey. It was designated a National Nature in 1961. The clan badge in ancient times was a sprig of Scots Pine, normally worn in the Balmoral or Glengarry headgear.

The Badge of Clan Grant.

The following History of Clan Grant is far from being comprehensive. Hopefully this work will at least give the reader an insight into Clan Grant and those that want to may undertake further research into what is one of Scotland's most formidable Clans.

CHAPTER 1. LEGENDARY BEGININGS.

The true origins of Clan Grant are lost in the mists of time and in the Legends of Scotland and those of the Celtic and Norse worlds.

There are three possible options for the origin of the clan:

1). **Norman**, largely on account of there being Grants, Le Graunts and Le Grande's in England and Scotland after the Norman Conquest of England. There are a number of Le Grants or Le Graunts named in documents in England immediately after the 1066 Norman Conquest.

However, William F. Skene (2) supports the tradition of the Gaelic origins. "For their Norman origin, I have in examination entirely failed in discovery any further reason than that their name may be derived from the French, grand, or great, and that they occasionally use the Norman form of de Grant."(3)

The Norman descent story goes as follows. In 1174 Richard 'the Lion Heart' future King of England visited Scotland to seek the support of the King William I of Scots, in a rebellion against his father. On this visit he was accompanied by members of the Bisset family, a powerful English/ Norman family at this time. William Le Grant had married the daughter of Lord Bisset and William Le Grant was in the accompany of his father-in-law. On this visit the Bissets were granted land by the Scottish King in Stratherrick and Beauly. It is possibly that after this that Laurence and Robert Le Grant, sons of Gregory Le Grant went to Scotland to seek their fortune administering the lands which had been given to the Bissets.

Another legend is that in 1261, King Henry III at the King of Scotland's suggestion, pardoned an offence against the forest laws committed by one of his subjects, William Le Graunt. Apparently he was caught shooting venison in the Royal Forest of Sherwood; a hanging offence. After being pardoned he left to return north with King Alexander of Scotland and was gifted lands in the north of Scotland.

2). **Norse**. This tradition on the origins of the Scottish Clan Grant is outlined in the Monymusk Text printed in 1876 but most of the documentation was compiled between 1705 and 1713. This claims that the Grants are descended from Wodine (Odin), a prince and god of the Norse and Germanic tribes of Northern Europe. Wodine was married to Freia, from whom Friday is named. She was another god. The couple had seven sons and because of their strength and courage in battle these sons were called 'Gyant' or Great.

The Grants are descended from Hacken Gyant, 3rd of that name, who was born in the 9th century AD and was the Earl of Trondelagen in Norway. He was the most renowned warrior in the Kingdom of Norway and, undefeated in battle. It is claimed that the Grant Clan motto, **'Stand Fast'**, comes from him. Because of his prowess and honesty he was appointed Protector of Norway during the minority of the young King Haakon I Haraldsson. He was also a strong supporter of the 'old gods', including his ancestor Wodine. He built a temple to Wodine and even sacrificed his eldest son, Erling, as part of the dedication ceremony. Eventually Hacken was murdered by one of his own servants, a man called Formod Carcart, around the year 960 AD.

The Norway Chronology has two lines which clarify that Hacken the Great was the progenitor of the Grants and other Scottish Clans:

"Hacken the Great Protector of the Dames,

Begat Grant, Kinnon, Rowin, Gregor, Thanes."(4)

Hemming Grant was the second son of Hacken the Protector. He married Tora, the natural daughter of Hathen Adelstein, the 1st Christian King of Denmark. His daughter Tora was also converted to Christianity and she convinced Hemming to ditch the old religion and become Christian. This enraged his father and he ordered his son to renounce Christianity for face exile. Hemming refused and his father banished him, his wife and children. They went to the Earldom of Orkney which was then part of the Kingdom of Norway.

Hemming and Tora had two daughters and four sons. The two daughters married Norwegian nobles and remained in that country. The four sons went with their father to Orkney. *"The Eldest was Andlaw or Allan Grant, of whom the name of Grant descended; Gregorie, whom the name of MacGregorie, of Glenstrue, in Scotland, descended (although some allege that MacGregorie is descended from Gregorious, King of Scotland), Rowin, because [of his] red hair was third son of Hemming, the representative and Progenitor of the name of Rowin or Ruthvin, in Scotland, and was after Earl of Gowrie. Fingone was fourth son to Hemming Grant, and of him descended the name of MacFingone or Mackinnon in Scotland, and to this day there is a warmness of heart betwixt these four names, as being descended of our Father Hemming."*(5)

Tora died soon after the exiles arrived in Orkney. After seeing his sons settled, Hemming eventually travelled to Ireland and married Isabella, daughter of the

Prince of Dublin, with whom he had several other children. His four sons remained in Orkney or the northern Scottish mainland then controlled by the Earls of Orkney. In this tradition the Grants are descended from Andlaw or Allan Grant.

At this time the Earl of Orkney was Sigurd the Stout and his lands included Orkney, Shetland, and large parts of Caithness and Sutherland. His lands may even have stretched into Morayshire, south of Inverness. The sons of Hemming would have fought for Sigurd in his struggle against Scottish domination. Around 990 AD Sigurd's lands in Caithness and Sutherland were attacked by the Scottish Earl of Moray, Findleach, the father of future King MacBeth. Sigurd gathered his forces, which would have included the sons of Hemming Grant, and outnumbered seven to one the Norsemen defeated the Scots.

Then in 1005 the Norwegians fought in the **Battle of Mortlach,** near Dufftown in Morayshire, where they were defeated and had to retreat north into Caithness. King Malcolm pushed into Caithness and although Sigurd the Stout successfully expanded his control of the Western Isles, he eventually had to 'bend the knee' to Malcolm II, King of Scots, for his lands on mainland Scotland.

Sigurd and Hemming Grant were both killed at the **Battle of Clontart**, which took place on 23 April 1014, near Dublin. This battle was between Brian Boru, High King of Ireland, against a Norse-Irish alliance comprising the forces of Sigtrygg Silkbeard, King of Dublin (who was either father-in-law or brother-in-law of Hemming Grant), the King of Leinster and a Viking Army led by Sigurd of Orkney and Brodir of Man.

The battle lasted from sunrise to sunset and it was estimated that up to 10,000 men were killed, including most of the leaders on both sides. The dead included Hemming Grant and Earl Sigurd. Andlaw Grant also fought in this battle but survived and was able to return to the north of Scotland. After this the power of the Vikings and the Kingdom of Dublin was largely broken. Sigurd was succeeded, eventually, by his youngest son, Thorfinn the Mighty, and Andlaw Grant gave him allegiance. Thorfinn was perhaps the greatest of all the Norwegian Earls of Orkney and on his death in or around 1065 he controlled Orkney, Shetland, the Western Isles and large parts of the Northeast Scottish mainland. It appears that during his reign the Grants may have established themselves on the Scottish mainland, specifically in Morayshire.

2). **Gaelic**. On account of Irish/Scotti Gaels who have the same name. This is in all probability the most likely true ancestry of Clan Grant. This ancestry may be the reason for the close link between Clan Grant and Clan MacGregor, who both claim descent as a branch of Clan Alpin. The supporters of this theory promote that the name Grant was derived from the Gaelic word 'grannda', meaning ugly, which they say applied to the original ancestor of the Clan. They also point to the fact that many of the Clan Chiefs and Lairds were given Gaelic names such as Patrick, Duncan etc, all common in both the Scottish and Irish Gaelic communities.

"In the old Irish treatise on the 'law of Adamnan' of date 697 AD, there is given a list of chiefs and notables guaranteeing the observance of his [Adamnan's] famous 'Law of the Innocent' exempting woman and children from the duty of fighting in battle, in which occurs the name of Conall Grant rii deisint Brig, or King of Southern Brega (Bray, near Dublin), who was slain in 718 AD."(6)

But the main connection with the Gaels and Clan Gant is through the Siol Appin, which is Gaelic for 'Seed of Alpin' and is a group of 7 Scottish Clans who traditionally claim descent from Alpin, father of Cinaed mac Alpin (Kenneth MacAlpin) first King of the Alba, which was formed from the amalgamation of the Kingdoms of the Picts and Dalriada.

Diagram 1. The Siol Alpin.

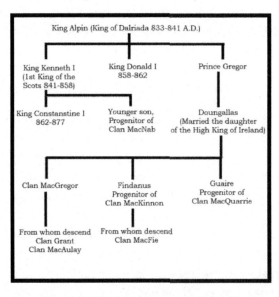

The seven clans that make up Siol Alpin are Clan Grant, Clan Gregor, Clan MacAulay, Clan MacFie, Clan MacKinnon, Clan McNab and Clan MacQuarrie.

The Siol Alpin tradition was so strong in the Clans Gregor and Grant that in the early years of the 18th century the two clans met at Blair Athol to discuss re-uniting.

In the discussions, which lasted 14 days, it was agreed that if the proscription against the surname MacGregor could be reversed then the new clan would take that name, otherwise MacAlpin of Grant would be used. However, there was a disagreement on who should be Chief and discussions eventually broke down. Despite this several branches of Clan Grant, including the Laird of Ballindalloch, "showed their loyalty to the ancient kinship by adding the MacGregor patronymic to their name."(7)

Clan Grant was also close to Clan Mackinnon. "Following the failed Jacobite rising of 1715, Iain Dubh, Chief of Clan MacKinnon, lost his lands under the Act of Attainder. His forfeited lands were then bought from the Government by the Chief of Clan Grant and then handed over to Iain Dubh's heirs. The author, Charles MacKinnon, claims that there can be no reason that a chief, so far removed from the Isle of Skye, bought another clan's lands and then gave them back – other than a belief in common ancestry. And that the two clans belonged to the same family Siol Appin."(8)

The belief in their descent from Alpin is also shown in the clan badges of the seven clans. These badges were worn in the bonnets of highlanders to help distinguish friend from enemy, and all seven clans of the Siol Alpin share the Scots Pine as their badge.

MAP 2. KINGDOM OF DALRIADA Circa AD 500.

Kenneth MacAlpin was initially the King of Dalriada. The first King of Dalriada was Fergus Mor (or Fergus the Great) who was initially a prominent Lord of the Scoti Tribe in Northwest Ireland. The name 'Scoti' was a generic name given by the Romans who applied it to all raiders from Ireland. The name was also used by them to differentiate them from the' Picti' of mainland Scotland.

Around AD 500 the famous Scoti warrior, Fergus Mor and his brother Loarn mac Eirc (some name him Erc but this is likely to have been both men's father), moved in strength from Antrim in Northeast Ireland and took over the area known as Argyll from the resident Picts and established the Kingdom of Dalriada. Fergus Mor became the first King of the new kingdom. The people were known as the Dal Riata and they soon started to expand their territory, led by several aggressive warrior kings. After Fergus Mor, his brother Loarn mac Eirc became King.

Probably the most famous of the Dalriada Kings was Aedain mac Gadhrain, who ruled Dalriada from AD 574 to AD 603, "whose recorded exploits included large-scale raids by land and sea against the territories of the Picts, the Britons of Strathclyde and the Anglians of Northumbria. He was eventually defeated and killed by the Northumbrians in AD 603."(9)

Dun Add Hill Fortress

The Dal Riata divided into four main kinship groups:

- The Cenel nGabrain (kindred of Gabrain) in Kintyre.
- The Cenel nOengusu (kindred of Oengus) in Islay and Jura.
- The Cenel Comgail (kindred of Comgall) in Cowal and Bute.
- The Cenel Loairn (kindred of Loarn) in Lorne, and possibly also in Mull and Ardnamurchan, who claim descent from Loarn mac Eire.

The Grants are descended from the fourth kinship group, the Cenel Loairn.

The capital was established at Dunadd at the southern end of Kilmartin Glen, just north of Lochgilphead. It is a massive natural rock which rears out of the Crinan Moss. At the top of the crag is a footprint which has been carved out of the bedrock and which points to the distant Ben Cruachan, the 'holy mountain' of Argyll. "Most commentators now agree that the carved footprint was used in the ritual inauguration of early Dalraidic kings: the new king would have placed one foot in the carving during the ceremony, in full view of his people gathered on the terrace below, to symbolise a royal 'marriage' with the land."(10) It is an extremely enigmatic and magical place.

The King's Footprint at Dunadd Fortress

Copyright: Eileen Sinclair 2022

The Kingdom of Dalriada was no backwater on the northern edge of Europe. The capital, Dunadd, was occupied for 500 years and "it was a place where skilled craftspeople fashioned high-quality jewellery and implements in bronze, silver, and gold. It was also a major trading centre in a huge Celtic network which stretched from Ireland, down the west coast of Britain and across the Mediterranean. Dunadd was clearly an important player in European trade, exporting commodities like hides, leather and metalwork and importing luxury goods from abroad."(11)

The area of north Dalriada became the heartland of the Cenel Loairn and from them became known as the lands of Lorn.

Lorn is bordered in the west by the Firth of Lorne, which separates it from the island of Mull. The famous Glen Coe and Rannoch Moor form the northern boundary, while in the east the border is the Bridge of Orchy hills. Loch Awe provides its south eastern border, separating Lorn from the rest of Argyll to the south. Lorn also incorporates the islands of Lismore and Shuna. Although the town was only created in the 19th century, Oban is the only large settlement in Lorn and is its modern-day capital.

The Cenel Loairn established their power base at Dun Olliagh Castle (Dunollie) located on the west coast of Lorn, just north of the town of Oban. Here the Cenel Loairn ruled as sub-kings of Dalriada for over two hundred years. "The Irish annals record that 'Dun Olliagh' was attacked and burned down three times, in 668, 698 and in 701. It was subsequently rebuilt in 714 by Selbach mac Ferchair (died 730), the King of Dalriada credited with destroying the site in 701."(12)

Dunollie Castle

This destruction was caused primarily by civil war within the Celtic Kingdom as the various 'Houses' vied for power. This was mainly between three of the great houses, the Cenel nGabrain who initially held the overlordship and who occupied Dunadd, and the lands of Kintyre, Cowal, Bute and Arran. The Cenel nOengusa and

Cenel Loairn were the two main houses who fought against them. "The relative importance of each of the three tribes is confirmed by the survey in the 'Senchus' outlining the manpower each could provide: Cenel NGabrain had 560 houses or clients and could muster 800 men; both the Cenel Loairn and Cenel nOengusa, which had 420 houses and 430 houses, could probably raise 600 men apiece."(13)

The dominance of the Cenel nGabrain was reduced in the 7th century when Dalriada suffered a series of military defeats, particularly against the Picts and the Briton Kingdom of Strathclyde. By the end of the 7th century the Cenel Loairn had taken over as overkings of Dalriada. However, this dominance only lasted for just over 100 years. First the Cenel Loairn King, Selbach, was defeated in a sea battle by the nGabrain in AD 719. This was the first recorded sea battle in the history of Britain. "Most seriously of all, they faced the brunt of a sustained period of aggression waged by Oengus, King of Picts, which culminated in the 'smiting of Dalriada' in 741. The result, it is likely, was the eclipse of Cenel Loairn ambitions. "(13) Yet, only 100 years later the House of Cenel Loairn would come to dominate Dalriada and Pictland through another of their sons, Kenneth mac Alpin. He was supported by the ancestors of the Grants in his successful wars to unify the Celts and Picts under one realm, Scotland.

Kenneth's father, Alpin II, became King of Dalriada in 830 AD. He was born in 778 AD and died in July 833 AD. He was only King of Dalriada for three years. As soon as he came to the throne, "he made an attempt to rule over the Picts, which, by Pictish law, he was quite entitled to do as his mother was a Pictish Princess."(14) He chose what he thought was a perfect time to attack. The Picts had just lost a great battle with the Viking raiders and their King, Angus II, and many of their other leaders had been killed. The young son of Angus was on the Pictish throne and Alpin took the opportunity to attack them on Easter day, 833 AD. Attacking on this most holy of days was seen as an unforgivable sin by the now Christian Picts and Celts alike. His initial attack was successful and he defeated all the Pictish forces raised against him. However, his victory did not last long, as in the autumn of the same year he was heavily defeated by a new Pictish army in Galloway in South West Scotland. Alpin was captured and the Picts showed him no mercy and he was beheaded on the battlefield. Alpin's head was fastened to a pole and carried before the triumphant Pictish army as it marched north. It was then displayed at Abernethy, their capital and principal settlement.

Alpin was succeeded by his eldest son Kenneth mac Alpin (Cinead macAilpin), commonly known as Kenneth I of Scotland, born around 800 AD. He was supported by his brothers Donald and Grigor in his successful wars to unify the Celts and Picts under one realm, Alba. Alpin had married a Pictish Princess and this allowed Kenneth and his brothers to unite the two kingdoms through the Celtic tradition of inheritance through the female line.

Kenneth became King of Dalriada around 833 AD and immediately sought to unite the Gaelic and Pictish kingdoms. Winning a series of battles all over northern and central Scotland, he was eventually successful and became King of the unified Alba around 845 AD. From then onwards he ruled the new kingdom from a royal fortress at Scone, Perthshire. This began the process which would eventually lead to the creation of the unified Kingdom of Scotland. For now, however, this northern Kingdom was known as Alba. The Grants would have fought for their leader and kinsman, King Kenneth mac Alpin.

MAP 3. DALRIADA AND PICTLAND UNITED AS ALBA AD 845.

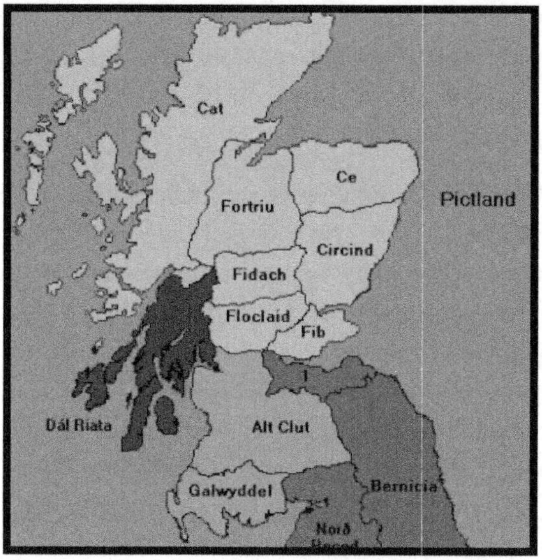

The main reason for the unification of the kingdoms was a new threat to both the Celts and the Picts, in the form of the 'Vikings'. "The historical record of their incursions into Scottish waters and territory began in 795 with a raid on Iona (the first of three such raids in ten years), and Scotland was then engulfed In the turmoil of what has come to be called the Viking Age (800-1050). While Danish raiders attacked the continent and southern England, Norwegian invaders established a Norse earldom in Shetland and Orkney which was to last for more than three hundred years, from the middle of the ninth century to the thirteenth."(15) After

16

Orkney and Shetland the Norsemen took over the entire Western Isles, from Lewis to Arran, and even established themselves in Dublin and the Isle of Man. In doing this they inflicted many defeats on both the Picts and the Celts.

The Kingdom of Dalriada was significantly reduced and it looked likely that it would be totally taken over by the new invaders. Given this threat the Picts and Celts started to come closer together. Kenneth Mac Alpin's mother was a Pictish Princess and his father a King of Dalriada. He had the perfect pedigree to unite the two kingdoms. He emerged as King of Dalriada around AD 834 and a few years later he became King of the Pictish Kingdom of Fortriu. "How exactly that came about in not known; according to a lurid folktale he invited the leaders of Pictish nobility to a feast under a flag of truce and had them all slaughtered, but that yarn is no longer given any credence."(16) The legend goes further to state in the banquet hall Kenneth had pits dug beneath the benches on which the Pictish leaders would sit. When they were all seated and feasting, a signal was given and the bolts securing the benches were removed and the nobles fell into the pit and were trapped, unable to get out and unable to defend themselves. In this perilous state they were all butchered.

Kenneth mac Alpin then moved his capital out of Dunadd and Dalriada and established the new capital of the unified kingdom in Forteviot, near Perth. He then established his supporters in key positions throughout the new Kingdom. It was the end of Dalriada as a separate kingdom. Kenneth was known as the first King of Scots and all Scottish Kings are numbered from him. He died at Forteviot in AD 858. Before this, however, he married off many of his Celtic Dalradian followers to Pictish Princess's and as inheritance in Pictish custom was through the female line he ensured that the local Picts would accept his supporters. This was probably when the ancestors of the Grants first moved to Moray which at that time was part of the Pictish Kingdom of Fortriu.

The historic lands of the Grants are in Speyside and around Loch Ness and there are many legendary traditions belonging to these area. They involve the local inhabitants and wherever the Chiefs of Grant descend from, what is clear is that the majority of those with the surname Grant come from the local indigenous population who have inhabited this area for centuries.

One is the local tradition as to the origins of Loch Ness, home of the Grants of Urquhart and Glenmoriston and also of the original Grant land holdings of Stratherrick. The legend goes that at in the days of the Picti, the Great Glen of Ness was a beautiful valley, covered by pasture and home to a large number of people. Through it ran a majestic river in which was found good fish. Many Picti lived in this valley and all had plenty of food. The men chased the boar in the valley and the deer in the hills. When they were not doing this they tended their cattle on the Plain of Ness.

In this Glen was a spring which was blessed by the Druid Daly. The spring had healing powers for every disease. "This holy well was protected from pollution by a stone placed over it by the Druid, who enjoined that whenever the stone was removed for the drawing of water, it should be immediately replaced. 'The day on which my command is disregarded'; said he. 'desolation will overtake the land'. The words of Daly were remembered by the people, and became a law among them; and so day followed day, and year gave place to year'. "(17)

Then many years later a woman left a young baby by the fireside and went to the well to draw water. No sooner than she had removed the stone from the head of the well, she heard her baby cry as it neared the fire. She rushed over and saved the infant but she forgot the order of the Druid and did not replace the stone. The waters soon flowed and soon covered the Glen. The people had to escape to the mountainside, lamenting the loss of their idyllic home. They cried, "Tha Loch 'nis ann, tha loch 'nis ann! And the lake remained, and it is called Loch Nis to this day."(18)

There is also another legend regarding the sons of Uisneach, from whom Loch Ness is named. In the 1st century AD the King of Ulster in Ireland was Conachar Mac Nessa. At this time in Ireland lived a man named Colum Cruitire, who had a daughter, Deirdre, who was renowned as the most beautiful woman of her age. King Conachar resolved to marry this woman and she agreed, but only after a year.

But before the end of the year the King was visited by his cousins, Naois, Ailean and Ardan, the renowned sons of Uisneach. Naois and Deidre fell in love with each other and the lovers fled to Scotland with Ailean and Ardan. On the shores of Loch Naois (Loch Ness) they built a tower close to the loch where they fished salmon and hunted deer, and here they lived in happiness for a year.

However, their location became known to King Conachar and he sent his servant Farquhar Mac Ro to them to give them assurances of friendship and an invitation to a great feast in his kingdom. Deirdre was suspicious and begged Naois not to go, but he would not listen to her. The King was his cousin and he trusted his word. All the brothers accompanied Farquhar Mac Ro to Ireland.

As soon as they arrived they were surrounded by the King's soldiers and immediately executed and their bodies laid in an open grave. "Then Deirdre looked into the open grave and said – 'Let Naois of my love move to one side: let Ailean press close to Ardan: if the dead could only hear, you would make room for me!' And the dead did make room for her; and she, laying herself by her husband's side expired. But the King would not have Naois and Deirdre lie in the same grave, and he caused her to be buried on the opposite bank of an adjoining stream; and a tender pine sprang out of the grave of Naois, and another out of the grave of Deirdre, and the pines grew and joined above the stream,"(19)

The lovers fame continued in Alban and from Naois comes the name Loch Ness, the Rive Ness and the town of Inverness. On the Stratherrick (south) side of the loch was a fort named Dun Dearduil (Deirdre) in memory of the faithful wife of Naois.

The true origin of the Scottish Grants is difficult to prove one way or another. Possibly it is a mixture of all three traditions; Celtic, Norse and Norman. But there is also another possible origin of the name, in that it could also come from 'Sliabh Grianais' which is a moor above Aviemore, which was supposed to be part of the first lands held by the ancestors of the Grants. Whatever the origin, the natives who took the Grant name would be composed of Pictish/Celtic natives.

The Clan Grant Society have the first chief of Clan Grant as **Amhlaim (Aulay) Grant** who was Chief of the Grants between 1174 AD and 1215 AD. Very little is known about Amhlaim Grant apart from that he was a loyal supporter of King William 'The Lion', who inherited the throne in 1165. Although an effective monarch, King William's reign was marred by his unsuccessful attempts to regain control of the English County of Northumbria. Amhlaim and the rest of the Grants supported this King throughout his long reign from 1165 to 1214.

In 1174 the English King, Henry II, was occupied fighting against his sons. King William took the opportunity and invaded Northumbria. The Earl of Moray called his forces together and Amhlaim and his men formed part of this force which joined the Scots army on the Scottish borders. The army soon besieged Alnwick Castle but King William then divided his army into three separate forces. The Earl of Moray and the Grants joined the force under the command of the Earl of Fife, Duncan II (Donnachaed II). This force left Alnwick and attacked the village of Warkworth where the Grants may have been involved in a murderous genocide.

The inhabitants of Warkworth fled and took refuge in the Church of St. Lawrence, where the Grants barricaded them inside and then set fire to the building, killing hundreds of innocent men, women and children.

Meanwhile the King's depleted force at Alnwick was attacked by a force of English knights and William himself was captured and imprisoned after his horse was killed beneath him. The rest of the Scots army soon fled north. The English then occupied much of Scotland after this. In order to be released from his prison, King William had to sign the Treaty of Falaise (1174), under the terms of which he had to swear allegiance to the English King and agree to the garrisoning of the major Scottish castles by English soldiers. During the 15 years which the Treaty lasted there were many revolts against King William due to his power being greatly diminished. Throughout this Amhlaim stayed loyal to the King.

The Treaty lasted until 1189, when the new English King, Richard the Lionheart (Richard I), renounced the Treaty and sold the castles back to William in return for funds for his forthcoming Crusade to the Holy Land. William almost immediately began to take action against his rebellious lords. He quickly took control of Galloway in the Southwest of Scotland which, previously, had been a semi-independent Earldom.

Amhlaim Grant then took part in putting down an insurrection in Inverness and then participated in a series of campaigns in the far north of Scotland to bring back Caithness and Sutherland under the power and control of the Scottish Crown. For more than a century this area had effectively been controlled by the Norwegian Jarls of Orkney. King William 'the Lion' died of natural causes in 1214 and was buried in Arbroath Abbey. He was succeeded by his eldest son, King Alexander II. Amhlaim died soon after in 1215 but the cause is unknown.

His eldest son, Gregor, married Mary Bisset a daughter of Lord Sir John Bisset, one of the most powerful Lords in the north at this time. From this marriage came at least two sons, one of whom was Sir Laurence Grant who became Sheriff of Inverness. He appears to be the eldest son. The other son was Robert Grant. There is also evidence that two Grants, William and Thomas were at the court of King Alexander II and accompanied him in his invasion of England against King John.

Gregory Grant is acknowledged as the 2nd Chief of Clan Grant. Their first major known landholding in the north was Stratherrick, a large estate on the south-eastern shore of Loch Ness, Invernesshire. Much of the area is dominated by Loch Mhor. Gregory Grant was known as the 1st Lord of Stratherrick.

When King Alexander II became King of Scots in December 1214 he was only 16 years of age. Immediately after his coronation two Highland Clans, the McWilliams (Meic Uilleim) and MacHeths, rebelled against control from the Scottish Monarchy. Gregor Grant and his forces joined the Earl of Ross who was a loyal supporter of the new King and they marched north and destroyed the forces of the rebels, bringing the heads of the two Chiefs south to be impaled on the gates of Stirling Castle.

MAP 4. STRATHERRICK AND SPEYSIDE.

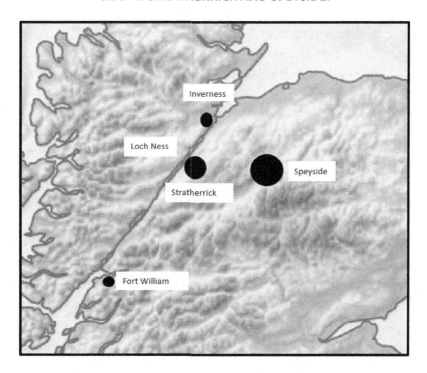

Secure in the north, the young King then got embroiled in a civil war in England between King John and his Barons. Hoping to have his family's old claim to the English County of Northumbria granted to him, Alexander joined forces of the Barons against King John. But King John reacted first, and sent an English Army to "hunt the red fox-cub from his lair."[20] They burned Berwick and many other border towns before retiring.

Alexander retaliated by invading England. In fact he is the only Scottish Monarch to take a Scottish Army through England to the shores of the English Channel, where he proposed to join up with the King of France. Within the army were William and

Thomas Grant. We do not know if Gregor was within the Army or whether he had sent the other Grants in his place. It may be that Gregor was told to stay in the north of Scotland to quell any potential rebellions while King Alexander was campaigning in England. Luckily, before any great battles were fought, King John died from dysentery and the Scottish Army returned home.

King John's eldest son became King Henry III of England and King Alexander II married his sister, Joan, in 1221. This only brought an uneasy peace between the two kingdoms as Henry III wanted Alexander to pay him homage as Overlord of Scotland, which Alexander refused. Indeed, at one point King Henry got the Pope's support and he sent his legate to Scotland to convince the King of Scots to do as the English King commanded. When the Legate entered the Scottish Court, Alexander had filled it with Highland Chiefs, dressed in their war gear, including Lochaber axes and long swords. Gregor Grant carried the now skeletal head of the MacHeth Chief tied to his belt. The Legate …. was told by the King: 'Untamed and wild men dwell in my land, they thirst for human blood, and if they should attack you I cannot restrain them'. The Legate's response went unrecorded, but he does not seem to have pressed the order from the Pope.

Eventually peace was secured with England and this gave the King the opportunity to tackle the unruly parts of his Kingdom. He put down two rebellions in Galloway, which had always considered itself at least a semi- independent part of the Scottish Kingdom and then with the help of Gregor Grant, the King turned on the unruly clans in Argyll and after a short campaign either destroyed them or obtained their oaths of allegiance.

The Western Isles and parts of the Scottish mainland were still part of the Kingdom of Denmark and Norway at this time. In 1249 the Grants joined the King as he gathered a large army and fleet at the harbour of Ayr, on the west coast of the Scottish mainland. They then sailed north up the coast and made a landing on the island of Kerrera (opposite modern-day Oban), ready to launch an assault on the Island chiefs who gave homage to the King of Denmark and Norway, Haakon. Unfortunately on the voyage the King became ill of a fever and died on Kerrara. The invasion fleet, including the Grants, dispersed and the army was sent home.

King Alexander III, was anointed King of Scots on his father's death in 1249 when he was only 8 years old. The reign of King Alexander III was generally considered a 'golden age' for Scotland when it was in relative peace with its neighbours, particularly England, and when it was therefore able to flourish without constant warfare. Gregory Grant may have also died in the same year as King Alexander II and was succeeded in 1249 by **Sir Laurence Grant 3rd Chief of Grant.**

While he was in minority there were no major escalation of the dispute over ownership of the Western Isles. However, when King Alexander III reached the age of 21, he laid claim to the Western Isles, as his father had done before him. King Haakon rejected these claims again and in response gathered a vast army to invade Scotland.

In 1258 Robert Grant, younger brother of Sir Laurence Grant, acquired land at Coulmony near Findhorn (now known as the Lethen estate in the county of Nairn). This is the first known written evidence of the Grants in this part of the country. The brothers, Sir Laurence and Robert Grant, were witnesses to an Agreement between John Bysset (Bisset) and Archibald, Bishop of Moray in 1258, regarding land in the Aird of Inverness. In 1263 Sir Laurence is recorded as being Sheriff of Inverness, and the Counties of Ross, Sutherland and Caithness in 1263. This was a huge area of Scotland and shows he must have been a man of great importance at this time and a supporter of the King. He may also have been given governorship of the Royal Castle of 'Invery', which may have been Blervie Castle, near Forbes in Aberdeenshire.

DIAGRAM 2. CHIEF OF CLAN GRANT.

Name	Chief Number	Title	From	Until
Amhlaim (Aulay) Grant	1		1174	1215
Gregory Grant	2	1st Lord Stratherrick	1215	1249
Laurence Grant	3	2nd Lord Stratherrick	1249	1275
John Grant	4	3rd Lord Stratherrick	1275	1295
Sir John Grant	5	4th Lord Stratherrick	1295	1320
Patrick Grant	6	5th Lord Stratherrick	1320	1362

The one major exception to the peace was the invasion of King Haakon of Norway. When the King Alexander III reached the age of 21, he laid claim to the Western Isles, as his father had done before him. King Hakon rejected these claims and in response gathered a vast army to invade Scotland.

In July 1263 the ageing King Hakon of Norway sailed a mighty fleet to Orkney and then carried on to the Isle of Skye intent on expanding his empire and giving the Scots a bloody nose. In Skye he was then joined by Magnus, King of Man and other

Norse and Celtic Chiefs from Ireland and the Western Isles who were obligated to Norway. The fleet then sailed down the Firth of Clyde where, fortunately for Scotland, worsening weather conditions made them take refuge on the Isle of Arran.

There was panic in Ayrshire which was only 20 miles across the Firth of Clyde from the Norwegian Fleet. King Alexander immediately assembled an army consisting of mainly lowland Lords and their vassals. Laurence Grant, who was Sheriff on Inverness, Sutherland and Caithness did not form part of this army. He was instructed to gather as many men as possible and march north to threaten the lands of Caithness which had many Norsemen loyal to Haakon living there. He did this very successfully and took a number of hostages for the 'good behaviour' of their Chiefs and Lairds. Few of Haakon's supporters from the north west mainland joined his fleet and army which invaded the Firth of Clyde.

On September 31, 1263, while the Norwegian force were moored off Arran, a mighty gale drove Hakon's treasure ship and 10 other fighting vessels full of troops ashore at Largs on the Ayrshire coast. On hearing of Hakon's misfortune at landing, the Scots army hurried to Largs. They reached the Norwegian force before nightfall and had time to unleash a storm of arrows on Hakon's force before darkness ended the fighting for the day.

At dawn the Scots divisions drew up on the ridge above the beach and launched a full scale assault. After much fierce fighting Hakon's force suffered heavy casualties and were slowly driven back to their ships after enduring horrific casualties. The retreat turned into a rout and the Scots hacked through the enemy as they ran to safety.

Hakon escaped and although he reassembled his force, he retired to Kirkwall in Orkney where he eventually succumbed to illness and died. Three years later, after some tough negotiations, Hakon's successor sold the Isle of Man and the Western Isles to Scotland for a sum of 4,000 merks of silver and an annual payment of a further 100 merks, which as it happens was never paid. Laurence Grant was one of the Ambassadors who travelled to Norway and concluded the peace agreement with the new Norwegian King. Although glorified by later writers, the **Battle of Largs** was decisive and led to the loss of Norwegian power in all the Western Scottish seaboard.

After the defeat of the Norwegians, King Alexander III sought to assert his power over the island and mainland Lords who had once given loyalty to Norway but who were now part of his Kingdom. Among those he sent to the north were Laurence and Robert Grant, who visited every Lord of Caithness and Sutherland and again took hostages for their good behaviour. Any who still refused to acknowledge Alexander III as their sovereign, the Grants took action against.

For his loyalty Sir Laurence Grant was also appointed Baillie or Governor of the Royal Castle of Inverquoich. Sir Laurence Grant married the daughter of Alexander Comyn, Earl of Buchan, a descendant of Donald III, King of Scotland. They had at least two sons, John and Robert Grant.

The Grants continued in their loyalty to King Alexander III who was a very popular King with his people and his early years were generally good for Scotland. However, his later years very filled with sorrow. His English wife died in 1275 and she was followed in quick succession by both of his sons. According to the Clan Grant Society Sir Laurence Grant died in the same year as the Queen and was succeeded by his eldest son **John Grant, 4ᵗʰ Chief of Grant.**

Then King Alexander's daughter, Margaret, who had married the King of Norway (Hakon's successor) in a bid to make peace with that Kingdom, also died in childbirth in 1285. John Grant was one of the northern lords who attended the important Government Council at Scone later in 1285 when King Alexander's grand-daughter Margaret (whose mother had died in giving birth to her) was recognised as his rightful heir. She was known as the 'Maid of Norway' and lived with her father, King Eric II of Norway.

In the same year as the Council of Scone, King Alexander married Yolande, the beautiful daughter of the French Comte de Dreux. Alexander loved her dearly and could not bear to be parted from her, and this was to lead directly to his death. On a wintry night in March 1286 Alexander dined with his Lords in Edinburgh Castle. After eating, and against the wishes of his noblemen, he left to join his wife across the Firth of Forth at Kinghorn. A great gale was blowing and after berating the boatmen for refusing to sail in such weather, the ship carried him over to the north shore. He landed at Inverkeithing where he again refused the appeals of his men to wait the night out in safety. Hurrying to be with Yolande he rode ahead of his men and somewhere along the way fell from his stumbling horse to his death. Scotland mourned its most likeable King.

CHAPTER 2. THE FIRST WAR OF SCOTTISH INDEPENDENCE – WALLACE.

Alexander III was succeeded by his grand-daughter Margaret, 'the Maid of Norway' in 1286 but owing to her young age (she was born in 1283) she remained in Norway for four further years. During this time a Treaty was signed by the Regents of Scotland, King Eric of Norway and King Edward I of England, betrothing Margaret to the King of England's eldest son, Edward of Caernarfon. If this marriage had taken place Scotland and England would have been unified by this marriage. However, on her voyage to Scotland to be crowned Queen of Scots in September 1290, she became ill on-board ship, and stopping at Orkney her condition worsened and she died. Rumours at the time suggested she may have been poisoned.

Her death was followed by a bitter power struggle for the succession between John Balliol and Robert Bruce (grand-father of Robert the Bruce, future King of Scotland). Both were descendants of daughters of King David I. Looking at it objectively, Balliol had the best claim to the Kingdom, although he was by far the weakest candidate.

It was Balliol (who was later to be known as 'Toom Tabard' or Empty Jacket) who became King of Scots in November 1292 after Edward I of England was asked by the Scots Parliament to judge between all the contenders. It is understandable why the ambitious and ruthless Edward chose this weak and ineffectual man in preference to the strong, robust and proven military leader, Robert Bruce: Balliol would easily became the English King's puppet. Balliol was a kinsman of the powerful Comyn family who ruled much of the North West highlands at this time, as well as large tracts of Scotland. The Grants were allies of the Coymns at this time and supported the crowning of John Balliol.

Three days after being chosen as King of Scotland, Balliol swore fealty to King Edward as his 'Overlord' in Berwick and then rushed to Scone where he was crowned King of Scots on St Andrews day, 1292. Meanwhile King Edward lost no time in asserting his control of Scotland. Almost immediately after his coronation, King Balliol was summoned to London by Edward, like any other common English nobleman called by his master. Indeed, it was soon obvious that Edward took great pleasure in humiliating the new King of Scots.

By this time John Grant was an elderly man and more and more of his duties were taken over by his eldest son, another John Grant. Indeed John the elder probably died in late 1295 or early 1296, as from this date his son John is recognised as Head of the Grant family and Chief of the fledgling clan. Around this time there was also a Patrick Grant who was Governor of Cluny Castle in Perthshire from 1291 and 1292 on behalf of the Coymn family.

Sir John Grant was the 5th Chief of Clan Grant (1296 -1325) was the 1st Grant of Inverallen in Strathspey. He bought these lands from a Lord John of Inverallen in 1316. This estate was on the grounds of what would become Grantown-on-Spey, the heartland of Clan Grant. However, prior to this he may have married Bigla Coymn of Glencairnie, a wealthy heiress of the Comyn family.

Records are very sketchy about the wider Grant family at this time, as well as his son and heir, Patrick. John Grant may have had at least three other sons, Robert, Sir Alan and Thomas (who may have been a churchman). Thomas had two sons who travelled to Normandy and stayed there. John may also have had a brother, Andrew Grant, who also fought with him in 1333 at Halidon Hill. Another member of the family may have been Maurice, who in 1340 was Sheriff of Inverness.

As supporters of the Coymn faction the Grants were given positions of power in the North.   John's son was given the Governorship of their Castle of Clunie, in Perthshire between 1291 and 1292 and a David Grant was Sheriff of Stirling in 1295.

Eventually King Balliol could take no more of Edward's humiliations and he refused to obey his commands and in 1295 he signed a Treaty of Alliance with France. This was a declaration of war against England and, in 1296, King Edward gathered a great army to crush the Scots once and for all. As he was doing this, however, the Scots had also begun to muster their own forces. The King of England was now determined to crush the Scots and marched his great army north to besiege Berwick. Now an English town, at the time Berwick was one of Scotland's most important settlements and its harbour the main trading port between Scotland and the North European countries. King Edward reached Berwick in March 1296 before a Scots army had even been assembled to meet him. However, Sir William Douglas, an experienced soldier, had brought a number of soldiers to garrison the Castle of Berwick against the English.

Despite the poor condition of Barwick's walls, the presence of the renowned Douglas 'the Hardy' gave the defenders heart and they taunted King Edward and his army across the fortifications. This show of defiance further enraged the English King and he ordered his men to advance and they soon poured over the weak defensive walls of the town. Edward proclaimed that no mercy be given and up to fifteen thousand men, women and children of Berwick were murdered. Blood flowed in the streets and after three days the stink of decaying bodies could be smelt twenty miles away.

Meanwhile, the Scottish Army assembled at Haddington, just outside of Edinburgh. Both John Grant and his brother, Robert, and their men obeyed the call to arms and joined the Scottish army. The Earl of Dunbar had, by this time, joined the King of England, and sworn fealty to him. His wife, Marjory, had a stronger back bone and she allowed the Scots to occupy his Castle. The English King was determined to take the fortress and sent the Earl of Surrey, with a strong force of mounted knights, to take the Castle by force. On learning of this the Scots marched south to meet them and the **Battle of Dunbar** took place on 27 April 1296.

The Scots Army, under the Earl of Buchan, occupied the Castle and then gathered on the heights above the town of Dunbar in a strong defensive position. The disciplined English army arrived at Dunbar on April 27, 1296. Brave though the Scot's army was, it lacked experience in warfare. The English made a tactical withdrawal and the Scots, assuming that they were fleeing, charged down the hill in disarray only to meet the regrouped English battle lines. Thousands of Scots were killed and quarter was only given to the Scottish Knights who could later be ransomed. It was a complete victory for Edward Longshanks (a nickname given to the English King because of his great height) Over 100 Scottish nobles and knights were captured, including John and Robert Grant. The Grant brothers were still fairly young at this time and were probably Squires in the force led by John Coymn of Badenoch, Earl of Moray.

Both were taken to England and held in Gloucester and Bristol Castles respectively. After a year they were released on bail, with the condition that they would accompany King Edward of England on his military expedition to Flanders (now Belgium). John Comyn of Badenoch and David Le Graham were sureties for their compliance.

Meanwhile, the rest of Scotland crumbled quickly. By 10 July, Balliol lay before Edward at Montrose and surrendered himself and his Kingdom, blaming evil counsel and his stupidity for resisting English domination. Still Edward was not satisfied and before all he further humiliated the King of Scots by having his embroidered Royal Arms torn from his clothing and thrown on the floor. Scotland, like Wales before it, was no longer to be a separate Kingdom but merely a province of a Greater England.

After a triumphant tour of the North of Scotland, sacking Inverness, Edward stopped at Scone and seized what he thought was the Stone of Destiny, upon which the Kings of the Scots were crowned, taking it with him to London where it lay until 1996 in Westminster Abbey. Fortunately, he only got a fake, an ordinary piece of local quarry stone and the real Stone of Destiny still lies hidden somewhere in Scotland waiting to be recovered. Not satisfied with this he then stole the Scottish Royal Regalia, including the Holy Rood which had been brought by St. Margaret from Hungary centuries before.

On the 28 August 1296 Edward held a Parliament at Berwick at which every landowner in Scotland was to attend and kneel before him and sign an act of submission. Called the **'Ragman Roll'** it was signed by nearly all Scots landowners including notable names like Bruce, Stewart and Coymn. Robert Le Gruant was a signatory to the Ragman Roll in August 1296. But this couldn't have been Robert, brother of the Chief of Grant, as he was in prison in England and must have been another relative. He is recognised as a Lord of Fife, both John and Robert Grant would have been designated as Lords of Inverness. Only a handful refused to sign, the most significant of whom was William Wallace. The submissions were made under duress, however, and Edward would still not trust his new Scots subjects.

Also captured at Dunbar was Andrew Moray (or Murray) and his father, Sir Andrew Moray of Petty, a leading noble from the Northeast of Scotland. The father was taken to the Tower of London, where he died in 1298. Andrew was taken to Chester Castle, but he escaped during the winter of 1296/97 and returned to his father's lands in the Black Isle, north of Inverness. There, at Avoch Castle he raised the banner of rebellion against England. He was joined by many Lords of the North and Northeast Scotland. An important ally was Euphemia Berkeley, Countess of Ross. Although her husband remained a prisoner in England she was a strong supporter of Scottish Independence and called on the nobles of Ross to arm themselves and join the rebellion.

This happened at the same time as the Grant brothers were released from their captivity and returned home. On hearing of the new rebellion they immediately agreed to break their parole and with their men they quickly journeyed to the Black Isle and joined with Andrew Moray.

Their first action was to ambush Sir William Fitz Warin, Constable of Urquhart Castle, on the northern shore of Loch Ness. He was returning to his Castle from Elgin, where he had attended a meeting of English supporting Lords. A few miles south of Inverness, Moray ambushed him. Although he escaped, most of his men were either killed or captured. He only got back to his Castle with three men. He then woke the next day to find Moray, John Grant, Robert Grant and Alexander Pilche (a magistrate of Inverness) and their men surrounding his fortress.

The Scots rebels did not have any siege equipment and decided to try and take the Castle by stealth. In the middle of the night John Grant and twelve of his men attempted to scale the castle walls, hoping to take the guards by surprise and open the gates to Moray and the men waiting outside. However, one of his men fell during the climb and the noise alerted the defenders, who were then able to repel the attack, but not before the Governor's son, Richard Fitz Warin, had been killed.

This initial failure did not stop Moray and he went on to raid and burn the lands of Sir Reginald Cheyne, the English supporting Scots Governor of Elgin. *"A very large body of rogues swept through the province of Moray towards the Spey, destroying the lands of Duffus, laid waste and captured the castle."*(21) Their campaign was an outstanding success and took many English held castles and towns across Moray and Northern Scotland. John Grant even returned to Urquhart Castle and successfully scaled the walls, took the castle and killed all the defenders. Next they attacked Aberdeen and burned several English ships which were moored in the harbour. By the end of the summer 1297 most of North and Northeast Scotland was in the hands of Andrew Moray and his small but determined army. Of the castles of the North, only Dundee remained in English hands and by September 1297 it was under siege by the Scots.

Meanwhile in the South the Scots were also having great success in their rebellion, under the command of William Wallace. *"In [1297] the famous William Wallace, the hammer of the English, the son of the noble knight [Malcolm Wallace], raised his head... When Wallace was a young knight, he killed the sheriff of Lanark, an Englishman who was dexterous and powerful in the use of arms, in the town of Lanark. From that time therefore there gathered to his side [like a swarm of bees] all those who were bitter in their outlook and oppressed by the burden of servitude under the intolerable rule of English domination, and he was made their leader."*(22)

Not much is known of the early life of William Wallace, but according to the Scots poet, Blind Harry, he was the second son of a small landowner named Sir Malcolm Wallace. He fell foul of the new English masters of Scotland early on, killing the son of the English Constable of Dundee, for which he was outlawed. His reputation quickly grew and he soon began a guerrilla war against the English in the Borders, Clydesdale and Ayrshire, killing them whenever he could.

The turning point in this small-scale insurrection came in May 1297. Wallace had secretly married a beautiful young lady, Marion Braidfoot, of Abington, Lanarkshire. One night he secretly visited her in Lanark. His presence became known to the English soldiers garrisoned there but after killing a number of them, Wallace escaped. The English Sheriff of Lanark, Sir William Hesselrig, furious at the villain's escape, promptly arrested Marion and executed her by cutting her throat.

"In a murderous fury of grief Wallace struck back at once. That very night he and his men infiltrated the town in ones and twos, then formed up for a surprise attack on the sheriff's residence. They burst into the castle, where Wallace slew Hesselrig in his bed; when Hesselrig's son rushed to his father's assistance Wallace killed him too, then he and his men went on a rampage of slaughter, cutting down every Englishmen in sight. William Wallace had 'lifted his head' with a vengeance."(23)

This started a widespread revolt all over Scotland. Wallace retired into the vastness of Ettrick forest in the Scottish Borders and it was here that he was joined by more and more men who were discontented with their new English masters. Wallace campaigned mainly in the South and Southwest of Scotland and gained victory after victory over the English and their Scottish born supporters.

King Edward I of England was busy preparing a military expedition into France and demanded that Wallace and Moray and other rebels be crushed by his two commanders in Scotland, the veteran Earl of Surrey and Hugh Cressingham, Treasurer of Scotland. He gave them powers to raise a large army from North England and march into Scotland, meet up with the garrison defending Stirling Castle and then to wipe out Wallace, Moray and his supporters. He then left for France thinking the Scots would be easily defeated.

On hearing of the English advance Wallace and Moray marched to Perth, where they met up and combined their forces. John and Robert Grant were by this time two of Moray's leading commanders. They then marched to Stirling and got there before the English. The Scottish Army was made up of 8,000-foot soldiers, but hardly any cavalry. There were virtually no great Scottish Lords with Wallace and Moray, only lesser gentry like the Grants and common townsmen and folk of the country. All were, however, Patriotic Scots.

The English army was made up of around 200 knights and mounted men at arms and 10,000-foot soldiers. Many were battle hardened experienced soldiers and they were confident of success. The Scots had not beat them in open battle for over a generation. A few Scottish nobles were with the English Army, including James the Steward and Malcolm, Earl of Lennox. On the evening before the battle, they volunteered to go and speak to Wallace and Moray to seek peaceful terms. They did so but were rebuffed. Two friars were then despatched to give offers of peace but again this was refused by Wallace: *"Tell your commander that we are not here to make peace but to do battle, to defend ourselves and liberate our kingdom. Let them come on, and we shall prove this in their very beards."*(24)

After hearing this the Earl of Surrey gave orders that the next morning, at dawn, the English infantry were to begin crossing the Stirling Bridge. **The Battle of Stirling Bridge** was fought on 11 September 1297. At dawn, as ordered, the English infantry started to cross the bridge but were eventually recalled because the elderly Earl of Surrey had not yet risen from his bed and the action was postponed awaiting the Commander. When Surrey eventually arrived, he viewed the lightly armed Scots awaiting him on the slopes of Abbey Craig, above the bridge, and became very confident of victory. The Scots in the force advised against marching across the bridge, arguing that because only two men could cross at the same time, it was death trap if a retreat was required. There was a ford a few miles upstream where the English cavalry could cross sixty abreast, and they should wait until this had been undertaken.

However, the overconfident Surrey rejected this and the slow process of getting 10,000 men across the bridge began. Meanwhile "on the north side of the river the Scots can scarcely have believed their luck. All they had to do was wait until a significant (but not too large) part of the English army had crossed onto the marshy meadowland on the north bank. At just the right moment a horn was sounded, and the massed ranks of Scottish spearmen surged down and along the causeway towards the bridge. The marshy ground hindered the deployment of the English cavalry, and neither the floundering horsemen nor their supporting infantry could withstand the onslaught. The end of the narrow bridge, quickly surrounded by Scottish pikemen, offered no escape for the packed mass of panicking troops, and the Scots had a field-day of slaughter. The Earl of Surrey could only watch helplessly as nearly half of his seasoned, powerfully-equipped host was cut to pieces or drowned in the deep waters of the Forth in the space of an hour."(25)

The English Commander, cutting his losses, ordered that the bridge be broken up and set on fire, lest the Scots cross it and annihilate the remainder of this army. "Among those who perished was Cressingham….. He had charged at the head of the vanguard, his mind no doubt filled with the dreams of that glory which the office of treasurer had denied him. Misguided, pompous, less than popular with his own army, he nevertheless met the sort of end which was more appropriate to such as Surrey. He was dragged down from his horse and died under the spears of the Scots infantry…… After the battle, the Scots, in a gruesome ceremony, flayed his obese body. Strips of his skin were sent throughout Scotland to proclaim the victory of Stirling. Other strips of skin were used to make saddle girths. Wallace himself had a belt made for his sword from what was left of Cressingham's skin."(26)

Overall, the English lost 100 Knights and up to 5,000-foot soldiers. Meanwhile, the Grants, when they were certain of victory, crossed over the ford on their mounts, and descended on the retreating English and plundered their English baggage train, capturing much of its great wealth.

Battle of Stirling Bridge. Victorian Depiction of the Battle

James Grant 1873.

The **Battle of Stirling Bridge** was the most significant victory of the Scots against the English for at least two centuries. It was done without any of the main Scottish noble families taking part. There was one major negative, Andrew Moray was mortally wounded in the battle and died soon after. Wallace's main confederate was lost, as a member of the Scots nobility, his continued support of Wallace may have helped to bring more of the Scottish nobility over to Wallace's side. Instead, his death left Wallace to rely on the support of minor lairds and the common people of Scotland. This was fine when he was successful. But one defeat would see his support dwindle.

John and Robert Grant were with their friend and commander Moray when he eventually died from his wounds a few days after the battle. Half the troops in the army gave their loyalty to Andrew Moray, but almost every one of them now swore loyalty to William Wallace. Many of the Grant men, however, now wanted to return north to their homeland, with the booty and riches they had gathered in their victories against the English and the Scots who had supported them. This was common among all Highlanders who were always unhappy about being away from their homes and family for too long. John let about half of them go home with his brother Robert, leaving him with about fifty men who were promised more riches in the coming battles with the English invaders.

Wallace immediately took the fight to the English and invaded their northern counties. John Grant was very agreeable to joining him on the expedition. They invaded Northumberland and Cumbria and pillaged everywhere, including Lanercost Priory, near Carlisle. Only bad winter weather, snowstorms and ice, brought their raid to an end but John Grant and his men returned with much wealth and many hostages to ransom. By Christmas 1297, the Grants went home, richer and wealthier for their support of Scottish Independence.

After these victories, Wallace was knighted, possibly by Sir Robert the Bruce, and then appointed Guardian of Scotland in March 1298. Meanwhile King Edward I had returned from his war in France and was determined to put down the rebellious Scots. He moved to York and there gathered a great army. He then marched north and crossed into Scotland on 3 July 1298 with his army of 1,500 mounted knights and men-at-arms, 12,000 battle hardened foot soldiers and a large contingent of Welsh and English archers. Wallace called on all his supporters to bring their men again to protect the Kingdom. On hearing the summons, John and Robert Grant again gathered their men and with about 150 clansmen quickly travelled south to join Wallace.

MAP 5. THE BATTLES OF STIRLING BRIDGE AND FALKIRK.

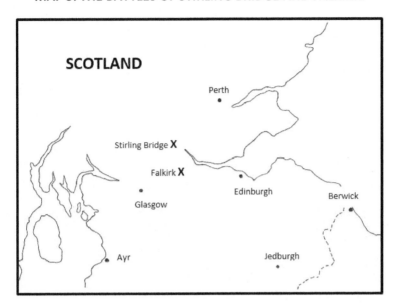

The Scots used a 'scorched earth policy', removing anything that could be eaten from Southern Scotland. Soon the English army was near to starvation and King Edward was about to order the retreat to England, when two Scots traitors, the Earl of Dunbar and the Earl of Angus, sent a messenger to the King advising that the Scottish army, under Wallace, was camped near Falkirk, only 20 miles away. The English King rejoiced at hearing this news and immediately mobilised his forces and marched towards Falkirk.

The Battle of Falkirk was fought on 22 July 1298. The Scots had a small cavalry force, commanded by John Coymn, younger brother of the Earl of Murray, but the majority of the army consistent of largely inexperienced foot soldiers. In addition, the Scots only had a small number of archers, especially compared to the large archer force with the English army. Wallace therefore organised his main force into four 'schiltons' of between 1,500 and 2,000 men each, which were " made up wholly of spearmen, standing shoulder to shoulder in deep ranks and facing towards the circumference of the circle, with their spears slanting outwards at an oblique angle. The hedgehog like appearance of schiltons would be frightening, as it was intended to be. The schilton could be switched from the defensive to the offensive, as Robert I was able to do at Bannockburn. The twelve-inch, iron-tipped spears of the infantry were a powerful deterrent to the cavalry and at Falkirk, as again at Bannockburn, inflicted severe injury on the horses themselves."(27)

On the morning of the battle, Wallace formed his troops in battle formation, protected by the Callendar Wood to his rear and in front by the Westquarter Burn. When the approaching English commanders saw the good defensible position which Wallace held, they advocated caution. However, the Earls of Norfolk, Hereford and Lincoln, who commanded the cavalry vanguard were impatient for victory and immediately assaulted the defensive schiltons. The Scots easily held off the mounted knights and men-at-arms of the English army and hundreds were killed on the steels points of their spears. Then treachery and disaster: the Scottish cavalry fled the battlefield. Some say this was pre-organised between the Scots traitors and King Edward. Whatever the reasons, it led to disaster. The cavalry was to be used against the English and Welsh archers if they appeared on the battlefield. Without the cavalry to chase them off, the Scots infantry, closely huddled together in their four schiltons, were an easy target.

It did not take King Edward long to realise this and he quickly ordered his mounted men to withdraw and brought up his archers. "The Scots cannot have been ignorant of what was to come. It is easy to imagine their despair as they stood impotent, to await the arrows. That they did not break speaks well for the discipline which Wallace had instilled in them. They died in large numbers. One English chronicler celebrated the slaughter: 'they fell like blossoms in an orchard when the fruit has ripened'. He goes on to relate that their 'bodies covered the ground as thickly as snow in the winter'. These images, while hardly original, convey the horror of the battle. When the archers and slingers had done their work, Edward sent the knights against the thinning, demoralised ranks of the schiltons."(28)

The fighting became a slaughter and eventually the remnants of the Scots army fled. The English cavalry pursued them and killed hundreds as they tried to escape. There are few contemporary accounts of the battle on the Scots side and we do not know how many Grants perished, but it extremely unlikely that the got away without a significant number of casualties. John and Robert Grant did escape, along with the wounded Wallace.

It was a total victory for the English, at least 2,000 Scots had been killed. Most of Wallace's commanders were also dead. The remaining Grants quickly headed back north and hid out with their kin. The renowned historian, Fiona Watson says:

"The problem has always been to explain the fact that Wallace could win a stunning victory at Stirling Bridge and then, less than a year later, lose so badly at

Falkirk. Personally, I think that Wallace was desperately unlucky. He was without his outstanding military commander, Sir Andrew Murray; and he was up against a new and devastatingly effective weapon – the long-range English longbow. Wallace took a gamble and lost; in 1314, Bruce would take a similar gamble and win. Sometimes you have to take the gamble – otherwise you can never win."(29)

King Edward then sacked a few towns and cities but then retired south to England via Carlisle, leaving English garrisons all over Scotland, who were to be supported by the Scots nobles who had sworn allegiance to him. The only castle which held out was Castle Urquhart which was commanded by Sir Alexander Forbes, with a garrison of his own clansmen and those of Grant. The English, therefore, settled down on the gentle slope that connected the Castle Rock with the adjacent Eagle's Height, resolved to starve the garrison into submission. Soon the garrison was starving and Forbes and his companions resolved to fight their way out or die in the attempt.

The drawbridge was lowered but the besiegers were surprised when one poorly dressed female came out, stating that she just happened to be in the castle at the beginning of the siege but as she was about to give birth, she had no choice but to leave the Castle. Her story was believed and she was allowed to pass. She then climbed to the top of the Eagle's Height where she watched the attempt of her husband, because she was no other than the wife of Sir Alexander Forbes, clad in beggars clothes to escape detection more easily.

The drawbridge was again lowered and the men of Forbes and Grant dashed across the drawbridge to confront the surprised English.

> "They fought together as brethren true,
>
> Like hardy men and bolde;
>
> Many a man to the ground they thrue,
>
> And many a harte made colde."(30)

But the Scots could not fight their way to freedom and over 100 men of Forbes and Grant were cut down to a man. Forbes' wife escaped to Ireland where she had a son, Alexander, who would eventually support Bruce when he grew to be a man. But he too died for a Bruce, King David II, at the Battle of Dupplin Moor in 1332.

After his defeat Wallace soon resigned as Guardian of Scotland. He did not give up, however, and continued a guerrilla warfare against the English with a hard core of loyal troops. At some point he also left Scotland for a while, seeking to gain support for the Scottish cause from both the King of France and the Pope.

Initially, the two most important nobles left in Scotland, John Coymn (the Red Coymn), Lord of Badenoch and Robert Bruce, Earl of Carrick were appointed joint Guardians of Scotland. These two men led the rival factions for the Scottish throne and after only a few months they fell out and resigned the Guardianship. The Coymn's were closely related to the former King John Balliol. Eventually Sir John de Soulis, of Liddesdale, was appointed Guardian of Scotland. He was seen as a neutral between the two factions, but in reality he supported the restoration of the exiled King Balliol and this led Earl Robert Bruce to seek peace with the English in January 1302. King Edward of England led another invasion force into Scotland in 1303, determined to crush the Scots. Some resistance was put up by a few Scottish nobles, most notably at the **Battle of Roslin Moor** in 1303, but generally the divided Scots crumbled completely against this new English army. Scotland eventually capitulated and its nobles surrendered in February 1304. The Grants had kept themselves to themselves and took no part in this final campaign.

Wallace on his way to Execution.

Copyright: Getty Images

38

Eventually, William Wallace was captured on 3rd August 1305 by the traitor, Sir John Menteith, who had been a close friend of his and had fought alongside him on many occasions. He lured Wallace to Glasgow on the pretence of organising a meeting with Sir Robert Bruce. At Robroyston, near Glasgow, he was overpowered by Menteith's men and captured. He was immediately handed over to the English and marched behind a pony all the way to London. There he was put on trial as a traitor to the English King. In his defence Wallace proudly proclaimed that he had never sworn fealty to King Edward, and never would he. This mattered not and he was found guilty and immediately executed by being hanged, drawn and quartered.

CHAPTER 3. THE SECOND WAR OF SCOTTISH INDEPENDENCE – BRUCE.

After the Scottish defeat at Falkirk, the Grants kept themselves out of the politics of the nation for several years, concentrating on holding onto their lands in North. Robert the Bruce began his rebellion against King Edward of England in February 1306. He met up with his arch Scottish rival, John Coymn, 3rd Earl of Buchan, in Greyfrairs Church, Dumfries. The meeting was supposed to heal the differences between the two Scottish factions and allow them to unite to face the English. However, here they argued and at some point Bruce drew his dagger and killed Coymn. This alienated half of Scotland against him as Coymn was either related to or supported by a great many of the Scottish Lords. Despite the sacrilege of killing in sacred ground, the Scottish Church supported Bruce. This was a brave decision by the Scottish Church as the Pope immediately excommunicated Robert Bruce for the killing of a nobleman in a church.

After the death of Coymn, Bruce rode immediately to Scone Palace, Perthshire, where he was inaugurated as King of Scots on 25 March 1306. At this time only a small number of Scottish nobles supported him.

Civil war now broke out in Scotland with the Coymns, supported by their English masters, against the small number of Bruce supporters. The Grants had been supporters of the Coymns at the beginning of Bruce's campaign. Initially, they stayed out of the conflict, not supporting any side, happy to remain in their Highland estates. King Edward gave his Lieutenant, the Earl of Pembroke, the power to 'burn, slay and raise dragon'. This meant that the normal rules of chivalry were suspended and any Scots Knights captured would be treated as traitors and executed, rather than held for ransom.

King Robert initially moved his small army to the south of Scotland to quash the opposition to his rule in Ayrshire and Galloway. After this he moved his forces north in an attempt to capture the town of Perth (known then as Saint John's Town of Perth) with an army of about 4,500 men. The Earl of Pembroke was in Perth with his forces, which although smaller than Bruce's, was experienced and well defended behind the walls of the town. Bruce had "neither the numbers nor the siege engines to invest the town so, resorting to an old chivalric tradition, he rode to the city gates and challenged Pembroke either to bring out his men to fight or to surrender the town. Pembroke replied that the day was too far advanced for combat but on the following morning he would accept his challenge."(31)

At this early period in his reign Bruce was naïve. He knew Pembroke personally from his time at the English Court and, regarding him as a man of honour, he accepted to meet in battle the next day. Pembroke was under immense pressure from King Edward to put this rebellion down quickly and therefore ditched any chivalric pretensions. Bruce's army had retired six miles away to Methven Wood, south of the River Almond. In his naivety he did not even set out sentries around his perimeter.

As the Scottish Army was resting, kindling fires or cooking their evening meals, the English Army attacked, taking them completely by surprise. Bruce ended up in a hand-to-hand fight with the Earl of Pembroke and slew his horse. In the fight, however, the King was unhorsed himself and was seized by the English knight, Sir Phillip Mowbray, who shouted, 'help, help, I have the new-made King'. The King knocked him down and tried to rally his men, but it was too late, the ambush had taken his army totally unawares and they were completely routed.

Bruce was unhorsed twice more and would have been killed or captured had not a small group of knights formed a circle around him and broke through the English line to escape.

It was total defeat for Bruce's fledgling rebellion against English rule. The King's main force had been destroyed. Many of his most devoted followers were either killed or captured. No mercy was shown and all who were captured were executed as traitors. The captured Scottish nobles were immediately beheaded and their bodies dismembered and distributed to all parts of Scotland as a lesson to others not to rebel against English rule.

Methven was a devastating defeat for the cause of Bruce. His main force had been destroyed and he and his remaining men were fugitives. Bruce, fled to the mountains of Athol and hid out there. He had about five hundred men left and decided to head west to reach the Western Isles where he still had friends, in the form of the MacDonalds of Islay.

Unfortunately, to get there he had to travel through the lands of MacDougall, Lord of Lorne, a supporter of King Edward, and who was the son-in-law of the murdered John Coymn. He had sworn revenge on Bruce and all his supporters. Near Tyndrum, Argyllshire, MacDougall barred the pass which Bruce would have to come through and waited for Bruce and his small force to appear. In the narrow pass, Bruce and his mounted knights could not manoeuvre and it was here that MacDougall attacked. With their broadswords and their Lochaber axes they charged down the hillside from both sides and in the melee many were killed.

Bruce fought a rear-guard action to allow the women, which included the Queen, the Countess of Buchan, Bruce's daughter and two sisters, time to escape. Eventually they retreated to safety and the MacDougalls, who had suffered significant casualties themselves, decided to call off their attack.

Fearful for his womenfolk, Bruce gave them his remaining horses and sent them north, hoping they could escape to Norway. With them he sent his brother Nigel Bruce. They were later captured and Nigel was hanged, drawn and quartered at Berwick and the Bruce women were put in cages and suspended from the battlements of Castles around the country. They would stay imprisoned for many years.

After escaping from the MacDougalls, Bruce eventually made his way to Kintyre and to Dunaverty Castle, the home of Angus MacDonald of the Isles, now Chief of Clan MacDonald. Angus was able to warn Bruce that a large English force was on its way to besiege the castle. So, after three days' rest, Bruce and his remaining supporters, slipped away by boat, and headed north where he visited his relative, Christina of the Isles, Chief of Clan Ruaidhri (MacDonald's of Clan Ranald), in her island fortress of Castle Tioram, off the mainland coast. She was instrumental in getting the clans of the Islands and Western Highlands to support Bruce. After the MacDonalds and MacLeods and other Clan Chiefs agreed to bring men the following spring, Bruce left to spend the winter at Rathlin Island, just off the coast of Northern Ireland.

By early 1307 Bruce was ready to renew his campaign and he decided to start in his own homeland of Ayrshire and Galloway. The details of this campaign are not required as the Grants took no part in this campaign but Bruce, his brother Edward and his able Lieutenant James Douglas first took Brodick Castle in Arran, and then they attacked and defeated the English forces who had occupied his old home of Turnberry Castle, although they were unable to take the castle itself.

At the same time, he sent two of his brothers, Thomas and Alexander, with several hundred men to land in Galloway. Here they were ambushed by the McDowalls and after a bitter battle Thomas and Alexander were severely wounded and captured. They were taken directly to Carlisle where, under the direct order of King Edward, they were found guilty of treason and then taken directly to the Gallows Hill where, like their brother Nigel, they were hanged drawn and quartered. Their dismembered heads were placed on spikes at the main entrance to Carlisle. Now three of the four brothers had been executed by the English.

When Bruce heard of this he began to have second thoughts and brought his commanders together to consult on whether they should continue or retreat. His remaining brother, Edward Bruce, was the first to view his opinion, saying, '*Sire I have nothing more to lose, nothing will make me about turn, here we either win or die*'.

The leaders of the rebellion reviewed their war strategy. Having few knights, little money and no heavy cavalry, they concluded the only way to defeat the English invaders was not in open battle but guerrilla warfare, concentrating on ambush, sudden raids, scorched earth and the dismantling of castles and towers. Bruce then defeated a joint English and MacDougall force at the **Battle of Glen Trool**, Galloway.

This was a small victory with massive consequences. It totally transformed the Scottish rebellion. News spread within both Scotland and England that a small band of Scottish foot soldiers had defeated a much larger force of experienced English knights. The invincibility of the English Knights had been severely dented and slowly but surely more and more Scottish nobles, with their men, began to join Bruce's force.

The Glen Trool Monument to Robert The Bruce.

Copyright: Eileen Sinclair 2021.

Bruce now felt strong enough to come out of the hills and he marched his growing force to Galston, Ayrshire, which he made his headquarters. A force of one thousand Englishmen set off to attack him from Lanark but was utterly defeated by a force under James Douglas. This brought more recruits to Bruce's cause. Percy was ordered by King Edward to attack Bruce and he marched his troops out of Ayr and headed for Galston in May 1307.

Bruce scouted the area around Galston to find ground where his largely foot army could get an advantage over the predominantly mounted English army. He found Loudon Hill. At the bottom of this volcanic crag the ground was wet and marshy and did not suit a mounted force.

Here he dug ditches and lined them with stakes to nullify the charge of the English Cavalry. The far superior English force drew up immediately opposite the Scots and charged. As the enemy approached quickly on their horses the Scots placed their pikes in the ground and pointed them towards the oncoming English. Just as the thunderous English charge was about to hit the Scots they met the trenches of the defenders and collapsed into them. Knights and horses were skewered on the stakes or thrown from their mounts. The Scots then charged and utterly destroyed the whole English force. It was a massive victory for Bruce.

MAP 6. Main Battles of Robert The Bruce.

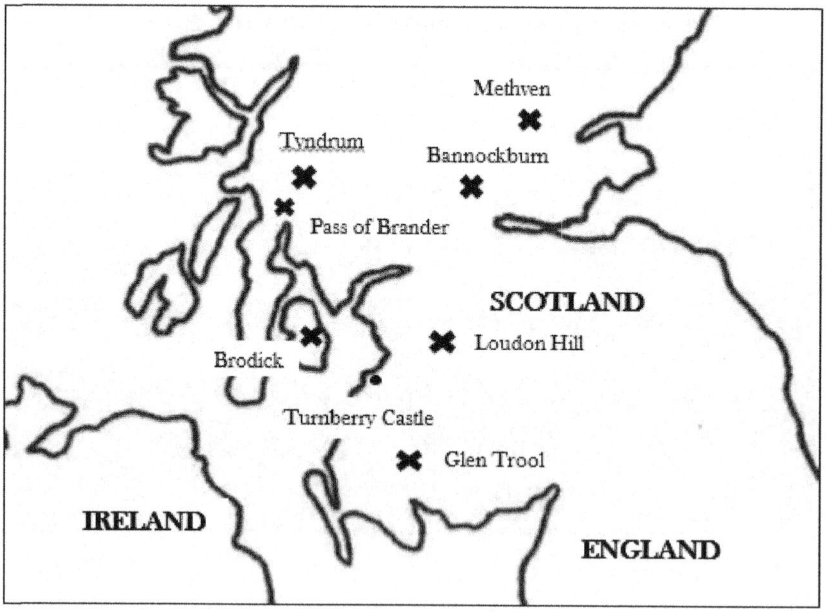

44

It was this victory which eventually persuaded John and Robert Grant to support the new King of Scots and they rode south to give him their oath of loyalty. Previous to this they had been allies of the Coymn's but the prospect of a successful rebellion against English rule under Bruce persuaded the Grants to change their allegiance.

After this the aged warrior, King Edward I of England, decided he must take up the fight against Bruce in person. Lifting himself off his sick bed he travelled to Carlisle where he assembled a great army, determined to destroy the Scots once and for all. Luckily for Scotland his illness was terminal and he died before he could bring his vengeance to the Scots.

Now Bruce had the freedom to tackle the Scottish nobles who opposed him. His main objective was to destroy the power of his rivals, the Coymns, before the new King of England, Edward II, could turn his attention to Scotland. His forces were still small but were now experienced in the art of total war.

The centre of the power of the Coymns was Aberdeenshire, Moray and Inverness. With a force of seven hundred men, Bruce marched north to confront them. At some point on the march north they were joined by the Grants. The Earl of Buchan gathered his forces to meet the threat of Bruce.

Bruce and his force first headed up the west coast and neutralised the forces of John MacDougall, Lord of Lorne. Then he headed east taking Inverness Castle and burning Nairn. He made a truce with the Earl of Ross and then headed into Coymn lands. During the campaign the Grants attacked Freuchie Castle and took it from the Coymns. "A rather macabre relic, in the form of the skull of one of the Coymns, was preserved and is still held and closely guarded today."(32) There is a legend/curse which goes along with the skull, that if the relic passes out of the possession of the Grants, then the family would lose all its property in Strathspey. There is also another legend regarding how the skull came into the possession of the Grants, "... that a Comyn was in love with one of the Grant ladies and abducted her. The couple were chased by four Grants; the Comyn was killed and his head brought back with the Grant lady."(33) However when the skull came into their possession it was at this time that the Grants first held Freuchie Castle as governors for King Robert Bruce.

It is said that the Grants were assisted by Clan MacGregor in the taking of Freuchie Castle. This again highlights the special relationship between the Grants and Clan MacGregor.

Coymn, Earl of Buchan, was not defeated yet and mustered his own troops. By this time, it was the dead of winter and the ground of Northeast Scotland was covered in snow. The two forces met at the **Battle of Inverurie** and for three days the two forces fought a running battle. The Grants fought hard for their King and eventually the Earl of Buchan had to withdraw to seek reinforcements. Bruce made Inverurie his base.

Bruce rested his force but did not receive any additional men. By January 1308, the Earl of Buchan had received both Scottish and English reinforcements and had a force numbering over one thousand men. Bruce's force now numbered only about six hundred men. There were only about fifty Grants in this force under John and Robert Grant, but most of these were cavalry and formed a large part of the Kings mounted force.

But Bruce had been taken seriously ill by this time and was confined to his bed. The Coymn force marched on Inverurie. Initially the Coymn attack was successful and it looked like the forces of Bruce would be destroyed. The King, however, rose from his sickbed and, putting on his armour, mounted his horse and rode to rally his men. Robert Grant, along with Edward Bruce and other nobles followed him and charged the enemy who were on the brink of victory.

In response to this charge the Coymn cavalry began to back up. When the foot soldiers and archers saw this they turned and fled. Then the cavalry, seeing the foot soldiers fleeing, also panicked and fled the field of battle, not stopping until they had reached the English held Castle of Fyvie, some twelve miles to the north.

The whole of Buchan now lay wide open to Bruce and his supporters. He meant to ensure that the Coymns could never again threaten his throne and he gave the order to his men to lay waste to Buchan and kill at will. It was genocide and the remaining Grants took a full part in it, killing Coymn men, burning farms and slaughtering or stealing any livestock found. The Grants took such booty home with them that it was said the whole clan feasted each night for a year. The Earl of Buchan fled to England in exile and was eventually killed at the Battle of Bannockburn in 1314 fighting for the English.

This **'Harrowing of Buchan'** is the reason why there are hardly any Coymn surnames left in Scotland today. It took two generations for the land to recover and that was only when the area was colonised by lowlanders and clansmen loyal to Bruce, such as the Grants. Indeed, Robert Grant led a force which besieged and took the Coymn Roy Castle, near the present day village of Nethy Bridge. This castle and its estate would eventually come into the possession of the Grants in 1560.

By mid-summer 1308 Bruce was now ready to march west and take on the might of Clan MacDougall. He sent for James Douglas and his men who had been fighting in the Scottish borders with great success. He was also joined by another large contingent of Grants, under John Grant. Robert Grant stayed in the north east to carry on the destruction of any remaining Coymn strongholds.

The army travelled to Argyll and Bruce sent out scouts to find out where the MacDougall army was waiting for them. The scouts reported that a force of MacDougall's was holding the **Pass of Brander**, which was a narrow path only a few metres wide bordered by the magnificent mountain of Ben Cruachan to the north, and by a sheer cliff which dropped into Loch Awe to the south.

The main MacDougall army of over two thousand men were hidden in the mountainside above the Pass while John of Lorne remained in one of his galleys on Loch Awe.

The Pass of Brander

Copyright: Eileen Sinclair 2021.

The King sent James Douglas with a body of archers above the MacDougalls holding the path. Bruce then attacked, sending his armoured knights to attack in front and his Highlanders to flank them along the hillside. John Grant and his men were in the vanguard of the assault. As the knights reached the poorly armoured MacDougalls,

Douglas let his archers rein arrows down on them. The MacDougalls put up a brave fight but one by one they were cut down. The final straw came when the men with Douglas, having run out of arrows, drew their swords and charged the MacDougalls from the other direction. The enemy broke and ran.

The Kings force quickly pursued the enemy, killing any stragglers they encountered. They caught up with the MacDougalls trying to destroy the last bridge over the River Awe. They quickly dispatched the remaining MacDougalls and captured the bridge which allowed the rest of Bruce's army to easily enter Argyll, the heartland of the Lord of Lorne. John MacDougall fled with his fleet all the way to England, where he submitted to King Edward II. Bruce and his supporters were now in control of the West Highlands. John Grant returned north with much booty and the thanks of a grateful King.

The Earl of Ross, the last major noble who held out against Bruce, now submitted and swore allegiance. The King then sent his brother Edward to Galloway in the very southwest of Scotland where Dugald MacDowall and his clansmen had joined forces with an English force under Sir Ingram de Umfraville and Aymer St. John. Edward Bruce met, fought and destroyed this force which was the last major army in Scotland fighting against the King.

Now the King and his men could concentrate on clearing the Kingdom of the English garrisons manning the many Castles and Towers throughout the Country. On 16 March 1309, at St. Andrews, King Robert the Bruce held the first free parliament in Scotland for eighteen years. Most of the nobility loyal to Bruce were in attendance, including John and Robert Grant.

For the next three years Bruce consolidated this power and by 1312 his forces were in control of the majority of mainland Scotland, apart from four major castles which were still under the control of English garrisons, namely Perth, Stirling, Edinburgh and Dunbar. His policy was to retake these strongholds and then to dismantle them completely so they could never again be held by his enemies and dominate the lands around them.

By 1313, only Stirling Castle still held an English garrison. The King gave his brother, Edward Bruce, the task of besieging the Castle and starving it out. Edward Bruce was an aggressive and impatient man who liked battle better than a siege. He entered into an agreement with the English commander of the Castle, that if an English relief force had not arrived at Stirling by mid-summer 1314 (24th June) he would surrender the Castle. This made the siege unnecessary.

The King was furious with his brother but could not disown the agreement he had reached. Barbour puts the words of the King on hearing the news as: *"That was unwisely done indeed. Never have I heard so long a warning given to so mighty a king as the King of England, Ireland, Wales and Aquitaine, with all under his seineury, and a great part of Scotland, and his is so provided with treasure that he can have plenty of paid soldiers. We are so few against so many. God may deal us our destiny right well but we are set in jeopardy to lose or win all in one throw."*(34)

Edward II was determined to meet this deadline and, further, once and for all, destroy the rebellious Scots. He gathered the most powerful army ever assembled against the Scots and headed north to Stirling. This led to the most famous battle in Scotland's history, **Bannockburn**.

The odds were greatly in favour of the English. Their manpower was five times that of the Scots. In addition, apart from the northern counties of England (which the Scots had periodically raided over the last few years) the country had been untouched by war and was one of the most prosperous in Europe. Ireland and Wales were at peace and the English, for once, were on friendly terms with France. Whereas Scotland had far fewer men and had been ravaged by eighteen years of war, including nine English invasions.

All the great nobles of England joined their King for, what they thought, would be the final defeat of the Scots. "Also serving in his army were Scotsmen who still opposed Bruce, among them John Comyn, son of the murdered Red Comyn; Sir Ingram de Umfraville, one-time Scottish Guardian, his brother, the Earl of Angus, and a host of knights from France, Brittany, Poitou, Guyenne and Germany."(35) In addition the remnants of the MacDougalls of Lorne also joined the English invasion army. The English army consisted of 2,500 heavy cavalry, 3,000 Welsh archers and 15,000-foot soldiers: well over 20,000 men in total.

In April 1314 Bruce made Torwood, five miles north of Falkirk, his headquarters and called on his supporters to join him in defence of the nation. John and Robert Grant called their vassals together and over 200 Grants and allies journeyed south to join the King. They reached Torwood in late April 1314. The Grants were not one of the major clans at this time but their contingent showed their loyalty to the King and the campaign for an independent Scotland.

King Robert grouped his men in four divisions led by Thomas Randolph, Earl of Moray, his brother Edward Bruce, now Earl of Carrick and James Douglas. "The fourth division had the double strength of 2,000 and was commanded by the King himself. Here, under his banner were gathered the ... Highlanders from a score of different clans, muting their feuds beneath his chastening eye and in the face of the common enemy."(36) The Grants joined the Division led by Thomas Randolph, Earl of Moray. Finally, the Scots army was supplemented by five hundred light cavalry under the Marishal Sir Robert Keith and a small number of archers. The total army amounted to less than 6,000 men.

Bruce knew he could not fight the powerful English cavalry with his own horse, as they had neither the numbers nor the power of their English counterparts. He based his strategy on his foot soldiers forming into 'schiltons' (a hedgehog of spears). However, he realised that the schiltons must not be static and defensive, but must be mobile and able to move to the offensive quickly. This was paramount as most of his troops were Highlanders, accustomed to wild charges rather than keeping defensive lines. They trained all through May and early June, learning how to move their 'hedgehogs' in an offensive manner.

The English King was aloof and distant from all but his highest nobles. King Robert, on the other hand, made sure he met all his men and this relationship helped to strengthen the resolve of his army to meet and defeat the invader. Bruce could even speak fluent Gaelic and this allowed him to speak to the common highlanders and helped earn their respect.

While the English marched into Scotland from Berwick, Bruce took time to choose a battlefield to suit his forces: after careful consideration he chose Bannockburn, near Stirling Castle. There he positioned his army on 23 June 1314

The three divisions of Randolph, Edward Bruce and James Douglas lined up to face the English advance with the King's own division behind, held as a reserve. Here the men of Grant must have been in a prominent position when the English army of twenty thousand men marched up to the field of battle around mid-day.

King Edward immediately sent his vanguard of over 1,000 mounted knights to advance towards the Scots position and either force them to retreat or to attack them in one of their famous heavy cavalry charges. One of the first Knights to arrive with the English vanguard was Sir Henry de Bohun, clad in full armour and lance riding a powerful war horse. He spied the King of Scots parading before his troops on a small grey pony with only an axe in his hand and a golden circlet around his helmet. Without waiting, De Bohun aimed his lance and charged at the King, whereupon he was slain by one powerful blow from the war axe of Bruce to the rapturous applause of the watching Scots Army. This put fear into the ordinary English soldiers.

Bruce Addressing His Men At Bannockburn.

Woodcut by Edmund Blair Leighton, c1909.

Meanwhile 600 knights under Sir Robert Clifford and Sir Henry Beaumont then attacked the Scots from a hidden position on their flank. Bruce immediately sent the Division of Randolph to stop their advance. Beaumont saw the Scots coming towards him and did nothing to stop them initially, thinking that he would be able to surround Randolph's schiltron and destroy it. When the Scots had advanced sufficiently the English did surround them on all sides but as they were not supported by archers, they could not break the hedge of Scottish spearmen. All the Grants were in this Scots force and for a while it looked as if they might be destroyed. The fight went on for some time but the English could not break through the long spears of the Scots to attack them properly. Meanwhile the Scots were taking down any English knight who got close to their ranks. John Grant, one of the few Scots dressed in full armour, stood at the front of his men and took down 6 English Knights with his own sword.

Eventually Randolph was able to split the English force and to save his men and the English were forced to retire. When the enemy had fled, Randolph's men sat on the ground and took of their helmets to fan themselves, for they were weary and soaked in sweat, and after a little while they followed their commander to Bruce's headquarters, and there the men of the other Divisions crowded round them with their congratulations. John Grant in particular was singled out for his courage and bravery. He had little time to rest.

The next day the battle proper was fought to its bloody conclusion. The Grants were at the front of the Earl of Moray's Division and fought on foot. The more prosperous wore light armour, steel helmets, steel gloves and either back & breast pieces or padded leather jackets. The poorer soldiers wore no armour at all. They were armed with twelve-foot-long spears with swords and axes.

The English, outnumbering the Scots at least four to one, had positioned themselves on the assumption that the Scots would remain behind their defensive field position to receive the English cavalry attack. Bruce, however, made the dangerous decision to take the offensive as the English cavalry was enclosed on three sides by the Bannockburn, the Pelstream and the Scots Army. The English Knights never expected to be attacked by such an outnumbered force of predominantly foot soldiers. The three Divisions of Edward Bruce, Thomas Randolph and James Douglas moved off with the King's own Division held in reserve. The English had not learned their mistake from the day before and had their heavy cavalry at the front ready to charge the Scots with their vast infantry behind. The Scots were able to pen the English cavalry in so narrow an area that they were no better than a seething mass of men and horses, effectively blocking any access for the infantry behind them to take part in the battle. The English archers at the rear could not fire for fear of hitting their own knights.

Edward Bruce's Division was the first to attack, quickly followed by those commanded by James Douglas and Thomas Randolph. The Grants fought with Randolph. When the battle was at its highest and the outcome still unknown, the King's own division reinforced the Scots frontline. Chiefly comprised of Highlanders, the King's Division roared their clan battle cries and surged into the fray in one of their famous highland charges.

The English infantry and Welsh archers could not break through the ranks of their own knights to take part in the battle and the knights, hemmed in on all sides, could not manoeuvre their own horses. The result was complete disaster for Edward II and his troops who were killed in their thousands, the rest being routed and chased all the way back into the heart of England.

MAP 7. THE BATTLE OF BANNOCKBURN.

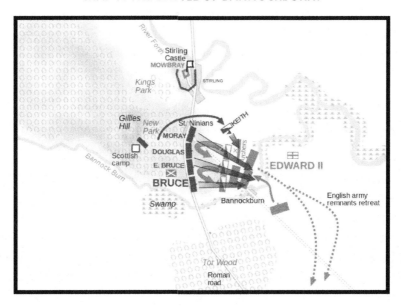

Copyright: Andrei nacu.

Edward II was forcibly removed from the battle by some of his loyal nobles and with a bodyguard of five hundred knights, sped south to safety. Although the battle was won, Bruce held back from ordering his army to chase the fleeing English as he was still wary of a counterattack from Stirling Castle. But he did allow his most trusted fighter, James Douglas, to take sixty horsemen and harry the English King during his escape south.

On their chase of the English King, they overtook and killed hundreds of fleeing English. They eventually caught up with the English King just beyond Linlithgow but even for James Douglas, sixty men against five hundred seasoned English knights was too much to take on. Instead, he shadowed them during their hurried retreat. If any Englishman fell behind he was taken or killed and they were so afraid to fall behind that they undertook their toilet whilst still on the saddle.

The English King and his guard eventually reached Dunbar Castle and they hurriedly jumped off their horses and rushed through the gates of the castle to safety leaving their horses behind. Douglas gathered all the horses and took them back to Robert the Bruce. Edward II eventually escaped by boat to Berwick and then home to London.

Meanwhile Stirling Castle surrendered to the Scots. So many English lords and nobles were captured that the Scots grew rich on the ransoms they received. John and Robert Grant and their men captured at least twenty English nobles or knights and received great wealth for their ransom. More importantly Bruce was able to obtain the release of his women folk held captive in England for all those years since 1306. The whole English baggage train, worth £200,000, was captured. Scotland was eventually cleared of its English oppressors. Although a great victory for the Scots, many of them were slain at Bannockburn, including a number of Grants, at least one being a close kinsmen of John and Robert Grant.

Bruce thought that the English King would agree to peace after this, but Edward II was so ashamed of his defeat, and so conditioned by his late father to hate the Scots that he refused to do so. Bruce therefore decided to mount attacks into Northern England to force the English Monarch to come to the negotiating table. In August 1314, under the leadership of Edward Bruce and James Douglas, the Scots mounted a large raid into Northumberland, County Durham and into Yorkshire, as far as Richmond, burning and pillaging wherever they went. John Grant sent a large contingent of Grants to take part in this expedition. They then returned up the west coast, raiding the County of Cumberland, burning Brough, Appleby and Kirkwold on their way home.

Then in December 1314 Bruce himself led a raid along the Tyne Valley, occupying and seeking tribute from the towns of Haltwhistle, Hexham and Corbridge, even getting them to acclaim him as their liege lord. In early 1315 James Douglas and Thomas Randolph, Earl of Moray, led a third raid into England reaching as far as Hartlepool which they burned. The Grants took part in all these raids.

Meanwhile still in 1315, King Robert and his brother Edward Bruce, hatched a plan to create a second front against the English which would drain their enemy of much needed men, materials and finance: they would invade Ireland and Edward Bruce would be its new High King. There was some legitimacy in this attempt: the Bruce family were descended from the High Kings of Ireland. The English had conquered much of the country but many of the remaining Irish sub-kings agreed to support Edward as High King if the Scots would help free them from the English. The main aim of the Bruce brothers was to create a Celtic Coalition against the English, first by taking Ireland and then by helping the Welsh to regain their freedom. There is no evidence that the Grants took part in this campaign but as seasoned warriors and strong supporters of Bruce it is likely that some members of the clan accompanied Edward Bruce to Ireland

After initial success the Irish expedition was embroiled in the internal conflicts of the opposing Irish Chieftains and it ultimately led to the defeat and death of Edward Bruce at the **Battle of Dundalk.**

Edward Bruce was a great warrior, but on occasion a very bad General. This was one of those occasions. He arranged his army into three columns but had briefed them badly and none were able to keep in contact with each other. Edward was in command of the third column. The English fought and defeated the first two columns without them being able to aid each other. When the remnants of these forces came running back to Edward's rear guard to report the destruction of two thirds of his army, his commanders urged him to retreat. But Edward would not hear of it, even though another Scots force of 1,500 men was only a few hours behind and would have aided the Scots numbers greatly. Then his Irish allies advised that they would not fight until reinforced by the other Scots force. Edward refused to listen to common sense. Headstrong as ever, he flew into a rage and swore that no man, while he lived, should ever say that an enemy had made him give way.

He then armed himself and the remaining Scots prepared for battle. The Scots were overwhelmingly outnumbered and were quickly overpowered. Edward Bruce was slain very early in the fight and at this his men lost heart. The remaining Scots fled to their Irish allies and the survivors eventually made it back to Scotland in small numbers.

"The death of Edward Bruce ended the attempt by the Scots to establish a sister regime in Ireland. But their invasion had to a large extent achieved the objective of Bruce's strategy. The authority of the English government had been shattered. Throughout the remainder of the Middle Ages it shrunk within the confines of the Pale [Dublin]. The greater part of the island reverted to its customary chaos of feuding kinglets. Never again could it be used by the English as a base from which to mount an attack on the western seaboard of Scotland."(37)

In 1316, John Grant was rewarded by King Robert Bruce who made him the Lord of the Inverallen estate which he had acquired some years previously. The Inverallen estate lies in Strathspey and this was the first estate in this area which belonged to the Grants. These lands had been the territory of the De Moravias family in the 13th century and then granted to the Church. They were then granted to a noble named Augustine. In 1316 John of Inverallen, son to Gilbert, brother of Augustine, disposed the lands to John Grant, Lord of Stratherrick.

King Robert the Bruce.

What Edward II of England could not win by war he tried to gain by politics. In 1320 he persuaded Pope John (a Frenchman from English held French territories) to renew the Bull of Excommunication on Bruce for the killing of Comyn in a church. To counter this deed an Assembly of Lords Temporal and Spiritual met at Arbroath Abbey and replied to the Pope with a plea for liberty unparalleled in its intensity for freedom until the American War of Independence. It is known as the '**Declaration of Arbroath'**.

The Declaration emphasised the independence of Scotland as a Celtic Nation under God and King and asked the Pope to intervene in Scotland's favour. One section of it reads, *"So long as a hundred of us remain alive, we will never in any degree be subjected to the English"*.(38) The Declaration was signed by 8 Earls and 31 Barons. The Grants were still not great lords of the realm at this time and therefore were not judged important enough to sign the document. It was, however, signed on their behalf by their Earl, Thomas Randolph, Earl of Moray.

The spirit and language of the Declaration persuaded the Pope to support the Scots and he advised the English King to make peace. Eventually Edward II was deposed and his son, Edward III was crowned King of England in 1327. He was a much shrewder and more intelligent Monarch. Having many troubles with his own nobles and those of his French territories he eventually agreed to peace which was acknowledged by the Treaty of Northampton in 1328. This renounced all English claims of sovereignty over Scotland. The Scots had finally won their right to independence and the Black Rood was restored to Scotland but not the fake Stone of Destiny. Bruce knew it was a fake and did not even ask for it back.

At this time John, Chief of Grant was still having problems with those of Clan Coymn who had not been forfeited or killed in King Robert's retribution on them years before. Remnants of the Coymns remained and they were defiant to the power of the Grants. John Grant wanted to end the disagreements with this Clan and thought of a way to get them into his debt. He got his father-in-law, the Chief of MacLean, to send his men to make a raid against the Coymns and drive away their cattle. The deed was done and the Coymns approached the Laird of Grant for help in recovering their cattle. They agreed to acknowledge the Laird of Grant in his possessions if he would help to recover their cattle. John Grant readily agreed and gathering his men set off after the MacLeans.

Unfortunately, one of the MacLean raiders did not know of the agreement between the Chief of MacLean and the Chief of Grant. As arranged, John Grant approached the raiders fast on his horse with his men following behind. The ignorant MacLean warrior, thinking that the Grants were attacking, took out his bow and arrow and fired at John Grant, wounding him in the ankle. The wound did not heal and John Grant bled to death a few days later. The Coymns, however, got their cattle back but Maclean was furious at the death of his son-in-law by one of his own men. The poor man was arrested and hanged from the nearest tree.

John was succeeded by his eldest son **Patrick Grant 6th Chief of Clan Grant.**

Unfortunately, King Robert Bruce did not get much time to enjoy his peace. His wife, Queen Elizabeth died in 1327. In October 1328 the Pope had eventually lifted his excommunication of the King and, indeed, the whole Scottish Nation. But the King was gravely ill by this time and knew he was dying and knowing this he undertook a pilgrimage to the shrine of St. Ninian in Galloway. St. Ninian was the first missionary to bring Christianity to Scotland in the fifth century and his name was linked in Bruce's memory with the first victorious clash at Bannockburn hard by St. Ninian's Kirk.

Although the King eventually made it back to his Royal Palace at Cardross on the north shore of the Clyde Estuary in June 1329, he died three days later on 7 June 1329, a little short of his 55th birthday. His heart was removed from his body, enclosed within a casket, and presented to Sir James Douglas, who had agreed to take it on a pilgrimage to the Holy Land. His body was taken to Dunfermline Abbey where he was buried next to his wife. Scotland's greatest King was eventually dead.

It was unfortunate for Scotland that he had chosen his greatest warrior to leave the country and take his heart on Crusade. Douglas would soon be sorely missed by his nation.

A particular problem with Scotland was that it was continually left with child Kings who had no real power. Bruce left his five-year-old son, King David II, as the new King of Scotland and with Randolph and Douglas as Regents. If these two men could have lasted the country may have been strong, but within a few years both old warriors and loyal supporters of Bruce were dead and the young David Bruce had to rely on men of lesser stature to support him.

The Bruce Monument at Bannockburn.

Castle Grant. The original castle was a small circular tower fort site on a small hill to the north of the original castle. It had initially belonged to the Comyns.

The oldest part of the existing castle was built in the 14th century. It was originally called Ballachastell, which means 'Castle of the Pass'. It was then renamed Castle Freuchie or 'Castle of the Heather'. Later it was renamed Castle Grant.

Babetts Tower is located in the oldest part of the castle and "is so called because of a tale that in the tapestry room at the top of the tower there was a hidden door leading into the 'blackness' into which a Barbara Grant – daughter of one of the chiefs- was thrust until she obeyed her father's wishes. It is a fact that there was a Barbara Grant who did not wish to marry the man her father proposed for her. However, no skeleton was found when the cupboard was opened in 1880, only hidden muskets, the racks for which could be seen until recently, under the linen shelves."(39) The fact that no human remains were found suggests that her father eventually let Barbara out of her prison, although she still gave her name to the tower. However, others claim that her ghost still haunts the Tower and her small apparition is said to be more sad than terrifying, indicating that she died from a broken heart.

Castle Grant from an 18th century engraving.

"Formerly, the castle was built to face the south, and the workmanship on that side is traceable to the fifteenth century, but at a later period, in the time of Sir Ludovick Grant, the principal face was made to front the north, and wings were then built out to the south. Among the internal features of the castle may be mentioned the magnificent dining hall, forty-seven feet in length, twenty-seven in breadth, and a proportional height, its walls adorned with numerous and rare works of art, and several of the numerous bedrooms are similarly ornamented."(40)

Another visitor in the 18th century wrote, "Everything within and without denotes the habitation of a chieftain, and brings to remembrance those days in which the head of every tribe was surrounded by his own clan. His castle was his fortress; his approbation was their pride; his protection was both their duty and their interest, for in his safety their own fate was involved. In his hall stood the board to which they were always welcome; there he sat with all the feelings of a father in the midst of his children; he acted as their general in the day of battle; their judge in the time of peace; and was at all times their friend."(41)

Castle Grant was captured by the Jacobites during the 45' rebellion but they spared its destruction and left it in one peace.

The castle was used by the Armed Forces during World War II. During the late 20th century the castle became derelict and went through a series of owners. A major refurbishment project was completed in 2008 and the castle is now a private home.

Roy Castle is a 12th century fortress built by Clan Coymn. It is situated on a small glacial mound north of the village of Nethy Bridge, Speyside. Clan Grant helped to take it from the Coymns in 1306 and in 1420 they eventually got the stewardship of the whole area surrounding the castle.

Aerial View of Castle Roy.

Copyright: 2013 Castle Roy.

It is now a ruin but it thick walls stand 25ft high, and still dominate the surrounding area. The castle is a simple four sided structure. "The main architectural feature is a tower on north-western corner which still has a window with a lintel. There is an entrance archway in the centre of the north-eastern side, with a small doorway on the western side for day to day use. In the garde-robe area is evidence of the chieftain's latrine at ground level and two latrines on an upper level."(42)

There is signature carved into a stone in the Tower area, WJG, possibly scratched there by a Grant?

The castle was opened to the public in 2022.

CHAPTER 4. THE THIRD WAR OF SCOTTISH INDEPENDENCE.

The reign of King David II was another turbulent time for Scotland. Initially, his experienced relative, Thomas Randolph, was appointed Regent of Scotland and as long as he was in charge the enemies of Scotland, both internal and external, were kept at bay. It would have been better for Scotland if James Douglas had not left to go on Crusade with the heart of Bruce and 900 experienced Scots warriors, as he and many of his men were killed at the Battle of Telba, Spain, fighting against the Saracens.

Robert Grant, the now elderly freedom fighter and brother of the John Grant was one of the Scottish warriors who accompanied James Douglas and the heart of Bruce on Crusade with a small band of similarly experienced Grant warriors. In early 1330 Douglas and his 900 men, the cream of Scotland's seasoned warriors, set sail from Berwick-on-Tweed and Bruce's heart was carried in a casket around his neck. He carried a safe conduct from King Edward III of England, and why not, the English King was getting rid of Scotland's most famous warrior and 900 of his most experienced soldiers. The English must have been jumping with joy. The Scots stopped in Flanders (modern day Belgium) and then carried on to Spain and the Kingdom of Castille and Leon, ruled by King Alonso XI.

Castille and Leon, in Southern Spain, had been invaded by the Moors from North Africa and the fight against them was seen as a 'Holy War'. This persuaded the Scots that King Robert's promise should be fulfilled by assisting in the fight against the Moors. James Douglas was now renowned, after the death of Robert Bruce, as the foremost knight in Christendom. Alfonso had numerous knights who relished the prospect of fighting with him against the Moors, many of them English knights who had previously feared meeting him in the war between the two countries.

He and his Scottish followers agreed to stay and help the Christians against the 'infidels'. Alfonso was preparing an assault on the Moorish capital of Grenada, some two hundred miles to the East. Before he could do this however, he needed to take the Castle of Telba, known as the Castle of the Stars, halfway between the two cities.

Then the great Moorish General Osmin advanced toward Telba from Grenada, intent on relieving it. He halted before reaching the citadel and spent the next few weeks sending out raiding parties, content to attack the Christians as they went out looking for water. Eventually Osmin gathered his forces for an attack on the main

Christian camp and Alfonso gave Douglas command of the vanguard sent to stop them. The Christian army marched to Telba and laid siege to the fortress.

"James found that the Moors had indeed crossed the river and were making for the town. The whole detachment charged and forced the Moors back across the water. They hit them so hard that they were soon in sight of the Moorish camp at Turron."(43) General Osmin soon realised that his attack on Alfonso had been detected and he had to concentrate on repulsing Douglas's attack on his main camp.

Douglas continued his attack, and for once his astuteness in battle was compromised. He acted like a young knight in his first battle and instead of waiting for reinforcements, continued to penetrate the enemy lines, accompanied by nine knights. As they hacked and killed the Moors, Douglas eventually realised he had overstretched himself and that he and his men were surrounded by Saracens. James rallied his small group and began to fight his way back to his main force, but once he got free of the enemy he realised "that Sir William Sinclair of Roslin was not with them. He looked back and saw that Sinclair was sorely beset, surrounded by the enemy, but doing his best to cut his way through them. James shouted to his few companions, and they wheeled round to go to Sinclair's aid.

Yelling 'Douglas! Douglas! and smashing into the Moors yet again, they cut their way towards Sinclair with mighty strokes, but the element of surprise had gone and the Moors closed in. He then took the casket containing Bruce's heart and through it into the Saracen horde, exclaiming, 'where Bruce goes fist, Douglas follows', and he then ploughed his horse into the enemy.

The Scots died bravely. When the battle was over, Keith of Galston and the surviving Scots scoured the field. James was found in the middle of a circle of dead Moors. Five mortal wounds pierced his body. Beside him lay Sinclair of Roslin and the brothers Robert and Walter Logan. The Christians reported that the Scots, on finding James's body, lamented like men gone mad."(44)

Alfonso treated him with great respect and "his bones were embalmed and sent to Scotland, and buried in the church of Douglas, called St. Brides Kirk"(45), on 20 August 1330. As minor landowners and common soldiers, history does not record how many of the Grants died in the sunshine of Spain, but we do know that Robert Grant never returned home with the remains of James Douglas and the Heart of Robert the Bruce. It is likely, therefore that he died alongside his commander.

Meanwhile back in Scotland, in 1330 Thomas Randolph, Earl of Moray, besieged Dunphail Castle, a tower house about 6.5 miles south of Forres, Aberdeenshire, which was a stronghold of the Coymns who had refused to give their loyalty to King David. The Grants formed part of the besieging force under Thomas Randolph. The attackers could not breach the walls of the heavily defended fortress but the Coymns were soon running out of food. They eventually sent out 5 defenders to steal food from the attackers and bring it back for the starving garrison. They did steal a number of bags of meal but were captured before they could get back within the walls and were executed by the hand of Patrick Grant, who then chopped their heads off and threw them over the ramparts, at which, he cried 'Here's some beef for your bannocks'. Soon after this the defenders surrendered.

Then, unfortunately, Thomas Randolph died suddenly in 1332 (he may have been poisoned) and Scotland was left leaderless. Randolph was the Earl of Moray and therefore the Grants held their lands under him.

The country was ripe for invasion and King Edward III of England supported a group of exiled Scots, led by Edward Balliol, son of the dethroned King John Balliol, 'Toom Tabbard'. King Edward III reneged on the Treaty of Northampton, calling it a shameful peace and reasserted his sovereignty over Scotland. Then, in the summer of 1332, supported by a large English army, Edward Balliol landed in Fife. The Scots rose to oppose him led by the Earl of Mar. Thomas Randolph, 2nd Earl of Moray (and son of the former Regent Randolph) gathered his men in the north and this included Patrick Grant who raised the men of Grant and followed the Earl south.

The Scots had a much larger army but the English and exiled Scots force was led effectively by the experienced warrior, Henry Beaumont. The Scots were led very badly by the Earl of Mar when they fought the **Battle Of Duplin Moor** in August 1332. After outmanoeuvring the Scots, the English archers piled arrow after arrow into the Scottish army until it eventually charged in a disorganised rabble and were met by the spears of the English. The Scots were slaughtered. Their bodies were piled so high on top of each other that they reached the height of a spear. Over 2,000 Scots died, including the Earl of Moray and a host of his men including most of the Grants. Patrick Grant survived and was able to escape north. He had, however, been wounded in the shoulder by an English spear. Thomas Randolph was succeeded by his younger brother, John Randolph, 3rd Earl of Moray, who for a time would become Regent of Scotland, loyal to King David II.

After the battle a triumphant Balliol marched to the Palace of Scone and there had himself crowned as King of Scots on 24 September 1332. He then gave fealty to King Edward III of England as his Overlord. It looked like Scotland's Independence had failed at the first hurdle after the death of King Robert the Bruce. The child King David became a fugitive and eventually found refuge in the largely impregnable Castle of Dumbarton. Along with the majority of Scots nobles, Patrick Grant refused to recognise the new King and continued to support King David II.

"Scotland was by no means finished, however. The Guardian who replaced the Earl of Mar was Sir Andrew Murray, the son of William Wallace's brilliant general at the Battle of Stirling Bridge and an uncle of King David II by marriage (he was third husband of Robert Bruce's sister Christina). It was Andrew Murray who now led the Scots into the third phase of the Wars of Independence, along with the teenage John Randolph (the next Earl of Moray) and King David's uncle, Robert Stewart (the Steward)."(46)

Satisfied that he was now in control of Scotland, Balliol dismissed most of his experienced English troops and let them head home. Balliol then moved down to his hereditary lands in Annan, on the Scottish side of the Solway Firth. He then preceded to send out a series of proclamations. The first was to announce that with the help of England, he had reclaimed his rightful kingdom. He also acknowledged that Scotland was, and always had been, a fiefdom of England. Next he then promised to give much of Southern Scotland to King Edward III of England.

Battle of Annan. While Balliol was sitting writing his proclamations at Annan, Archibald Douglas, John Randolph, 3rd Earl of Moray, Robert Stewart (the future King Robert II) and Sir Simon Fraser gathered a large force of men from their lands in the Scottish Borders at Moffat. Here the force was joined by the men of Clan Grant, commanded by Patrick Grant. They made a night march south and, at dawn on 16 December 1332, descended on the town of Annan, in a surprise attack on Balliol and his force. Balliol's army was completely routed and most of his men were killed. Edward Balliol only narrowly managed to escape, through a hole in a wall, and fled naked on his horse to Carlisle and the safety of England. Patrick Grant chased after Edward Balliol, keen to get revenge for the death of his friend the Earl of Moray only a few months earlier. Balliol's brother, Henry, turned to confront Patrick Grant and he was killed by the thrust of Patrick's sword: revenge.

The victory at Annan changed the cause of Balliol and Bruce and the whole country reverted back to supporting King David Bruce. Balliol had to lick his wounds back in

England. It was after this battle that Sir Archibald Douglas was appointed as Governor of Scotland. Patrick Grant was given the task of organising the defence of Moray from any future English attack.

King Edward III of England was furious that his puppet, Balliol, had been so easily thrown out of Scotland after seemingly having it in his grasp. He raised a large army, and in summer 1333, invaded Scotland himself. He immediately attacked Berwick and put it under siege.

On learning of the invasion Archibald Douglas immediately called all the nobles together in Edinburgh to agree what to do against this new threat. Archibald, the Governor, was immediately made General of the Scots Army. Many of the nobles advised him to do exactly what Robert Bruce and James Douglas had done faced with the same threat: invade and waste northern England from the west coast to force the English invaders to return home and defend their lands. Initially Douglas agreed to this strategy. As the army marched south it was joined by the men of Grant, under the command of Patrick Grant.

However, unbeknown to the Scots leadership, Sir Alexander Seton, Governor of Berwick, had made a pact with King Edward to surrender the town if it had not been relieved by the Scots by the 1 August 1333. As a condition of this agreement Seton had to give up his son and heir as a hostage.

On hearing the news of the Agreement at Berwick, Douglas changed his mind and against the advice of his other commanders, he marched the Scottish Army towards Berwick. As this was happening the English had also captured Seton's other son, who had ventured out from Berwick to harass the English surrounding the town.

Fearing that he would have to lift the siege, King Edward demanded that Seton surrender the town immediately or his two sons would be hung from a gibbet right in front of their father. Seton's answer was to remind the English King of their agreement and that as it had not expired yet, he could not surrender the town. Edward was enraged by this refusal and immediately ordered Seton's two sons to be executed. Their bodies soon hung from the gibbet in full view of both their mother and father. A cruel act by a cruel King.

A few days later the Scots army arrived and made camp at Halidon Hill, a few miles from Berwick.

The Battle of Halidon Hill, July 1333. It is said that Archibald Douglas made bad decisions in this battle because of his rage at the murder of Seton's sons. He should have known better and learned the lesson from his brother James Douglas: only to fight a pitched battle against the English on ground of your own choosing.

King Edward moved his army and positioned it on Halidon Hill, two miles north of Berwick. This hill gave the English a good strategic position and Douglas, stupidly, decided to attack, pressed by the need to relieve Berwick. The Scottish Army was badly led and formed up below the English. Here they launched a massive charge but were quickly bogged down. Seeing this, the feared English and Welsh archers loosed arrow after arrow into them, killing hundreds. Then the English knights, mounted on their war horses, charged down the hill to crush the remaining Scottish Army. It was an annihilation: the worst defeat the Scots had ever had. They lost thousands of men killed, including Archibald Douglas himself and five other Earls. King Edward ordered that no quarter was to be given and all those who surrendered were killed. The next day a hundred Scots who had been captured were beheaded.

The Battle of Halidon Hill.

Patrick Grant escaped the battle unhurt and was able to lead most of his men home. However, his cousin, Gregory Grant, had been unhorsed and captured by the English and he was one of the men beheaded after the battle at the insistence of the English King. After the defeat and his escape Patrick Grant was knighted by a grateful King David II of Scotland.

Seton surrendered Berwick as promised, despite the murder of his sons. Scotland was at its lowest ebb again, Edward annexed the Scottish Borders to become an English County and reinforced sub-king Balliol with English troops at Perth. He then returned to England. King David escaped to France where he was to remain for seven years.

For the next few years Scotland was to endure almost continual civil war as the forces of Balliol and the English fought to conquer the remaining supporters of Robert the Bruce. Under the Treaty of Newcastle 1334, Edward Balliol ceded the whole of the Scottish Borders and Lothian to England. For a short while he ruled the remainder of Scotland from Perth, but he had little support in Scotland.

Balliol was kept busy trying to retain control of Central Scotland and the Northeast and the annexed Scottish Borders was garrisoned by English soldiers who delighted in lording it over their new Scottish subjects. Patrick Grant was able to repel any incursions into Moray and Invernesshire and neither the English nor the Scottish Balliol supporters were able to get any foothold in the area.

The Bruce cause was taken up by Andrew Murray, John Randolph, Earl of Moray and William Douglas, Lord of Liddesdale (and the bastard son of Sir James Douglas). In early 1334 word was brought to the Earl of Moray "that there was a great army of the Guelders [now part of the Netherlands] coming through England, to join up with Edward [Balliol], and help him against the Scots. Wherefore Randolph passed over into Lothian, to try if he could to conveniently intercept them, and cut them off before they could join with the King."(47) He was joined by a host of Lords and Lairds, including Patrick Grant with his clansmen. The Scots force lay in wait for the army of Guelders at Boroughmuir, near Edinburgh. When the Dutch force came into view the Scots attacked immediately and after a great battle the Dutch were defeated and the remnants of the force was chased to a little hill with a ruined castle on it. They were then besieged and after a nervous night they agreed to surrender to the Scots.

Apparently Patrick Grant and his men were not involved at the start of the battle. They had been allocated to the division of William Douglas who had been charged with taking his force round behind the Dutch and, just when the Guelders force were appearing to get the upper hand, Douglas and Grant attacked them from the rear, which tipped the battle in the Scots favour.

There is an interesting tale of the courage of a woman in the Guelders army, "who at the beginning of the battle, stepped forth before her company, and encountered, in a single combat or duel, A Scottish squire named Robert Shaw, who she slew, and afterward beat down her enemies on each side, till at last, after a good time, she was compassed about, and so slain."(48)

The Duke of Guelders himself was in command of the Dutch army. After surrendering he was treated with honour and courtesy. His baggage train was even returned to him. The reason for this was because Randolph had been brought up in France and knew that the Duke was a personal friend of the King of France. He therefore decided to be shrewd and treat the Duke kindly. Before he was released, however, he and his remaining men had to swear never to aid the English against the Scots again.

The Earl of Moray dismissed many of his warriors, including the Grants, who were allowed to go back north to their homeland. Unfortunately, as the remaining Scots escorted the Dutchmen south they were ambushed by a force loyal to Balliol. Randolph was taken prisoner. After this Douglas and Andrew Murray became the main leaders of the opposition to Balliol and they led a largely guerrilla war against him and his Scottish and English supporters.

Eventually, by early 1335, after many skirmishes the forces of King David Bruce began to get the upper hand and King Edward III raised another English army and marched north to help Balliol again. The Scottish Lords had learnt their lesson by this time and did not face the English and their dreaded archers in open battle. Instead, they burned the countryside before the English army passed through it and hid all the crops and cattle. As the English sent out more and more foraging parties hunting for food they ambushed and killed as many as they could. King Edward was forced to retire back to England, his army on the verge of starvation. He was followed soon after by Balliol, who would never again return to Scotland. Patrick Grant and his clansmen were not involved in harrying the English army as they had been tasked with keeping an eye on the Moray Coast, lest the English navy attempted a landing in this area.

The turning point was the **Battle of Culbean**, which is located near Ballater, in Deeside. This battle took place on 30th November 1335. Nearby Kildrummy Castle was held by Bruce supporters and Balliol sent David of Strathbogie, a formerly exiled Scottish Lord, with a large force to capture it. Balliol had granted Strathbogie the Earldom of Atholl.

He besieged the Castle and it was on the verge of surrendering when Regent Moray arrived with a large force, including the Grants under Patrick Grant, surprised Strathbogie and destroyed his army. David of Strathbogie fled but was eventually surrounded and hacked to death with his son. From this time on Balliol was on the defensive and continued to lose support. Eventually he was chased out of Scotland and exiled himself in France never to be seen again.

The last English held stronghold left in Central Scotland was the town and castle of Perth, commanded by the English knight, Sir Thomas Uhtred. A large Scottish force was gathered together which included many of the clans north of the town, including the Grants, Frasers and Camerons. The Scots surrounded the town but it was strongly fortified and easily supplied by ships which could sail up the River Tay. After two months the defenders still held out but eventually five French warships sailed into the Tay Estuary and blockaded the river. At the same time, to the growing dismay of the defenders, the Scots commander, the Earl of Ross, drained the moat surrounding the town.

The Scots set the attack for the next day, 7th July 1339, however, on this morning there occurred an eclipse of the sun. In this age such an occurrence was thought to herald a great disaster but for which side it was not known. To be safe the Scots decided to put off their attack until the following day.

However, by this time, Sir Thomas Uhtred had decided he had had enough and surrendered to the Scots but was permitted to march out of the town with all honours. The Scots then removed all the fortifications of Perth.

The Scots were now confident enough to ask King David Bruce to return from exile and he landed at Inverbervie in Fife on 2 June 1341. He was still only seventeen years of age. By the end of 1342 all the English had been expelled from Scotland, apart from a few castles which they continued to hold.

Patrick Grant was then part of a force which invaded Northern England while Edward III of England was fighting in France. On their return they besieged and retook Stirling Castle. Patrick Grant was now titled Lord of Inverallen and Stratherrick. There is a surviving charter which shows that he was in possession of Stratherrick between 1357 and 1362.

Stratherrick "stretches along the south-eastern shore of Loch Ness, parallel with, but separated from it by a narrow ridge of hilly country which screens the valley from the loch."(49) It contains the famous Falls of Foyers, part of the river Foyers just before it reaches Loch Ness. Around 1420 these lands passed to the Frasers.

Patrick also appears as a witness to a charter in 1345 by John Randolph 3rd Earl of Moray, bestowing upon Sir Robert Chisholm certain lands in Urquhart. Patrick Grant owed military service to the Earl of Moray.

The Earl of Moray was eventually released from English captivity in 1341.

There were other Grants involved in the war against Balliol and his English supporters. A Sir John Grant was Castellan of Darnaway Castle in 1346 and Lord of Dunphail in Strathspey. He was also given the Keepership of the Earl of Moray's 'Forest beyond the Park'. This John Grant was probably a younger brother of Chief Patrick Grant.

In 1346, King David II made a disastrous decision. To assist France, he agreed to invade northern England. Patrick Grant again showed his loyalty to the King and brought his men south to join his army. The King assembled his forces at Perth. The army was not unified and many quarrels occurred between the various factions. Many of the Lords tried to dissuade the King from his invasion of England but the King spurned their advice and, marching into England, penetrated as far as Durham. Here they were met and defeated by a Northern English army. King David was captured, along with many of the Scottish nobles and thousands of Scots were killed. The Grants under Patrick, fought on the right wing of the army, under the Earl of Moray, who was killed in the first English attack. Luckily Patrick Grant and his clansmen were able to escape and return home, although many were killed.

Robert Stewart, King David's uncle and nearest heir, now assumed the office of Guardian of Scotland on behalf on the absent Monarch. He used his time as Regent to accumulate more and more lands for himself and his immediate family. The now ageing Patrick Grant stayed out of national politics at this time and concentrated on preserving and enhancing his own lands in the North.

Eventually after agreeing to pay a large ransom, King David II was released from captivity in October 1357 and he made it known straight away that he resented the incursions of Robert Stewart into lands in the Central Highlands, which he considered were his right to grant and give out. For the rest of his reign King David was at loggerheads with his uncle and heir and on a number of occasions their disputes almost led to civil war. The Grants kept out of these disputes neither siding with one faction nor the other.

King David was not a Scottish hero like his father but a rather self-centred and isolated monarch. He was childless and at one point was prepared to acknowledge one of King Edward of England's sons as his heir to gain more reasonable terms for the repayment of his ransom. His father would be turning in his grave.

This, of course, did not go down well with his true heir, Robert Stewart. In addition to this there were rumours that King David was using the ransom tax to feed his own coffers. In 1364 the Scottish Parliament rejected his proposals to make Lionel, Duke of Clarence, heir to the throne of Scotland.

King David II died unexpectantly in February 1371, childless after a reign of 41 years. Despite his faults he left a nation is reasonably good health. Before this, however, in 1362, Patrick Grant was killed.

There is a legendary tale relating to the death of Patrick Grant "... while he was on a visit to the Baron of Kincardine, which place is in Abernethy Forest, near Aviemore, he was attacked and killed by a party of Coymns. A 'taille' of Grants then materialised .... and pursued the murders, who took sanctuary in Kincardine Kirk .... The Grants could not break the sanctuary so one of them hit on the bright idea of shooting a fire arrow into the thatched roof. The Kirk and the Coymns were then burnt, except one tall Coymn, who managed to flee, but was caught by an athletic Grant, who removed his head with a blow from his two-edged Sword, possibly a claymore."(50)

Patrick left one daughter, **Maud** and she is said to have married Andrew Stewart, Sheriff of the Isle of Bute, who changed his name to Grant, or so some historians have said. Information is very confused at this time and other evidence suggests that his only daughter was named Elizabeth Grant, who married Sir William Pylche, one of the main ruling families of Inverness, and it was their son Malcolm Grant, who was the next Grant heir. Other evidence points to Malcolm being Patrick's son and the father of Elizabeth himself. For this history I have taken the later as the truth.

Patrick, sometime between 1351 and 1362, granted his son-in-law William Pylche, burgess of Inverness, half of his lands around Inverallen, to be held by William Pylche and his heirs of his marriage to Maud (or Elizabeth), his daughter. But from another charter of the time it is clear that Elizabeth is a grand-daughter of Patrick

Grant and that he was actually succeeded by a son, **Malcolm Grant, 7th Chief of Clan Grant** "who appears among the barons of the neighbourhood, in a court held by Alexander Stewart, Earl of Badenoch, the 'Wolf of Badenoch' on 11 October 1380."(51) His name also appears in an agreement between Thomas Dunbar, Earl of Moray and Alexander MacDonald, Lord of the Isles, signed at Nairn in September 1394.

Elizabeth (or Maud) would then have been his daughter. With her the lands of Stratherrick eventually went out of the ownership of the Grants, going to her son, James Mackintosh from her second marriage. Her second husband was probably James Mackintosh of Rothiemurchas who was killed at the Battle of Harlaw in 1411. The lands of Stratherrick eventually passed to the Frasers. By her marriage to William Pylche she had two daughters, Elizabeth and Marjory Pylche and they inherited the half lands of Inverallen, Strathspey. These were eventually again brought into the lands of Clan Grant when Duncan Grant of Freuchie purchased them in 1453.

Meanwhile, Sir John Grant, Governor of Darnaway Castle, younger brother of Patrick Grant, had a son, Thomas. He was also given the Governorship of Darnaway Castle and the surrounding estates by King David II in November 1370. The charter refers to the great service that Sir John Grant gave to both King Robert the Bruce and King David II both within and out with the realm. He seems to have had allegiance to the Earl of Mar in the 1340's and 1350's. In October 1357 and again in 1358 he journeyed to both the continent and then to England on behalf of the Earl.

By 1361 the Earl of Mar fell out with King David and his lands were forfeited by the Crown and the Earl was forced into exile. For a time John Grant may have accompanied him. Evidence is that in December 1363, King Edward III of England granted John Grant a safe conduct and the King specifically stated that John Grant has been 'taken into his protection'. This protection even included his wife and 10 retainers. Under this protection John and his wife visited Scotland and then returned to England.

But by October 1366 Sir John Grant was back in Scotland and back in the King's favour. He was sent on another ambassadorial task by King David, and was given another safe-conduct by the King of England to pass through his country and 'go beyond the seas', the passport to last for one year.

His last known appearance was in 1368 when he again witnessed a charter by the Earl of Marr, at Cavers. Sir John probably died between May 1368 and January

1369. He was succeeded by his eldest son, Thomas Grant. Apart from inheriting his father's estates, little is known of him apart from being a witness to a number of charters and official documents, such as the charter which made him Castellan of Darnaway Castle in November 1371. He in turn was succeeded by his brother, Robert Grant.

Darnaway Castle was also known as Tarnaway Castle and is located in the Darnaway Forest, 3 miles southwest of Forres in Moray. This area was initially Comyn land but was granted to Thomas Randolph, Earl of Moray by King Robert the Bruce. Randolph probably built the first castle and appointed Sir John Grant as its Governor. Eventually the castle went to the powerful Douglas family around 1430. It then passed to the Murrays and from them to the Stuarts, and it is still owned by their descendants. Nothing remains of the original Castle which the Grants governed in the 14th century, and the Castle was rebuilt into a fine house in 1810.

Darnaway Castle in 1804 Before it's Reconstruction in 1810.

Copyright: John Claude Nattes.

The old Castle was the scene of a bitter feud between the Grants and the Gordon, Earl of Huntly in November 1590, when John Gordon, brother of the Laird of Cluny, was killed.

In 1625 the Earl of Moray moved into his new Stuart Castle near Inverness and left Darnaway Castle as his second home. Later in the 17th century the Castle was garrisoned by a troop of Cromwell's soldiers. In 1810 the old castle was completely demolished apart from Randolph's Hall.

CHAPTER 5. THE GRANTS AND THE EARLY STEWART KINGS.

Malcolm Grant appears to have died in 1370 and was succeeded by his son, **Robert Grant, 8th Chief of Clan Grant** 1370 – 1394. He was known as **The Ambassador** due to the active part he played in public affairs and in the service of his country. In addition to being highly thought of in the Scottish Court he was also in good favour with King Edward III of England who gave him a safe conduct to journey through England on a number of occasions.

On the death of King David II in 1371 Robert Stewart as heir to the throne, became King Robert II. During this time there was much fighting on the border Marches between Scotland and England and to try and foster better relations a Chivalric Contest (tournament) was organised between the two countries in 1380 at Liliot or Liliattecross in the English borders. Robert Grant was chosen as one of the competitors and was matched against a famous English Knight, Thomas de I' Strother of 'great courage and valour'. He won this contest.

MAP 8. THE BORDER MARCHES OF SCOTLAND AND ENGLAND.

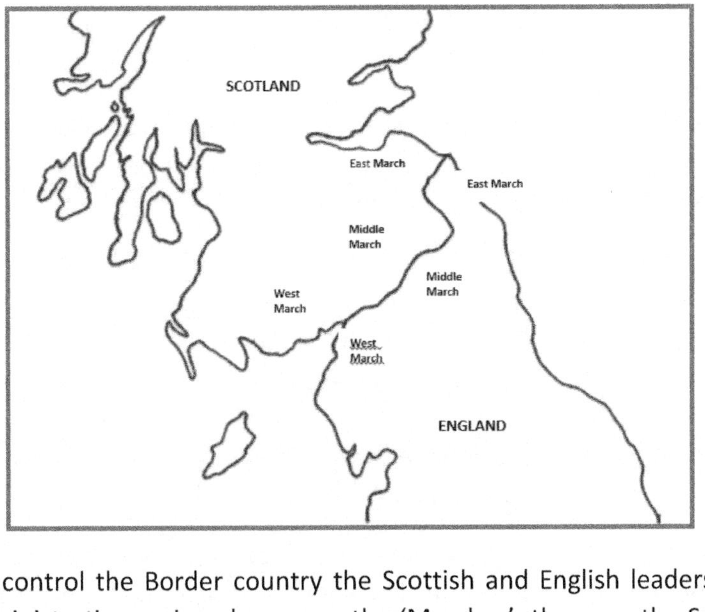

To try and control the Border country the Scottish and English leaders divided it into six administrative regions known as the 'Marches', three on the Scottish side and three of the English. Each one has a governing officer known as a 'Warden'. Each country had an East, Middle and West March. As far back as 1248 a conference took place between the six wardens of the Marches where they agreed the 'Laws of the Marches'. As part of these laws was the agreement to occasionally have 'Days of Truce', where complainers and accused could gather before the Wardens to settle complaints arising out of raids, theft and killing between the two nations.

DIAGRAM 3. CHIEFS OF CLAN GRANT.

Name	Chief Number	Title	From	Until
Malcolm Grant	7	6th Lord of Stratherrick	1362	1370
Robert Grant	8	7th Lord of Stratherrick	1370	1394
Malcolm Grant	9	8th Lord of Stratherrick	1394	1400
Sir Patrick Grant	10	9th Lord of Stratherrick	1400	1411
Sir John Roy Grant	11	10th Lord of Stratherrick	1411	1434
Sir Duncan Grant	12	1st of Freuchie	1434	1485
John 'Bard' Roy Grant	13	2nd of Freuchie	1485	1528
James Grant	14	3rd of Freuchie	1528	1553
John Grant	15	4th of Freuchie	1553	1585
John Grant	16	5th of Freuchie	1585	1622

"In the following February, however, there was a protection extended by the English King to Robert le Gaunt of Scotland, permitting him to pass into England to speak and treat with the King's treasurer, Robert of Hales, Prior in England of the Hospital of St John of Jerusalem, regarding certain affairs of the Hospital."(52)

In 1384 Robert Grant was sent to France as Scotland's Ambassador to renew the truce between Scotland, England and France which was to last until 1392. For these services he received, in 1385, a share of 40,000 francs of French Gold which was to be paid by the French to the King of Scots and his Barons. It was only shared out among 22 Lords and Knights. As Robert Grant was one of these men his role in the Peace Treaty must have been important, although his share was very small in comparison with the great lords and nobles of Scotland.

Despite this Peace Treaty there were a number of large scale raids by both countries into the other's territories and eventually even the Grants from Speyside joined Border Lords in a massive raid in 1388 which led to the **Battle of Otterburn.**

By this time King Robert II was an old man in ill health. The King, and his eldest son John (later King Robert III), wanted to stop the raids into England but could not control the more warrior-like younger sons of the King, particularly the Earl of Fife.

Both the Earl of Fife and James, Earl of Douglas became frustrated by the lack of action from both the monarch and his eldest son. They secretly called on their friends and allies to bring their men south for a great raid into England. The Earl of Moray called on his men and vassals. One was Robert Grant and he gathered together a company of around 200 mounted Grants and quickly travelled south. Without the King's knowledge the force met near the border in the summer of 1388. However the English found out about the forthcoming raid and prepared themselves to surprise the Scots when they did attack.

The Scottish camp was in Teviotdale, near the border, and the English sent a spy into the Scottish camp. This spy heard all the Scots plans for a single assault into England. When he tried to escape, however, he was suspected and captured. He was brought before Scottish leaders who threatened him with the 'Rack' if he did not confess. The man quickly confessed all and revealed the English plans to counter the Scots assault.

Knowing this the Scots changed their plans, instead of attacking in one force, they now divided themselves into two. The largest part of the army headed to Carlisle, led by two of the King's sons, the Earls of Strathearn and Fife.

The other part of the Scots army was led by the Earl of Douglas himself. He had between two and four thousand men, including Robert Grant and his men. This force attacked down the east coast and marched all the way to Durham before the English knew they was there. They then burned all the countryside around the city.

Percy, the Earl of Northumberland, was by this time an old man, but sent his two sons, Henry and Ralph, to Newcastle with a large army, with the intention of intercepting the Earl of Douglas on his return north. Henry Percy was known as 'Hotspur'. By mid-August 1388, the Scottish force headed home.

When the English saw the size of the Scottish force they concluded that discretion was the better part of valour and decided to stay behind the walls of Newcastle Castle. Douglas rode to the walls of the castle and challenged Percy to a duel by single combat which the Englishman readily agreed to. They fought outside the city wall and after a fierce fight Douglas eventually got the upper hand, unhorsing Percy who was concussed from his fall.

Douglas let him live, but captured his pennon, which was a banner attached to his lance which bore the Percy Coat of Arms (a blue lion rampant). Douglas mocked the injured Percy and, grabbing the pennon, said he would take it to Scotland and fly it from his Castle.

Despite this victory, the Scots could not take the formidable Castle of Newcastle and soon broke off the siege and headed north. On 19 August 1388 the small Scots army was camped about a mile from the village of Otterburn, still on the English side of the border. By this time Percy had gathered a large army and was hurrying to catch up with the Scots. They met the Scots where they camped and here the **Battle of Otterburn** took place.

Percy arrived about 7pm and took the Scots by surprise. Had he attacked immediately his force would have totally destroyed the unsuspecting Scots. But he took his time deploying his forces and this gave the Scots time to get their men into battle formation. With superior numbers the English were confident of victory and commenced a full-frontal assault on the Scots. Douglas led the initial Scottish defence and single-handedly killed six men with his great sword. Despite this the English were getting the upper hand, but Douglas then took three hundred of his best warriors and, flanking the main English position, was able to attack them from the rear.

MAP 9. THE BATTLE OF OTTERBURN.

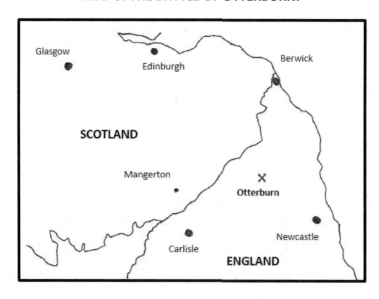

The English were now being attacked on both sides, and fierce hand to hand fighting broke out all along the battle line. Robert Grant and his men were in the thick of the fighting and many were killed or wounded. The Scots were eventually successful and come the first light of dawn, they held the field and the English retreated. Unfortunately the Earl of Douglas was mortally wounded in the battle and died soon after his last victory.

"But whilst he was thus fighting in the midst of them, before his friends could come at him, though they pressed forward to have seconded and assisted him with all the force that might be, they found him lying on the ground with three deadly wounds. There was lying dead by him Robert Hart, and the priest called Richard Lundie..... that had ever stood fast by his side, defended his fainting body with a halbert from injury; he being in this state, his kinsman James Lindsay and John and Walter Sinclair came to him and asked him how he did:

'I do well (said he) dying as my predecessors have done before; not in a bed of languishing sickness, but in the field. These things I require of you as my last petitions: first, that you keep my death close from our own folk and from the enemy; then that ye suffer not my standards to be lost, or cast down; and last that ye avenge my death, and bury me at Melrose with my father. If I could hope for these things, I should die with the greater contentment: for long since I heard a prophecy, that a dead man should win a' field, and I hope in God it shall be I."(53)

Douglas then died and his men wrapped his body in a cloak to hide it. They then raised his standard and crying, 'A Douglas, A Douglas, they rallied the Scots army and won the battle. Both Sir Henry Percy and his brother Sir Ralph Percy, and many other English knights were captured and the wealth of many Grants families was greatly enhanced by the ransoms they received from these prisoners. In all 1,800 English were killed and 1,000 were wounded. The Scots also took 1,000 prisoners. The toll for the Grants was high with almost half of their 200 men either dead or wounded.

A famous verse from the time quotes Douglas as saying:

"My friends you ask me how I do?

My soul is now prepar'd to go,

Where many wounds have made ther way.

Conceal it, till you have won the day;

Pursue your hopes; this said he dy'd.

Then the whole ranks 'A Douglas' cry'd,

And charg'd afresh, that thou might'st have,

Revenge and honour in the grave."(54)

Then in 1389 Robert Grant was again one of the Scottish Ambassadors who negotiated and renewed the alliance between Scotland and France. In 1391 he then again went to France, accompanying the Bishop of St Andrews (Walter Trail) on a 'special mission'. They spent a year in France and concluded another peace agreement which this time was to last until 1399. For his efforts ".... he received £20 per annum for life, in recognition of his services from the Deputy Chamberlain of Scotland."(55)

King Robert II died in 1390. Prior to his death he had lost control of his wayward sons, particularly Alexander Stewart, Earl of Buchan, known as the 'Wolf of Badenoch'. In 1388 he had elevated his son the Earl of Fife to the Duke of Albany and made him Regent of Scotland. Alexander Stewart's activities caused resentment and distress in the highlands, particularly the activities of his 'cateran' war bands which raided across the highlands with impunity. Robert Grant and his successor spent much of their time and efforts either befriending the 'Wolf' or fighting off raids from his warriors. The Duke of Albany immediately curbed the power of his brother by removing his title of Justiciar of the North and gave it to his own son Murdoch Stewart. The assaults on Buchan's power continued into the 1390's and this was very gratefully received by the clans of the north, including the Grants. Robert Grant and his son, Malcolm became firm supporters of the Duke of Albany.

Robert II was succeeded by his eldest son who took the name King Robert III who was 53 years of age when he became King. He was a weak and timid man, unlike his more aggressive brothers such as Robert, Duke of Albany (formally Earl of Fife) and Alexander, Earl of Buchan. There was a fierce rivalry for power between Albany and the new King's eldest son, David Stewart. If Albany could get rid of the sons of King Robert III, he would be next in line to the throne of Scotland.

Robert Grant died in 1394 and was succeeded by his eldest son, **Malcolm Grant, 9th Chief of Clan Grant.** He was only Chief for a short period of time between 1394 and

1400. Little is known of this Chief except that he was a gentleman of rank and that he was a member of the convention to settle a dispute between the Earl of Moray and the MacDonald Lord of the Isles. He was succeeded by his son, Patrick Grant.

With the reduction in power of the Earl of Buchan, the MacDonald Lord of the Isles began re-establishing their prominent position in the mainland of the Highlands from their base on the west coast and islands. By the end of 1395 Donald MacDonald, 2nd Lord of the Isles had control of Urquhart Castle, just over Loch Ness from the Grant lands of Stratherrick.

Sir Patrick Grant 10th Chief of Clan Grant from 1400 to 1411. He continued the Grant support of the Duke of Albany. Meanwhile on the national scene the fierce rivalry for power between the Duke of Albany and David Stewart, Duke of Rothesay, the Kings eldest son and heir to the throne continued. In February 1402 when David Stewart was travelling to St Andrews to meet one of his mistresses, he was ambushed by a joint force of Albany and the Earl of Angus and was then held captive in Falkland Palace, which was owned by Albany. On his journey to Falkland Palace, David is said to have been blindfolded and mounted backwards on a mule to ridicule him. At the Palace he was starved to death by his uncle. The heir to the throne was only twenty-four years of age and in good health when he died. By all accounts, however, he was not a man of good morals, and in some respects Scotland was well rid of him.

In March 1402, the Duke of Albany and the Earl of Angus were summoned before Parliament to account for the death of the heir to the throne. Patrick Grant journeyed south to attend this Parliament and provide support to the Duke of Albany. Because they were the two most powerful men in the country at this time and Scotland was being threatened by the English the two men were acquitted of any wrongdoing and Parliament decreed that the Prince had died from natural causes. The weak and ailing King Robert III did nothing. Patrick Grant returned north to take command of his clansmen against the ever growing threat of the Lord of the Isles and his MacDonald clansmen.

After the death of Prince David, the King's remaining son, James, became the heir to the throne. But by the winter of 1405 King Robert III knew his health was failing and he resolved to send his 11-year-old son to safety in France, away from the clutches of his brother Albany and his ally, Earl of Angus.

After a skirmish with a force of Angus's men, James and his guardian, the Earl of Orkney, hid out on the Bass Rock, an island within the Forth Estuary, for over a month. They then boarded a ship to take them to France but on 22 March 1406, the ship was captured by English pirates who then sold the heir to the Scottish throne to King Henry IV of England. He remained a captive for 18 years. Meanwhile, Robert III moved to Dundonald Castle, Ayrshire, where, on hearing of his son's capture, he died on 4 April 1406. The imprisoned James became the uncrowned King until 1424 when he was ransomed. He was treated well in England and had a great friendship with King Henry V and even went on campaign to France, occasionally fighting against his own subjects.

In the meantime, the new Kings uncle, Robert Stewart, Duke of Albany, became Regent of Scotland. In the power vacuum in the North, Donald MacDonald, Lord of the Isles, took over the Earldom of Ross and asserted his powerful position in the North. Around this time, Patrick Grant took as his 2nd or 3rd wife, the daughter of MacLean of Duart, a powerful West Highland Chief but also a strong supporter of the MacDonald, Lord of the Isles. This brought the Grants onto the side of the MacDonalds who were against the Duke of Albany.

A Clan Grant Warrior.

The Scottish Government, under Regent Albany, refused to recognise MacDonald's right to the Earldom of Ross. But Donald MacDonald had control over the principal seat of the Earldom of Ross and with the support of the imprisoned heir to the Scottish throne, Donald rebelled in 1411. At Christmas 1410, Donald held a great gathering of his clansmen and supporters at his castle of Ardtornish, on the Sound of Mull. There, according to tradition, he selected six thousand of his best fighting men and sent the rest home. Among the selected men were the MacLeans of Duart. He then sailed for the mainland, landing at Inverlochy, where another 4,000 supporters joined him, including Patrick Grant, with about 200 Grant clansmen. They then marched up the Great Glen to Inverness and then invaded north into Ross, meeting with little resistance, at least initially.

However, when the army reached Dingwall they were met by a large body of clansmen from Sutherland, under Angus Dubh Mackay. The fierce **Battle of Dingwall 1411** ensued, but the MacKays were eventually routed and Angus MacKay was taken prisoner and his brother Roderick slain. After keeping MacKay in prison for a few weeks he then released him and married him off to one of his daughters, thus procuring the support of the MacKays.

He then marched back to Inverness, invaded Moray and ravished the lands of Strathbogie and Garioch, belonging to Alexander Stewart, Earl of Mar. The main aim of the campaign was now to win an independent kingdom for himself and the MacDonald clan or at least to get recognition of his right to the Earldom of Ross. All of the North of Scotland looked as if it would fall into the hands of the MacDonalds and that the Grants had picked the right side to support. The army then marched on towards Aberdeen which the Lord of the Isles had promised to burn.

The Provost of Aberdeen prepared to abandon the city, but the Earl of Mar, who commanded the Government forces in the north, refused to retreat. He then gathered a small army of around 3,000 men.

Twenty miles from the city, the Highland army, including Patrick Grant and his clansmen, were met at the village of Harlaw by the Earl of Mar and his army, much smaller in number, but composed of Lowland gentry, who were better armed and better disciplined than the Highland followers of the Lord of the Isles. Although Mar was heavily outnumbered he was resolved to fight. Most of the Highlanders wore no armour, if anything they would have a padded jacket, known as a 'cotun'. The wealthier lairds and chiefs would have been equipped with long padded jackets, called 'gambesons', mail 'haubert' (shirts) or, for a very few, plated armour.

The Battle of Harlaw was fought on 24 July 1411. It was seen as a battle between the Gaels and the Sassenachs, Celts verses Teutons, Highlands against Lowlands.

The Earl of Mar placed a number of his heavily armoured and experienced Knights and men-at-arms in front and then drew up the rest of the army behind them. The Lord of the Isles placed himself at the command of his army and led from the front. He divided his army into three divisions, commanding the centre himself, with the Chief of Mackintosh leading the left and Red Hector MacLean of the Battles commanding the right wing. Patrick Grant fought alongside his MacLean father-in-law.

MAP 10. THE BATTLE OF HARLAW.

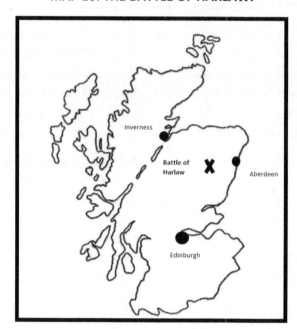

"On a signal being given, the Highlanders and Islemen, setting up those terrific shouts and yells which they were accustomed to raise on entering into battle, rushed forward upon their opponents; but they were received with great firmness and bravery by the knights, who with their spears levelled, and battle-axes raised, cut down many of their impetuous but badly armed adverseries. After the Lowlanders had recovered themselves from the shock which the onset of the Highlanders had produced, Sir James Scrymgeour, at the head of the knights and bannerets who fought under him, cut his way through the thick columns of the Islemen, carrying death everywhere around him, but the slaughter of hundreds by this brave party did not intimidate the Highlanders, who also kept pouring in by the thousand to supply the places of those who had fallen.

Surrounded on all sides, no alternative remained for Sir James and his valorous companions but victory or death, and the latter was their lot. The Constable of Dundee was amongst the first who suffered, and his fall so encouraged the Highlanders, that seizing and stabbing the horses, they thus unhorsed their riders, whom they dispatched with their daggers." (56)

Meanwhile, the Earl of Mar with the largest body of men, penetrated into the heart of the enemy ranks. Hundreds of his men were killed but they kept fighting until dusk. It was disastrous for many of the families and clans of the Northeast, particularly those of Angus and the Mearns, who lost not only their Chiefs, but also every male in their House. Lesley of Balquhain is said to have fallen with six of his sons.

The two armies only stopped fighting when it was too dark to see each other. Thousands were left killed on the field of battle, hence why the conflict got the name 'Red Harlaw'. Donald's army lost 900 men, including the Chief of MacLean, who was slain in single combat with Irvine of Drum, when both men fought until they had killed each other. At least 100 Grants were killed, including the Clan Chief, Patrick Grant, who died alongside his father-in-law. In all Mar lost 600 men, fewer in number, but a much larger proportion of his force.

Battle of Harlaw 1411.

Too tired to retreat, Mar and his surviving men camped on the battlefield, expecting to resume combat the next morning. But at dawn they found that Donald's army had retreated back to Ross. The amount of dead on both sides meant neither side had won, but Mar had kept Donald from Aberdeen, his main objective and the rebellion soon petered out after this. Patrick's eldest son, John Roy Grant, survived the battle and the following day he abandoned Donald MacDonald's army and returned home with the body of his dead father and his remaining clansmen.

Why Donald MacDonald did not resume battle the next day is unknown. He still had a great army in the field and would surely have won the battle the next day. Possibly, he thought that Mar was going to be reinforced with another army. Whatever the reason, he retired north to Ross where he sought to recover and regain his strength and more men, claiming Harlaw was a great victory for him. Many other highlanders advocated that Donald actually won the battle. "Patrick, Earl of Tullibardine said as other men were talking of the battle of Harlaw, we know that MacDonald had the victory, but the Governor had the printer."(57) If Donald had fought on the next day and won, as he surely would have done, he may have been able to establish a separate Kingdom in the North of Scotland and the Western Isles.

On hearing of the retreat, the Duke of Albany, Regent of Scotland, raised another, largely Lowland army, and marched north in autumn 1411 to defeat Donald. The Lord of the Isles declined to give battle and headed back to his island strongholds. Albany recovered possession of the Castle of Dingwall and using this as his base, set about taking possession of the whole of the Earldom of Ross.

Donald MacDonald refused to surrender, however, and hostilities were renewed in the summer of 1412 but this did not last long. Eventually peace talks were held at Lochgilphead and Donald was compelled to give up his claim to the Earldom of Ross, to become a vassal of the Scottish Crown and to deliver hostages to secure his future good conduct. Meanwhile, while the northern rebellion was disintegrating, John Roy succeeded his father as Chief of Clan Grant.

Sir John Roy Grant 11ᵗʰ Chief of Clan Grant 1411 – 1434 who was Sheriff Principal of Inverness. He married Matilda (or Bigla) of Glencarnie, a very rich heiress who owned the lands of Elgin, Rothes and Fochabers. She was also a Coymn, bitter enemies of the Grants. "It is at this period that the alliance of the Grants with the powerful family of Coymn, connecting together the two houses and putting an end to a long feud between them, is said to have taken place. The heiress of the Coymn's is stated to have been the mother of Sir Duncan Grant, first of Freuchie...."(58) She was also related to the Earls of Strathearn.

This marriage secured the rights of the Grants to their lands in Strathspey. Matilda's father was Gilbert Coymn of Glencairnie. Her son Duncan Grant inherited much of the lands of Strathspey. Legends of Bigla (Matilda) are still told in Strathspey. In the area there is still 'Bigla's Key Stone', near Duthil, which is alleged to be the stone under which Bigla hid the keys to her castle while she was in church.

It was John Roy Grant who consolidated the position of the Grants as masters of Strathspey when he concluded an agreement with the Frasers to swap his land interests in Stratherrick for the Fraser lands in Speyside, making the Grants by far the largest landholders in the whole of Speyside. He moved the majority of his clansmen to his new home but some remained on the south side of Loch Ness. "According to tradition, the Church estate of Foyers was their last possession in Stratherrick, and they lost it in this manner. The young bride of Gruer Mor of Portclair went forth, as was then the want of newly married woman, to receive the presents of her friends. At Foyers she was grossly insulted by Laurence Grant; and she reported the outrage to her husband, who resolved to punish the offender, and sailed from Portclair with galleys full of fighting men. Grant and his followers rowed out to meet him, and a desperate fight took place in the bay to the west of Foyers, which to this day is known as Camis Mharbh Dnaoine – Bay of the Dead Men. Defeated, and unable to reach the Stratherrick shore, Laurence made for Urquhart, followed by Gruer. At Ruigh Lauris – Laurence's Slope- above Ruiskich, he was overtaken and slain; and Gruer seized and retained all his lands in Foyers."(59)

In early 1424 King James I was finally released from English captivity and was crowned King of Scots on 22 May 1424 at Scone Palace. Straight away the new King was determined to assert his authority over the leading nobles of the land and, in 1425, he arrested and imprisoned twenty four of them. By this time, the Duke of Albany had died and was succeeded by his eldest son, Murdoch Stewart. He and two of his sons were also arrested, found guilty of treason and immediately executed.

King James had shown himself to be very determined ruler and after the destruction of the Albany Stewarts he turned his attention north where he was determined to curb the power of the Clan Chiefs and the MacDonalds in particular. In 1428 the King travelled north and requested all the main Clan Chiefs to attend his Court in Inverness, including John Roy Grant and Alexander MacDonald, Lord of the Isles. As soon as they appeared at Inverness they were all arrested and imprisoned in the Tower of Inverness Castle. The King then prosecuted a few minor

87

Chiefs and Lairds and had them executed to show his power. The Highland Chiefs all quickly pledged their allegiance to him and John Roy Grant was soon released along with many others. Alexander MacDonald, however, was kept a prisoner but he soon escaped and came out in rebellion against the King.

In the spring of 1429 Alexander MacDonald's army advanced on Inverness and burned it to the ground, although he failed to take the Castle. Meanwhile the Grants and the Frasers, now loyal to King James, had gathered their forces and had disrupted his advance, causing him much trouble. Once MacDonald had taken and destroyed Inverness, he was determined to punish the Grants and the Frasers and he sent out a strong force of MacDonalds to ravage their lands. They decided to deal with the Frasers first and laid siege to Lovat Castle, near Beauly, north of Inverness.

However, while they were doing this the Frasers gathered all their men and that of their allies. John Roy Grant brought a force of over 300 Grants to assist. They then besieged the force of MacDonalds and attacked, forcing them to abandon the siege and retreat. As they marched back to Inverness the combined force of Frasers and Grants continued to attack the MacDonald rear guard. By the time the MacDonalds reached the Moor of Caiplich, only a few miles from Inverness, they had had enough. They stopped and gave battle to the Frasers and Grants. Both sides fought with great courage and determination and the MacDonalds were eventually defeated before the main MacDonald force could reach them from Inverness. The engagement is known as the **Battle of Mamsha.** John Roy Grant was wounded in the battle and although he survived his health never fully recovered.

Sacking Inverness was enough for the MacDonalds at this time and they soon returned to the West at the end of June 1429. However, as Inverness was burning, the King gathered a great army, under his own command, and they caught up with the MacDonalds on a moor somewhere in Lochaber, close to Inverlochy (now Fort William) on 23 June 1429. John Roy Grant was still recovering from his wounds and gave command of the Grant contingent in the Royal Army to his eldest son, Duncan Grant.

Alexander MacDonald had 10,000 men but when the royal standard was unfurled the Mackintosh and Camerons (Clan Chattan) switched sides and fought for the King against the Lord of the Isles. This changed the course of the battle and Alexander was defeated and fled. Some say it was only the MacMartin Cameron's who defected and Cameron of Locheil stayed loyal to the Lord of the Isles; hence to that clan it was known as the **Battle of Split Allegiances**. It is highly likely that the defection was concluded in advance by bribes as the MacMartins were soon after granted land in Lochaber which had formally belonged to the Lord of the Isles uncle, Alexander of Lochalsh. The young Duncan Grant fought with courage and valour and was personally knighted by the King immediately after the Battle. The Grants lost around 50 men, including 5 lairds who were close kinsmen of Chief John Roy Grant. However, they had proved their loyalty to King James I.

The Kings force then marched up the Great Glen and seized the Castles of Urquhart and Dingwall, which were still in the hands of the MacDonalds. The King then sought to either capture or kill Alexander and sent a large expedition force with artillery into the Western Isles. Alexander had fled to Islay and the force was not strong enough to take him in his stronghold. However he knew his rebellion had failed and he decided to surrender to the King and ask for mercy. The King refused to negotiate with Alexander and he knew he was in serious threat of being eventually captured and executed as a traitor. He travelled virtually alone to Edinburgh and on 27 August 1429 presented himself to the King at Holyrood Abbey, Edinburgh. There he "knelt in front of the high altar in his shirt and drawers, handing his sword hilt-forwards to the king"(60)

Obviously, all this had been pre-arranged, as Alexander would never have given himself up without a fight unless he knew that he would be saved. He then went on with the charade and begged for his life and then Queen Joan, duly prompted, vocally urged her husband to show mercy and spare the life of the Lord of the Isles. King James was persuaded by his Queen not to have Alexander executed and he was sent to Tantallon Castle, North Berwick, under the guard of William Douglas, 2nd Earl of Angus, King James' nephew.

The King now sought to take more control in the North and Western Isles. He sent the Earl of Mar against Alexander Carrach MacDonald, the uncle of the Lord of the Isles. Mar gathered a great army and marched down the Great Glen intent on destroying Lochaber and Strathnaver. Again John Roy Grant gave command of the Grant contingent to his son, now Sir Duncan Grant.

The MacDonalds and their allies rallied around Donald Balloch MacDonald of Dunnyveg and Alexander Carrach MacDonald of Lochaber, who both refused to 'bend the knee' and they defeated the Kings army, commanded by the Earl of Mar, at the **Battle of Inverlochy**.

Donald Balloch gathered all the loyal MacDonalds on Islay and then sailed to Carna, an island in Loch Sunnart and there met with Allan MacDonald of Moidart and his brother Ranald Ban. They agreed to join him with 600 men and then they all sailed for Inverskippinish, two miles south of Inverlochy.

Meanwhile the Royal Army, under the Earl of Mar, was camped just to the east of Inverlochy, close to its castle with 3,000 men, including around 300 Grants.

At the same time Alexander Carrach MacDonald of Lochaber was to the east of Inverlochy, and on hearing of the main MacDonald landing he marched his men and hid them on top of the hill above the Royal army but did not engage.

Donald Balloch then marched his army up to the Royalist positions and organised his men. As the combatants faced one another, Alexander Carrach and his 220 archers poured down the brae of the hill on which they had planted themselves, and shot their arrows so thick on the flank of the Royal Army that they were compelled to give way.

Donald Balloch then charged with the main MacDonald force and the result was a total rout of the Royal Army. Mar escaped on foot back to Kildrummy Castle, Aberdeenshire but the Sinclair Earl of Caithness and 16 of his personal retinue died. In total the King's army lost 990 men. The MacDonalds lost 27 men. Sir Duncan Grant also survived. We do not know how many of his clansmen perished but it must have been considerable. The remnants of the Clan fled eastwards over the hills and glens.

After this Donald Balloch raided the lands of Clan Mackintosh and Clan Cameron in revenge for their betrayal at the Battle of Lochaber.

Initially King James wanted to raise another army but he could not find the money to do this and he also had troubles with his Lords in Central Scotland. The tax he proposed was such that, 'in all lands of the realm where the yield of twa pennies was raiset, there be now ten pennies raiset'."(61) The great lords of the country refused to pay this tax and King James had to climb down. He was therefore forced into a reconciliation with Alexander MacDonald, still held at Tantallon Castle, who was pardoned and released from captivity. The Lord of the Isles was also granted the Lordship of Lochaber, which had, on his forfeiture, been granted to the Earl of Mar.

Alexander was good to his word and never again rebelled against the King and he returned to the Isles and remained subdued for the next few years. However, luck was on his side, the King's main supporter in the north, the Earl of Mar, died in 1435 and his only son, John Stewart, Earl of Buchan had predeceased him in 1424. John was Alexander's main rival for the Earldom of Ross but was killed fighting for the French against the English at the Battle of Verneuil, France . When he died the Earldom reverted back to the crown and Alexander was able to rightfully claim the Earldom through his mother. Furthermore, when the Earl of Mar himself died, King James' control of the North collapsed.

James finally acknowledged Alexander as the only noble who could control the north, and formally granted him the Earldom of Ross to win his support. Not only did he get control of Dingwall, but also Inverness, which he held until at least 1447.

Bigla Grant (ne Coymn) died prior to 1434 before her husband and the Coymns did not take kindly to a Grant inheriting all their lands in Strathspey. They gathered with the MacLeans and raided the Grant lands and John Roy Grant was killed in the ensuing fight although the Coymns were defeated and had to flee after much slaughter.

With Bigla (Matilda), John Roy had at least two sons:

1. Duncan Grant, afterwards Sir Duncan Grant of Freuchie.
2. Patrick Maclan Roy Grant, who married Janet, daughter of the Chief of Mackintosh.

Patrick got the lands of Auchanarrows, Pownan and the Point of Dalfour, all in the Barony of Freuchie. It seems Duncan and Patrick got half the lands of Freuchie each. Patrick died in 1508 but had a son, Patrick Reoch Grant, who was killed at the Battle of Flodden in 1513. This Patrick's lands eventually came into the possession of John Grant, 5th Laird of Freuchie in 1589.

Sir Duncan Grant 12th Chief of Clan Grant and 1st Laird of Freuchie. He was born on or before 1413 and he inherited the extensive lands of both his father and his mother in or around 1434. There is a document dated 1453, where Duncan is described as 'of Freuchie', but there is no record as to how he obtained the lands of Freuchie. He also reunited all the lands of Inverallan back to the Chiefs of Clan Grant. Another name for Freuchie was Ballachastell, which in Gaelic means, 'the town of the castle'.

He married Muriel, daughter of Malcolm, 10th of Mackintosh. The history books are a bit confusing at this time and it may be that John Grant, his son, was actually married to Muriel Mackintosh.

During the 1430's the King continued to alienate his Lords and the remainder of his extended family by grabbing their lands when he could and taxing them when he could not. In particular, the King was loathed and hated by his uncle, Walter Stewart, Earl of Athol. Sir Duncan Grant remained loyal to the King when other Lords began to talk of rebellion.

A General Council was held in Athol's heartland in Perth on 4 February 1437 and crucially for the conspirators, the King and Queen were also in the town at their lodgings in Blackfriars Monastery. On the evening of 20 February 1437, the King and Queen were in their rooms and separated from most of their servants. Athol's grandson and heir Robert Stewart, the King's Chamberlain, allowed around thirty men, led by Robert Graham, to access the building. King James was alerted to the men's presence, giving him time to hide in a sewer tunnel but, unfortunately its exit had recently been blocked off to prevent the King's tennis balls getting lost. James was trapped and soon uncovered; he was then unceremoniously murdered. Although in some respects a great King, James failed in one requirement of Kingship: keep your nobles' content or kill them. The murderers were soon rounded up and after being cruelly tortured, were executed. Sir Duncan Grant took part in the search for and captured some of the conspirators.

James I's six-year-old son succeeded him as King James II. He was crowned in Holyrood Abbey on 23 March 1437. The death of King James I and the crowning of his 6-year son changed the whole political situation in Scotland and the North in particular. The Regents of Scotland reaffirmed Alexander MacDonald as Earl of Ross and at the behest of his ally, Archibald, Earl of Douglas, Alexander was appointed 'Justiciar of Scotia, which made him the chief legal official in the Kingdom of Scotland. He used this new power to harass his enemies in Lennox and to take revenge on the Camerons who had deserted him at Lochaber.

The minority of King James II was a time of turmoil in Scotland as the powerful Lords of Southern Scotland vied for control of the young King. Sir Duncan Grant kept well out national politics at this time and consolidated his position in the new lands of Strathspey. During the minority of the King the MacDonalds were virtually defacto rulers in the North and Sir Duncan made sure he kept on the good side of the Lord of the Isles. For the next decade the Grants stayed out of national politics while the Lords of Douglas, Crichton and Livingstone vied for power in the South.

Although this next story had nothing to do with the Grants, the tale of the **Black Dinner** shows the murderous nature of Scottish politics at the time. The Lords Crichton and Livingstone were scared of the men that William Douglas could bring to his banner and also his friendship with the young King. They hatched a plot. In the name of the King they invited the young Earl of Douglas to a dinner with the King at Edinburgh Castle on 24 November 1440.

The young King knew nothing about the conspiracy. The Earl of Douglas, for some unknown reason, decided to allow his ten year old brother to accompany him as David Douglas was also a good friend of the King. His men begged him to send his brother back home, mindful of the precept of their father's, 'that they should not come together in one place, where themselves were not masters. Lest they should endanger their whole family at once'. The young Earl, however, had been totally taken in. They arrived with their friend Malcolm Fleming. At dinner the two Douglas brothers were sat at the same table as the young King who was delighted to be in the company of his young friends.

Then one of the most diabolical acts of treachery in Scotland's history took place as the four young friends were enjoying their evening. As the dinner was ending, Crichton nodded to the servants and a "black bulls head was served on a dish- traditionally a symbol of doom."(62) The three youths (William and David Douglas and Malcolm Fleming) were seized, despite the King protestations, and quickly given a mock trial for treason which lasted a matter of minutes. All three were then taken from the hall into the castle courtyard where an executioner's block had already been set up and the executioner waiting with his axe.

William Douglas pleaded for the lives of his brother and friend urging Crichton to be merciful to them as they had nothing to do with his crimes. When this fell on deaf ears he then asked that his young brother be executed first, so that the boy did not have to witness his death before his own. This again was refused and the little ten-year-old cried as he watched first Fleming and then William Douglas being beheaded by the stroke of the executioner's axe. Last, he then suffered the same fate.

"There was no rallying cry of 'Douglas'. The clan's blood was thick, but family envies were strong, and unexpected good fortune was welcome from whatever source it came. The successor to the Earldom was James the Gross, great uncle of the dead, and he may have been party to the conspiracy, for he took no revenge. "(63) This is pure speculation, however, as there is no evidence and none of the conspirators were to know that both the Earl and his younger brother would attend the dinner. It is more probable that the new Earl, having been elevated to the position unexpectantly, had to spend his energies consolidating his power and status as Earl during the first few years, and did not feel strong enough to take vengeance. In fact, his son, the next Earl had a hatred of both Crichton and Livingstone, and this was, at least partly, due to their murder of his cousins.

The terrible event has been known as the 'Black Dinner' ever since and is commemorated in a popular rhyme of the time:

"Edinburgh castle, towne and toure,

God grant thou sink for sinne!

And that even for the black dinoir

Earl Douglas got therein."(64)

The Black Dinner also served as the inspiration for the 'Red Wedding' in George R.R. Martin's 'A Song of Ice and Fire', part of the Game of Thrones Series of novels and television series.

It was clear that Sir Duncan Grant did well to keep himself and Clan Grant out of nation politics and he remained in the north developing the power base of the Clan.

Eventually King James II took control of the Government himself but he was still being advised by Crichton. Eventually, he personally killed the new Earl of Douglas at a dinner in Stirling Castle in 1452. Sir Duncan Grant 1st of Freuchie was one of the Kings loyal guests at this dinner. The King and Earl William Douglas had once been good friends but over the years this friendship had waned and the King saw Douglas as a threat, particularly with the 5000 men he could bring to battle. He eventually persuaded the Earl of Douglas to meet him at Stirling Castle. William Douglas agreed and travelled north with a small retinue of followers.

After an initial meeting all seemed well and they retired to have dinner with the rest of the court. After they had finished the meal the King asked Douglas to come with him into a separate chamber, where they could talk privately. William should have been suspicious when the only man who accompanied them was Sir Patrick

Gray of Foulis, his sworn enemy. Once in the chamber the King berated Douglas for his offences against him and the number of times he had to pardon him. Douglas was initially submissive, saying that he had not acted against the King but against his advisors, particularly Livingston and Crichton, who were the King's real enemies.

The King then demanded that the Earl of Douglas dissolve the union he had entered with Alexander Lindsay, Earl of Crawford and John MacDonald of Islay, Lord of the Isles. When Douglas refused the King stabbed him and then his retainers did likewise, and Sir Patrick Gray, whom Douglas had made his enemy months before, brought out his giant pole axe and striking William in the head, struck out his brains. During the commotion the rest of the King's party entered the chamber and seeing Douglas slain, they each took out their dagger and stabbed the dead man, hoping to take some of the blame away from their Monarch. Sir Duncan Grant of Freuchie was one who drew his own dagger and plunged it into the body of the Earl of Douglas. After this his body was thrown out of a window to fall on the rocks below the castle heights. Where he was buried, or what was done with his body, there is no record in history. The date was 13th February 1452.

William Douglas died without issue and the Earldom passed to his brother James Douglas, 9th Earl of Douglas and 3rd Earl of Avondale. He immediately rebelled against King James with his allies, the Earl of Crawford and John MacDonald, 4th Lord of the Isles. Sir Duncan Grant immediately returned north to prepare the defense of the north against the impending revolt of the MacDonalds who were allies of the Douglas Clan.

The new Earl of Douglas, James, immediately rebelled and almost took the Kingdom but was eventually defeated and forced to flee into exile to England. Before this, however, he invoked the terms of the alliance with the MacDonalds and the Lord of the Isles, still only aged twenty-one, led 10,000 MacDonalds onto the mainland and seized the Castles of Inverness, Urquhart and Ruthven and declared his independence from the Scottish Crown. He demolished Ruthven Castle to the ground, but he was defeated in battle by the Earl of Sutherland, who brought with him Sir Duncan Grant and his clansmen who remained loyal to King James II. There was much slaughter on both sides. John MacDonald escaped but never again would he take personal command of his troops in a rebellion.

This was the last venture of Sir Duncan Grant into the national affairs of Scotland. Meanwhile King James's ambitions to increase Scotland's standing saw him besiege Roxburgh Castle in 1460, one of the last Scottish castles still held by the English after the Wars of Independence. For this siege, James took a number of large cannon imported from Belgium. On 3 August, he was standing near one of these cannons, known as 'the Lion', when it exploded and killed him. The Scots continued with the siege, led by George Douglas, 4th Earl of Angus, and the castle fell a few days later. Once the Castle was captured James's widow, Mary of Guelders, ordered its destruction. James's son was crowned as King James III and his mother functioned as Regent until her own death three years later. James III became a very unpopular monarch in Scotland due to his unwillingness to administer justice, his disastrous relationships with all his extended family and his 'ill-treatment' of the nobles of mainland Scotland.

In terms of Duncan Grant, however, "on the 26th March 1479 he was one of the arbitrators who gave decree in the dispute between the Mackintoshes and Roses of Kilravock as to the lands of Urquhart and Glenmoriston. His son, John Grant, was also an arbitrator."(65)

Meanwhile the reign of King James III was as turbulent as his father and grandfather. Like his father his early years saw him as a hostage to the leading nobles of the land who sought to rule in his name. Much of the fighting and intrigue occurred in the South and did not initially affect the Grants in the North.

However in 1480 the King had both of his brothers arrested and imprisoned in Edinburgh Castle. Soon after, the younger brother, John Stewart, Earl of Mar, died, supposedly of a fever but it was widely suspected that he had been murdered at the instigation of Cochrane, one of the King's advisors. The elder brother, the Duke of Albany, was determined not to suffer the same fate. One evening he killed his jailers, and with a rope provided by his page, both men scaled down the rock face of Edinburgh Castle. The page had broken his legs in a fall when near the bottom and the Duke personally carried him all the way to Leith Docks, where a ship was waiting to take him to France. Cochrane was rewarded by being created Earl of Mar by the King.

Eventually, in late 1481, an anticipated English attack came and they crossed the border with a vast army and sacked much of the borders before returning home. At the same time the Duke of Albany journeyed from France to England to seek the aid of the King of England. In return for this aid Albany agreed to do homage to King Edward IV for the Kingdom of Scotland and, in addition, he also agreed to surrender Berwick (once more in Scotland's possession) and large parts of the

Scottish borders to England. The English King gave Albany a great army, under the Duke of Gloucester, and it marched north to gain the throne for Albany.

The King's position in Scotland was not good. "James antagonised his barons by barring them from his Secret Council, the little committee of intimates who helped him shape his policies. Bad harvests, famine, the plague and rising prices angered a restless people who believed their King did nothing but sit at Stirling with his masons and fiddlers, counting his gold. In this hostile atmosphere, James went reluctantly to war with England. His brother Albany was there, marching northward to seize the throne, with an English army under Richard of Gloucester..."(66)

In 1482, despite the unpopularity of the King, a large Scottish army mustered on the Borough Muir of Edinburgh and marched south, resting at the town of Lauder. Sir Duncan Grant was an elderly man by this time but he and the Clan remained loyal to their King and he sent his only son and heir, John Grant, with over 400 Grants to join the Kings Army.

At the evening Council of War meeting King James III proposed to enter England at the head of the army and meet his brother head on. But the nobles, led by Archibald Douglas, Earl of Angus, refused to march under his banner unless he dealt first with their grievances. John Grant was not part of this rebellion and gave his wholehearted support to his monarch. The King was angered by this perceived disloyalty and refused to even hear what the grievances of his nobles were, and dismissed them from his royal tent.

The grievances were essentially two-fold. "One demand was that the copper money which the king had issued be withdrawn from circulation. The coin was so depreciated in value that no-one would accept it, and in consequence great misery existed among the poor classes, who could not purchase food."(67)

The second grievance was against the King's low born favourites, and the Lords demanded that he dismiss them and rule the kingdom with the advice and guidance of his nobles, as all other Kings had done.

When the King refused to hear their grievances the nobles reconvened in the command tent of the Archibald Douglas. John Grant was not invited. After a short discussion they all agreed to now obtain their demands by use of force. Archibald Douglas, Earl of Angus, stood up and made a lengthy speech to his other nobles, urging them to be rid of the King's favourites.

"In answer to this a confused murmur of assent arose, when Lord Gray told of a well-known story of mice who were agreed as to the policy of hanging a bell around the cats neck to warm them of the approach of their enemy, but were doubtful as to who should tie on the bell. To this parable Angus suddenly responded, **'I will bell the cat'**, and under his guidance measures for executing their purpose were at once taken."(68)

They then made their way to the King's tent but on route met the King's favourite, Cochrane, who had been sent to placate them. He was seen by the nobles as the main reason for the introduction of the copper coinage and for the King's mistrust of his nobles and he was, therefore, hated more than any of the other favourites of the King.

Archibald Douglas immediately grabbed Cochrane by his heavy gold chain and pulled it from his neck, remarking that a rope would suit him better. His kinsmen, Douglas of Lochleven then snatched away Cochrane's hunting horn which would have allowed him to forewarn the King of danger. Cochrane was then arrested and put in chains.

The noble rebels then marched on the King's own tent and entering, arrested five other low born favourites of the King, apart from James Ramsay who hid behind James and, because the nobles would not endanger the King, he was able to escape arrest.

On hearing of what they thought was an attempt on the King's life his loyal supporters soon grabbed their weapons and gathered round the King's tent ready to fight to free James. John Grant was one of the leaders of the King's faction and berated the Earl of Angus and the others for their disloyalty. However, Angus was able to placate them by convincing them that the King was in no danger and that their quarrel was with his advisors.

The King was confined to his quarters, 'for his own safety' and a mock trial was held immediately where Cochrane and his five associates were found guilty of treason. Archibald Douglas, showing no mercy, had them immediately executed by being hung from the Bridge of Lauder, within the grounds of Thirlestane Castle.

The whole army then returned to Edinburgh and King James III was confined in Edinburgh Castle. The nobles made a hasty peace pact with Albany, offering to make him Regent, and the English army withdrew, thinking they had achieved their objective without losing a single man.

Later evidence has shown that the Earl of Angus and many of the other nobles had been in collusion with the Duke of Albany throughout this period and were aware of the obligations he had agreed with the King of England. However, this must be seen in context; in any internal civil dispute in Scotland, the aggrieved party usually ended up in England, seeking the support of the English King, but they were almost always happy to agree homage to England when it suited but knowing that they would never fulfil such agreements, not least because their subjects, at that time, would never follow them. For Great Britain to happen required a Scottish King on the throne of England and the bankruptcy of the nation before Scotland agreed to union with the 'auld enemy', England.

The Grants and the other Highland levies returned north. John Grant was not only in command of the Grants but also the whole contingent of Clansmen from Morayshire. He died on the way home, although we do not know if this was from natural causes or from some incident. As the only son of the Chief of Grant his death was mourned by the whole clan. His wife is unknown but they left three sons;

-   John Grant, who succeeded.
-   Patrick Grant, younger twin of John, ancestor of the Grants of Ballindalloch.
-   William Grant, ancestor of the Grants of Blairfindy.

Their daughters were:

-   Catherine Grant, who became the 3rd wife of Lachlan Mackintosh, called 'Badenoch'; and
-   Muriel Grant, who married Patrick Leslie of Balquhain.

Sir Duncan Grant did not live much longer than his son and died in 1485. He was succeeded by his young grandson, John Grant. He was very young at this time and the Grants lived quietly for a number of years keeping out of national politics.

Meanwhile, Albany could not keep the peace for long and shortly afterwards he again fled to England, giving up Dunbar Castle to the English before he left. An uneasy peace between the King and the Earl of Angus lasted until 1488, when the Earl of Angus again rebelled against the King, but this time he was the main leader.

During the five years of peace in the Kingdom (1483 – 1488) the King continued to take the advice of his favourites over that of his nobles. James Ramsay, whose life had been spared at Lauder by his hiding behind the King, persuaded the King to create him Earl of Bothwell. This incensed the Earl of Angus and other nobles and their anger increased when an order was given out that Ramsay was the only person who was allowed to carry arms within the precincts of the royal residence.

Angus was determined to take matters into his own hands and this time he had the support of the majority of the Scots nobility. They proposed to remove King James III and replace him with his fifteen year old son, the future James IV. In order to achieve this they captured the Prince. The two factions gathered their forces. The King travelled north where most of his supporters resided.

Through the King's supporters, the Earls of Huntly and Crawford, a peace conference was organised in spring 1488 at Blackness Castle on the Firth of Forth. The rebels were represented by the Earls of Angus and Argyll and Lord Hailes and Lord Lyle. A peace treaty was agreed and the King's army was dismissed and he retired back to Edinburgh Castle.

It seems the King soon after violated the terms of the Peace Agreement and some of his remaining supporters such as the Earls of Huntly, Errol and Marishal, with Lord Glamis renounced their allegiance to King James III and joined the rebels.

The King went to Fife, gathered his northern supporters and marched south to Stirling. But by now, particularly with the loss of support from Huntly, the King's forces were greatly depleted. The rebels marched north and they fought the **Battle of Sauchieburn** on 11th June 1488, near Stirling. To aid him the King brought with him the sword of Robert the Bruce. It did him little good.

The Grants did not form part of this loyalist force. With the recent death of both Duncan the old Chief and his son and heir John, they had not organised themselves quickly enough to come to the aid of King James III. Reportedly the rebels were only 18,000 strong and were led by Archibald Douglas, 5th Earl of Angus, Alexander Home, 2nd Lord Home, Patrick Hepburn, 1st Earl of Bothwell and Lord Gray. "At Sauchieburn on the Stirling plain, near the site of Bruce's great battle and in the same summer month, he [the King] watched as his Highlanders and burghal levies were slaughtered by border lances and Douglas spears. He turned and fled, but was thrown from his horse near Beaton's Mill. He asked a cottage-wife to find him a priest. She brought him one, or at least a man who said he was a priest, and when James asked for absolution this stranger drew a knife and killed him."(69)

The young James IV had specifically ordered that his father was not to be harmed. For the whole of his life he continued to have intense guilt for the indirect role he had played in the death of his father and he did penance every year as a result.

Each Lent he wore a heavy iron chain around his waist, next to his skin. He added extra weight every year.

On the death of King James III, his son was immediately proclaimed James IV, King of Scotland.

CHAPTER 6. KING JAMES IV AND KING JAMES V.

John Grant 13th Chief of Clan Grant and 2nd Laird of Freuchie was Chief of the Clan between 1485 and 1528. John was known as **Am Bard Ruadh** (or Red Bard). He married Margaret Ogilvie of Deskford in 1484. Her family were the Earls of Findlater who later became the Earls of Seafield.

After the death of King James III, John Grant quickly swore loyalty to King James IV. During his lifetime he greatly extended the Grant Estates by the acquisition of further lands at Tullochgorm, Mulben, Urquhart, Glencarnie and Ballindalloch. "He was on good terms with the Earl of Huntly, and from him received the life rents of lands at Kinrara and other lands in Badenoch."(70) John Grant was also the arbitrator in a number of disputes between Mackintoshes, Dunbar's, Innes, Kilravocks, and others, so he clearly took an important part in public affairs in the north.

The death of King James III and the Coronation of his son as King James IV in June 1488 at the age of fifteen led to the usual turmoil in the South of Scotland. This allowed the MacDonalds to again flex their muscles in the north again, this time led by Angus Og, son and heir of John MacDonald, 4th Lord of the Isles. He was a formidable warrior who had even fought and defeated his father at the Battle of the Bloody Bay, Mull. He immediately took the opportunity to raid into the mainland again and ravaged Urquhart and Glenmoriston before capturing Inverness. He never left as "... he was murdered soon afterwards in a brawl in his rooms in the town by a wandering Irish harper called Dermid O'Cairlore, who was punished by being dragged behind a horse till he died."(71) With this the MacDonald revolt dissipated and they all went home with their booty.

After this the Earl of Huntly wanted a strong clan to look after the lands around Loch Ness and this is why he turned to the Grants and gave them control of Urquhart and Glenmoriston. The Grants also knew the area as until 1420 they had held the lands of Stratherrick on the south side of Loch Ness.

After the death of Angus Og, the King and his Scottish Court entered into dialogue with many of the Chiefs including John Grant. In the early days of his rule he had limited success, despite rewarding many with money and grants of land. But the King continued to pursue pledges of loyalty from the Clan Chiefs. In addition, he wanted the eldest sons of the Chiefs to be educated in the south, so they could be civilised. John Grant was one of the first chiefs to agree to this.

"John Grant, as early as 1488, must have acquired an interest in Urquhart, as in a dispute between the Laird of Freuchie and Alexander, Lord Gordon, the rents (270 merks) of the lands of Urquhart, and Glen Moriston are stated, 28th January, 1492-3, to be four years in arrears."(72) He then became keeper of Urquhart Castle. The lands of Urquhart are about 10 miles south-west of Inverness and formed the outlying province of the Grant possessions. Urquhart suffered badly from being on the route of the clans between the West and Inverness and were plundered many times. Because Urquhart was remote from Strathspey, it was usually administered by a Chamberlain, whose house and offices were at Balmacaan.

Urquhart Castle, Loch Ness.

Copyright: Eileen Sinclair 2023.

At Urquhart, Clan 'Ic Uian fiercely resisted the authority of the Grants for many years and there was much fighting between the two clans. They also refused to pay any rents to their 'superiors' the Grants. In one incident they chased a Grant from Speyside down the hill of Clunemore and he only escaped their swords by leaping the swollen river Coilty where it forces its way through the gorge which is now spanned by the 'Bridge of the Leap'. In another incident, they killed a party of Grants, chopped off their heads in Mac Uian's Pool, at the Bridge of Drumnadrochit and then sent them back to John 'the Bard' Grant as a 'gift'.

At Glenmoriston, the MacDonalds also opposed the Grants for years, but slowly but surely Laird John Grant brought peace and security to the area.

"In 1493, when John was in Edinburgh, he formally resigned all his lands into the hands of King James IV, who then re-granted them, and united them by Royal charter into one barony to be called the Barony of Freuchie. This barony continued until 1694 when, with other baronies, it was absorbed in the Regality of Grant."(73)

Map 11 . Grant Lands of Glenmoriston and Urquhart.

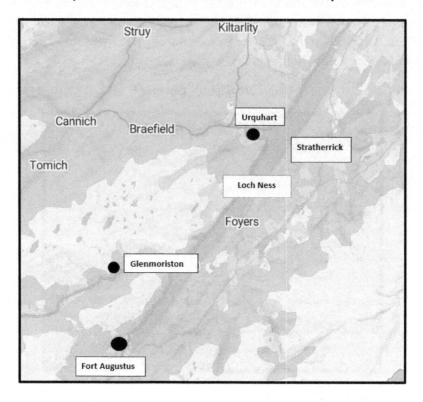

In 1498 the King confirmed John Grant in the estates of Glencarnie and Ballindalloch and also appointed him Sheriff in order to help maintain the King's peace. At the time there was much trouble when Alexander MacDonald of Lochalsh led a force of Islemen to Lochaber and Badenoch to try and recover the Lordship of the Isles and the Earldom of Ross for Clan MacDonald. This led to much fighting. The Mackintoshes and Kilravocks joined the MacDonalds and stormed Inverness Castle. They then raided into the Black Isle but then at Strathconan they were defeated by the Mackenzies at the Battle of the Drumchatt. The Mackenzies then went on to take revenge against the MacDonalds and their allies.

The killing between the MacDonalds and the Mackenzies was so great that although the Mackenzies had helped put down the insurrection of the MacDonalds, the Earl of Huntly, as Lieutenant of the North, was given a Commission of Fire and Sord against them and John Grant was one of those called to assist Huntly in the name of the King.

In 1505, John Grant acquired more lands in Cromdale. Then in 1509 the King bestowed on John Grant the outright ownership of Urquhart and Glenmoriston. This was given because of the loyalty which John Grant had given to the King in previous years. As we have seen these lands were in a strategic position in the Highlands and he needed men he could trust in command of the area: the Grants. The Laird of Freuchie also had a large number of clansmen to help protect the King's position. "It was believed, and with good reason, that, if the territory was absolutely made over to himself and his family …. their interest in the preservation of peace would be increased without ….. loss to the Crown. And so the Charters of 1609 passed the Great Seal, and the Castle and Lordship of Urquhart for ever ceased to be the property of the King.(74) The Charter was signed off in December 1509. Part of the charter obliged the Laird of Freuchie to provide 15 horsemen for Royal Service in time of war as well as all the remainder of his clansmen as foot soldiers. He was also obliged to maintain and improve the defences of Urquhart Castle.

At the same time the Barony of Corrimony was granted to his 2nd legitimate son, Iain Og (Young John) and the Barony of Glenmoriston on his illegitimate son Iain Mor (Big John). He also owned the estate of Culcabock near Inverness.

On the national scene, King James IV married Princess Margaret Tudor, daughter of King Henry VII of England. It was hoped that this marriage would bring peace between the two kingdoms, and an end to cross-border fighting. The two kingdoms even signed a new Treaty of Perpetual Peace in 1502. James IV was generally thought of as a reasonably just King: for a Stewart King of Scotland that is.

Good relations with the English could not last. When Henry VII died in 1509 he was succeeded by his son, Henry VIII. The new King was an extremely arrogant and intolerant character who had little respect for the Treaty of Perpetual Peace. He was generally bad news for Scotland. There followed several incidents between the two kingdoms with James's navy clashing with the English. Matters were not helped by the fact that the English Queen was at the time childless and, therefore, James's son was heir to the English throne.

Eventually the restless King of England turned his attention to war with the French. The French King, Louis XII, turned to the Auld Alliance and pleaded with the Scots to attack and distract the English. To impress upon King James the plight of France, the French Queen even sent James her glove and ring, appealing to his chivalry and begging him to attack.

The Scots King's greatest weakness was his 'honour', a luxury few Scots Kings could afford and it was to eventually lead to disaster for Scotland. He could not refuse the French Queens' plea and assembled the greatest army Scotland had ever produced, somewhere between 60,000 and 100,000 men.

With this force were Chief John Grant, all the leading men of the Clan and a substantial body of up to five hundred men. The army headed for the border and confidently sent the English Commander, the Earl of Somerset, word that they were coming, challenging him to meet in two weeks' time.

Initially the invasion was successful with the Castles of Norham, Wark and Etal falling before them. After much delay the English army was eventually reported to be on the march and James led his men to take up a strong position on the ridge of Brankston Edge, above Flodden Moor, in the Vale of Till.

The veteran English Commander was not stupid and ditched any pretence at meeting the Scots head on in a chivalric fashion, deciding instead, to use more devious methods. In this he acted more like King James's great forebear, Robert the Bruce. Somerset sent a small decoy force under his son to needle the Scots rear and James countered this by sending a large part of his cavalry force under Lord Home off to rout them, which they duly did.

In the meantime, the rest of the English army moved to a position under the hill where the Scots cannon could not get at them and where the Scots could not fight without coming down the hill to meet them. The Grant forces were grouped on the left wing of the Scots line, under the Earl of Huntly, where they waited impatiently for battle. Huntly placed his most heavily armoured men in the front rank, which would have included John Grant, so that the English archers would have little impact. The two armies met and fierce fighting ensued. The English began to fall back and were in serious trouble of being completely routed. But Surrey sent his light horse brigade to assist the retreating English and this helped stop the rout. The result was a stalemate, and both sides took no further part in the battle. According to later accounts, Huntly later suggested that their division rejoin the fighting but his overall commander, Lord Home replied, 'the man does well this day who saves himself: we fought those who were opposed to us and beat them; Let other companies do the same'.

Depiction of the Battle of Flodden 1873.

Meanwhile the other Scots grew impatient and this was matched by that of the King who, wanting to get into action, ordered the abandonment of the Scots superior position and they advanced down the steep hill to attack the English. The steepness of the slope prevented them from using their ten thousand horse and seventeen large cannon and the men, lords and commoners alike, rushed to battle on foot.

The result was outright disaster, the blackest day in Scots history. What made it worse was that it was mainly the fault of Scotland's most loved King, who acted more like a youthful squire eager for his first taste of battle as opposed to general of his forces. To make matters even more desperate, King Louis of France supplied the Scots with thousands of 18-foot-long pikes to help them in their fight. They may have been a great help against a cavalry attack but to men running ever faster down a rugged steep slope they were totally useless, helping the enemy more than their users. The Scots tripped, overbalanced, and their pikes broke, splintered, pierced and generally got in the way of the charging men who, when they reached the foot of the slope were utterly disorganised to be met by wave after wave of English arrows. Thousands died before they reached the enemy but the battle could still have been won in the hand-to-hand battle. But the English had the ultimate weapon of the time, the Bill, a weapon with a long shaft mounted with a broad blade, perfect for slashing through both men and spear shafts.

MAP 12. FLODDEN AND SOLWAY MOSS.

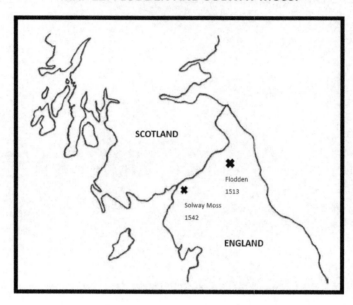

Against this weapon the Scots died by the thousand. The King and his accompanying nobles rashly stormed into the midst of the battle with their men and suffered the same fate: death. King James IV and his 17-year-old illegitimate son Alexander died bravely in the thick of the fighting. James is said to have killed five men with his sword, standing over the body of his beloved son, before his sword was shattered and he was eventually felled by an arrow and a gash from a Bill.

The nobles of Scotland died with their King, as did the manhood of the nation. Up to 20,000 Scots died including one Archbishop, two Bishops, two Abbots and 24 Earls and Lords. Many Grants died in this battle but Chief John Grant survived, although he narrowly escaped the charge of Sir Edward Stanley in the rear of the Highlanders as they fled.

Scotland was shattered by the defeat and there wasn't a home in all the land which did not mourn its dead. The country was wide open for invasion but thankfully Henry VIII was busy in France and could not spare the men to attack a sorry Scotland.

On 21 September, a mere 12 days after his father's death on the bloody field of Flodden, Prince James was crowned King James V at Stirling in a ceremony conducted by James Beaton, Archbishop of Glasgow. The new Monarch was 17 months old. Despite this, the nation rallied to the new King and prepared to defend the country against an impending English invasion which never came.

The death of King James IV put all of Scotland, but particularly the Highlands, into a state of confusion and turmoil. As ever the MacDonalds in particular took the opportunity to try and regain their lands and titles that they had lost over the last century. "On All Saints Day, 1513, Sir Donald MacDonald of Lochalsh, who had been proclaimed Lord of the Isles, invaded Urquhart, seized the Castle, plundered the neighbourhood, and held the lands for 3 years."(75) The Grant garrison were all either killed in the assault on the castle or executed immediately afterwards.

The Earls of Huntly and Argyll were directed to proceed against MacDonald who was declared a rebel but little was done. However the death of Donald MacDonald at the end of 1519 brought the rebellion to a sudden close.

One result of the invasion was that the Laird of Freuchie sought an alliance with Ewan Allanson Cameron of Locheil, Captain of Clan Cameron and they entered into a bond of friendship on 22 October 1520. The Treaty specifically provided that the Camerons would defend the Grant lands in Urquhart and Glenmoriston, and that the Grants would defend the Cameron lands in Lochaber. To seal the deal young Donald Cameron, son of the Chief, was to marry the Laird's daughter, Agnes Grant.

"The Laird of Freuchie and his clan appear to have been summoned to muster under the Duke of Albany, as Regent on 20 October 1523 to march against England. But owing, no doubt, to advanced age, and probably also to the example of the Earl of Huntly, neither the Laird of Freuchie, nor any of his name, responded to the summons, as appears from a remission under the Great Seal, dated 13 February 1527/28."(76)

Chief John Grant's last public act was to take part in the peace agreement, called a 'Letter of Slains', which ended a bloody feud between the Grants and the Farquharson's of Strathdee. This feud had caused much killing and looting between the two clans. A 'Slain' was a letter, written to the King or Queen by the family of someone who was killed, agreeing to forgive the person who did it and asking for them to be pardoned. The King or Queen could not forgive the person without the family's agreement.

John Grant, 2nd of Freuchie, died on 1 May 1528. By his wife Margaret Ogilvie, he left two sons and at least six daughters:

1). James Grant, who succeeded, known as James of the Forays (Seumas nan Creach).

2). John Grant of Corriemony.

3). Margaret Grant, who married Thomas Cumming of Ernside.

4). Anne Grant, who married Hugh Fraser, Master of Lovat around 1512, later 3rd Lord Fraser of Lovat. Her husband and son, Simon Fraser, were killed in 1544 at the Battle of the Shirts. There may also have been another daughter, Muriel, who married a brother of Hugh Fraser, Master of Lovat, thereby increasing the links between these two clans.

5). Agnes Grant, who married Donald Cameron, Chief of Clan Cameron.

6). Elizabeth Grant, who married John Mackenzie, 9th of Kintail around 1526.

7). Christiana

8). Another daughter, said to have married Hector Mackintosh, 'temporary' Chief of Clan Mackintosh.

He also left an illegitimate son, **Iain Mor Grant** (Big John) who came from Kincardine, near Boat of Garten. His mother was a daughter of the Baron of Kincardine. Iain Mor was renowned for his height and his strength and there are many tales of his bravery and valour. His father gave him the lands of Glenmoriston and other estates, including Carron, Wester Elchies and Kinchurdy by Boat of Garten.

This Glenmoriston sept of the Clan would become almost independent of the Clan Grant Chiefs and would follow the lead of the Grant Lairds of Glenmoriston, rather than the Clan Chiefs on many occasions, particularly during the Jacobite Rebellions. When the main family of Clan Grant supported the Government, the Grants of Glenmoriston were much more independent and often sided with the likes of the MacDonalds and other rebellious clans.

Formerly Glenmoriston had belonged to the MacDonald Lord of the Isles and were held by them by Macianruaidh, a vassal ,chief, and cadet of the MacDonalds. Macianruaidh, as to be suspected, initially resented losing control of his lands but

Iain Mor took the time to befriend him and his kinsmen and they eventually accepted him as their new laird. So much so that Macianruaidh eventually became Tutor to Patrick, Iain Mor Grant's eldest son.

By 1509 Iain Mor Grant received a Charter from King James IV of the Barony of Urquhart, confirming his position in these lands. He was soon in trouble with the authorities though for harbouring and receiving rebels and was forced to pay compensation in order to avoid forfeiture. Then in 1532 he again greatly expanded his lands by gaining the estates of Culcabock, Criocantionail and the Haugh, in the Parish of Inverness, which had belonged to the family of Hay. Then in 1541 he got the lands of Carron, Wester Elchies and Kincardine in Strathspey. These lands were considerable and firmly established him as the largest landowning Grant apart from the Chief.

At some point he divorced his first wife, Isabella Innes and even got a papal disposition for this. The reason may have been that she could not conceive. He then married Isobella or Agnes, grand-daughter of Fraser, Lord Lovat.

Isobella was the widow of Allan McRory MacDonald, Chief of Clanranald. "After the Chief of Clanranald died she left Moydart for the Aird, her father's residence. On her way, she and her retinue camped at Torgyle, in the Braes of Glenmoriston, and sent a message to the laird, then living at Tomantouil, craving his protection. To this request he responded in the most gallant style, and invited her and her party to his residence, where, after a week's festivities, they were united in the bonds of Wedlock."(77) This marriage would have severe repercussions for Clan Grant as Isabella had a son and heir with Allan McRory MacDonald, Ranald Gallda, who they would try to help in gaining the Chieftainship of Clanranald.

Iain Mor (Big John) Grant's eldest son, Patrick, succeeded to Glenmoriston and from him the branch were often called Clan Patrick. John Grant of Glenmoriston also had two illegitimate sons; John Roy who got the estates of Carron; and James, who got the estates of Wester Elchies.

Back to the main branch of Clan Grant of Freuchie.

James Grant, 3rd of Freuchie, Chief of Clan Grant succeeded his father in 1528 and was Clan Chief until 1553. One of the great Chiefs of Clan Grant, he was known as **'James of the Forays' (or Seumas nan Creach).** He was a very strong supporter of the Earl of Huntly, the King's Lieutenant of the North. However, he did not always do the King's bidding. In 1528 Clan Chattan, under the leadership of Hector

Mackintosh, had made trouble in Morayshire. A Commission of Fire and Sword was issued to burn out the clan, and to transport their woman and children to Norway. "The writ commanded them to invade the territories of the proscribed clan, and to utterly destroy them by slaughter, burning and drowning, and to leave none of them alive except priests, woman and children."(78) The women and children were to be transported to Norway, Zealand (Holland) and other distant countries as slaves.

However, the other Highland Lords, including James Grant, were slow to execute this extreme Commission and Clan Chattan were saved. For his inaction James Grant and other leading Grants were fined £1,000 merks. Hector Mackintosh continued in his old ways of raiding and stealing.

Clan Chattan did not learn its lesson and again raided and destroyed the Ogilvie properties in Strathnavin and Daviot, including Daviot Castle in 1531 and again in 1534. In the first raid they killed 22 of Clan Ogilvie, including woman and children. "Once more James did nothing to hinder them, and he was again ordered by the king to assist Huntly in a raid against them. James took little action, for he was related to Hector Mackintosh, their leader, so his inaction is understandable. For these faults, and also for his failure to send clansmen to join the King's army in an attack on England, James was, rather surprisingly, given a pardon and discharge by the King in 1536."(79) One major reason for James Grant refusing to aid the King's men against Macintosh was that he and his clansmen had actually taken part in the raid.

The King was desperate for the loyalty of Clan Grant and even went as far as providing James Grant with a royal letter exempting him, his friends and vassals from the jurisdiction of the Highland Courts and Judges, except the rule of law from Edinburgh. Basically James Grant and his men were now virtually independent of the law for the rest of their Chief's life.

However, before this exemption was granted by the King Clan Grants part in the attack on Ogilvie came to the King's attention and on 11 May 1536 James Grant of Freuchie, John Grant of Ballindalloch and John Grant of Culcabock had to find surety for assisting Hector and William Mackintosh in the raid against the Ogilvies.

The years of King James V's minority were a time of almost civil war in the South of Scotland with one faction fighting with the other for control of the young King. The Grants, in their highland fortress of Strathspey, largely kept out of this bitter fighting and concentrated on consolidating their power in the north and fighting off

112

rival clans. Then in the early 1540's King Henry VIII of England was seeking to win over King James to his new Protestant religion and his fight against the Pope and the French. In this regard he had a lot of support from the growing Protestant faction at the Scottish Court.

In 1541 the two Kings had agreed to meet at York to discuss another peace treaty. King Henry travelled north to the meeting but unbeknown to him, King James's Catholic advisors had persuaded him not to go. Henry was furious with James and was now determined to put him and Scotland to the sword until they agreed to come under his domination. Diplomacy was out the window, now the English would use only force.

Jedburgh Abbey, destroyed by the English in 1542.

Copyright: Eileen Sinclair 2020.

Late in 1541 Henry sent raiders into the Scottish Borders where they destroyed and pillaged everything they could find. As soon as the English had returned home the Border Clans retaliated with a raid on English territory. But the 1541 English raid was just a preliminary foray for a much bigger expedition in 1542. Henry sent three thousand raiders into the Borders, under the Warden of the East March, Sir Robert Bowes, burning villages and towns as they went.

At this time King James V had nominated the Earl of Huntly to command his army on the borders, consisting of 10,000 men. Huntly called on his northern allies and James Grant sent two hundred men of the Clan, under his eldest son, John Grant, to support the Earl. This force was relatively small as it was made up only of cavalry and not many of the highlanders owned a horse. Initially the English campaign went well and destruction was evident everywhere they went in the Scottish borders.

Then the English made a fateful mistake and split up their forces to better escort their stolen cattle and sheep back to England. The Scottish scouts found out that the English were intending to attack and burn Jedburgh and Kelso on their way home. On the night of the 23 August 1542 the Scots army marched to intercept the English force as it headed for Jedburgh.

When the English roused in their camp the next morning they were astonished to see a Scots army between them and their destination. Master John Grant and his clansmen formed part of this force. However, the English commander, Bowes, was still confident of victory and refused to retreat. The stage was set for the **Battle of Haddon Rig**.

The Scots army at the battle consisted of only two thousand men (only a small part of the overall army of 10,000) compared with an English force of three thousand. But many of the Scots were very experienced warriors who had spent many years on the Continent, in the army of the French King fighting the English. The two armies fronted up to each other. While they were doing this, the Grants, who had come predominantly on horseback, mounted their horses and stole round behind the English force.

The Scots did not wait for an English assault and stormed the English lines. The charge was so furious that they immediately broke the English formations. Meanwhile at the same time John Grant and his clansmen attacked on their mounts from the rear and totally overwhelmed the mounted English knights, striking them in their backs with their swords and battle axes. The English broke and ran. Of the three thousand Englishmen, over two thousand were killed and six hundred taken prisoner, including their leader, Sir Robert Bowes and over sixty northern English noblemen. The Scots losses were very small. Although this was a great victory for Scotland, its only real effect was to awaken the English sleeping giant. King Henry was furious and even more determined to obliterate Scotland. He raised an army of 20,000 men under the command of the Earl of Norfolk. He crossed the border on the 21 October 1542 with orders to destroy everything and everyone Scottish.

King James and the Earl of Huntly, the new saviour of Scotland, gathered their forces to oppose Norfolk. This force include John Grant and his clansmen. The English commander was a cautious man and after again destroying much of the

Border lands he used the excuse of having insufficient supplies to justify retreating back to England.

King James V wanted now to attack England but the nobles in his army would have none of it, thinking they had done enough by chasing the English off Scottish soil. But King James was not to be dissuaded, he wanted to invade England and restore it to the Catholic faith. On his return to Edinburgh, Cardinal Beaton, newly returned from France, helped him to make his quest a religious one and he soon had another army of over ten thousand men. James Grant and his son John were fully supportive of his King and they raised the Clan again to support the Scottish cause.

James Grant and 300 clansmen and vassals formed part of this force. Unfortunately, this army was devoid of many of the experienced Scottish leaders who hated the influence of the King's inexperienced 'favourite', Oliver Sinclair. The army left Edinburgh in November 1542 but by this time the King was gravely ill of some unknown disease. The further south they marched the worse the King got and the morale of the army deteriorated with the health of King James. Eventually they reached Solway in the West March, where James, hardly able to ride his mount, left for Lochmaben Castle, declaring that he would return to cross the sands into England when the tide ebbed. But he never did return and went to his sickbed in the Castle.

To the annoyance of his remaining Lords, the King appointed Oliver Sinclair as Commander of the Army. Fury erupted, the like had never been heard of before, and unpopular and inexperienced young man, with no large force of men of his own, being given command in the field over all the Earls and Lords of Scotland. Unhappy, the Scots marched over the Solway Moss into England on 24 November 1542.

At the same time a much smaller English army of three thousand men under Sir Thomas Wharton advanced to meet the invaders and they fought the **Battle of Solway Moss**. When the Scots got within arrow range Wharton attacked, letting loose, first his bowmen and then charging with his cavalry and driving the Scots into the bog of Solway Moss.

Over 1,200 Scots were captured, including Oliver Sinclair. The total Scots dead only amounted to around 500 men, and most of the dead were drowned seeking to escape across the River Esk. The Grants did not lose many men and slowly returned north to their homeland in Strathspey. But overall, the scale of the defeat was overwhelming. The news of the disaster was brought to an ailing King James who cried 'Fie, fled Oliver, is Oliver taken? All is lost.' It was the final nail in his coffin, sick in body and in spirit he returned to Edinburgh and died there on 14 December 1542.

"Before he died he is reported to have said 'it came wi a lass, it'll gang wi a lass' (meaning 'It began with a girl, and it will end with a girl'). This was either a reference to the Stewart dynasty accession to the throne through Marjorie Bruce, daughter of Robert the Bruce or to the medieval origin myth of the Scots nation, recorded in the 'Scotichronicon' in which the Scots people are descended from the Princess Scota".(80)

Urquhart Castle, Loch Ness has been a fortified site was over a thousand years. It guarded the western shore of Loch Ness and also the entrance to Glenmoriston. "The Castle is built on the rocky promontory of Strome, which is separated from the hill of Croc-na-h-Iolaire by a low-lying neck of land."(81) The original castle had a dry moat about 80 feet wide, and a considerable depth, varying from 30 feet to 50 feet. The approach from the drawbridge to the gate does not strike directly on the doorway, but on the northern tower, which commanded the approach and prevented a direct assault on the gate.

Urquhart Castle.

Copyright: Eileen Sinclair 2019.

In the 2nd half of the 13th century a new stone wall and gatehouse was built round the site. It was then owned by the Durwards and then the Coymns until destroyed by Robert Bruce around 1307.

"Urquhart was one of the many properties granted to Thomas Randolph, whom Bruce had made Earl of Moray and his Deputy in the north, and it was assaulted by the English in 1334. It passed to the hands of the Alexander Stewart, Earl of Buchan, by 1384, who was married to the Countess of Ross, meaning he controlled the North. When his wife died, however, the Earldom of Ross was claimed by the MacDonald Lord of the Isles, and in 1395 the MacDonalds captured Urquhart, enabling them to significantly increase the severity of their raiding in support of their Ross claim. Urquhart was recaptured and money spent on upgrading it, but it continued to be a target for the MacDonalds through the first half of the 15th century, until James II, probably in frustration as much as anything else, granted it to the MacDonald Earl."(82)

Eventually the MacDonald Lord of the Isles was forfeited and the Castle given to the Earl of Huntly who then leased it out to Sir Duncan Grant. The Grants brought order to the area and they built the new Tower House in 1509 when the Lordship of Urquhart was granted to them. This did not stop the MacDonalds seizing the castle in the confusion which occurred after the disastrous Battle of Flodden in 1513. The 'Great Raid' of 1543 by the MacDonalds was the last attack on the Castle for nearly 200 years. This raid removed 8,500 head of livestock from the lands around Urquhart Castle.

The Castle was then attacked by the Covenanters from Inverness in 1644 when it was again sacked and everything of value stolen. It was garrisoned again in 1689 and briefly besieged by the Jacobites before they were forced to retreat. When the Government garrison left in 1691 they blew part of the Castle up, to ensure it could not be used by rebels in the future.

It is believed that there are two secret chambers underneath the ruins of the castle, one filled with gold and the other with the plague. This is the reason no attempts have been made to find the treasure.

Part of the Grant tower collapsed in 1715 during a violent storm. The Castle remained in a state of decay until its ownership changed to Historic Environment Scotland, who have now made significant improvements and repairs. The property is open to the public and is probably the most visited historic castle in the north of Scotland.

CHAPTER 7. MARY QUEEN OF SCOTS.

Mary, the only surviving legitimate child of King James V was only six days old when her father died and she acceded to the throne. The death of King James V threw the country generally, and the north in particular, into a state of anarchy and confusion. Two factions immediately emerged to try and take power in Scotland. One faction favoured peace with Protestant England and the other faction were supporters of the Roman Catholic Church and good relations with France.

After much in-fighting, James Hamilton, the Earl of Arran, a supporter of the Protestant faith and of appeasement with England, became Regent. He was opposed by the Catholic faction headed by the Earl of Lennox and the Earl of Huntly. Negotiations commenced for the marriage of the young Mary Queen of Scots to Edward, heir to the throne of England. However, many opposed the marriage including the Earl of Huntly and James Grant of Freuchie and the agreement was never ratified by the Scottish Parliament.

James Grant was by now a very powerful lord and at this time a supporter of the French or Catholic faction at Court. "On 24th July 1543 he was one of those who signed the secret bond by Cardinal Beaton and others, which was directed against the designs of our *awld enemies of Ingland*"(83) against Queen Mary and the Queen Regent.

After this he was made Baillie of the Abbey of Kinloss before June 1544. This gave him great wealth as he now had all the rents of these lands. In 1544 the Earl of Huntly, as Lieutenant of the North, ordered a force to proceed against and punish Clan Ranald of Moidart, and the Mackenzies of Kintail, who were also rebellious at the time. The Earl's army, however, which was composed mainly of Grants, Rosses, Mackintoshes and Chisholms, clans all more or less allied to the Mackenzies, were slow to move against them.

Meanwhile, King Henry VIII of England decided that force was only way to get the Scots to agree to the marriage of their young Queen to his son and heir. His strategy was known as the **'Rough Wooing'**. In May 1544, Edward Seymour, Lord Hertford, began his first major raid into Scotland.

Hertford was given the following orders by King Henry VIII : "*...to put all to fire and sword, to burn Edinburgh town, and to raze and deface it; when you have sacked it, and gotten what you can out of it; as that it may remain for ever a perpetual memory of the vengeance of God lighted upon it, for their falsehood and* disloyalty. Do what you can out of hand, and without long tarrying, to beat down and overthrow the Castle, sack Holyrood House, and as many towns and villages about Edinburgh as ye conveniently can; sack Leith and burn and subvert it, and all the rest, putting man, woman, and child to fire and sword, without exception, where any resistance shall be made against you; and this done, pass over to the Fife land, and extend the extremities and destructions in all towns and villages whereupon you may reach conveniently, and not forgetting amongst all the rest to spoil and turn upside down the Cardinal's town of St. Andrews, and the upper stone may be the nether, and not one stick stand by another, sparing no creature alive within the same, specially such as in friendship or blood be allied to the Cardinal."(84)

His force landed at Granton, near Edinburgh and the Capital and Leith were sacked and burned by the English, as were many other settlements on both sides of the Firth of Forth. Instead of capitulating, however, the Scottish Lords settled their differences and sent Ambassadors to France to offer the young Scots Queen's hand in marriage to the Dauphin of France, heir to the French throne.

This infuriated King Henry VIII of England even more but the English army had to retire from the Capital and the Lothians but they still controlled much of the Scottish Borderlands. They continued to make raids into Central and South Scotland. At last the Scots, under the Earl of Angus, mustered a force and eventually defeated an English army at the **Battle of Ancrum Moor** on 27 February 1545. The Grants did not take part in this battle as they were busy in the north trying to keep the peace between the warring clans. The Scottish victory put a temporary halt to the English raiding and harrying of Scotland and there was relative peace for a time. King Henry VIII died soon after in January 1547 and the Rough Wooing ceased for a time. News of the Scottish victory was celebrated in France and King Francis I soon sent over 3,000 French troops to assist the Scots, although they did not achieve very much except antagonise the Scottish Protestants.

Over the next few years allegiances and loyalties continually changed with the French faction getting the upper hand and then the English faction. The Grants kept largely out of this as they had enough troubles of their own in the Highlands.

After the death of King James V the Highlands again became disorderly, particularly the Camerons, MacDonalds and the Mackenzies. Huntly, as Lieutenant of the North, proceeded against them with a force of Grants, Rosses, Mackintoshes,

Chisholm's and Lovat Frasers. But they were all allied in some way to the rebellious clans and the punitive action was slow and ineffective.

Then came the civil war within the MacDonalds of Clanranald. In 1530 Alexander Allanson MacDonald, 7th Chief of Clanranald died. Next in line to the Chiefship should have been Ranald Galldha, whose mother was Isabella Fraser, daughter of Lord Lovat, who had eventually married Iain Mor Grant of Glenmoriston. 'Gallda' means 'Foreigner' and he was so named by Clanranald because he had been brought up at his Fraser uncle's home at Lovat and was unknown to the men of Clanranald. The elders did not accept him and they offered the Chiefship of the Clan to John Moydartach MacDonald, who was a great warrior and the nephew of Ranald Gallda (although despite being a nephew he may have been older and more experienced)

"Lovat, however, espoused his nephews cause, and along with the Grants and Mackintoshes, under the leadership of Huntly, then Lord-Lieutenant of the North, an army was dispatched to Moydart to overawe the usurper and his followers, and put Ranald Gallda in possession of the Chieftainship. In this they were apparently successful, for they met with no opponents."(85) This occurred in October 1544.

John Moydartach had been imprisoned by King James V at this time, but immediately on his release from prison and return north the whole of Clanranald again acknowledged him as their Chief. Ranald Gallda, never liked by the clan, was expelled from Moidart and he again took refuge with his uncle, Lord Lovat. It happened as follows.

"A day or two after Ranald's arrival at Castletirrim, preparations were made for a feast to be given to the clan on his succession. Many sheep and cattle were slaughtered, and Ranald, observing a great number of fires in the courtyard of the castle, and the busy faces of the cooks employed in dressing immense quantities of victual, inquired the cause of such a scene, when he was informed that the 'feast of welcome' was to be given on that day, in honour of his succession, and, unused to the sight of such feasts, and having no idea of such preparations, he unfortunately observed that 'a few hens might do as well'. Such an observation was not lost upon the clan, they despised the man who could for a moment think of departing from the ancient practice, and they were confirmed in their belief of his weakness and want of spirit."(86) When John Moydartach returned they immediately expelled him and Lord Lovat from the Castle and the feast, instead, was given to the returning John.

The MacDonalds decided to take revenge on the Frasers and their supporters and John Moydartach, along with Ranald MacDonald Glas of Keppoch and their Clan Cameron allies, raided east into Fraser lands. "They soon overran the lands of Stratherrick and Abertariff, belonging to Lord Lovat, the lands of Urquhart and Glenmoriston, belonging to the Grants, and even possessed themselves of the Castle of Urquhart. They plundered indiscriminately the whole district, and aimed of a permanent occupation of the invaded territories."(87)

The Grants and the Frasers were incensed by the attack on their lands and swore revenge. Chief James Grant gathered his Speyside and Urquhart men and Patrick Grant of Glenmoriston gathered his men ready to march on the homeland of the MacDonalds of Clanranald. In April 1545 the combined Royal force marched west against Clanranald. The force was commanded by the Earl of Huntly, and he was accompanied by The Frasers and Grants. Hugh Fraser of Lovat also brought his grandson, Ranald Gallda. Gallda was also related to both James Grant of Freuchie and Patrick Grant of Glenmoriston, who was his step-brother.

Lord Lovat, James Grant and Patrick Grant had marched down the Great Glen to Inverlochy (Fort William) where he met with the Campbell, Duke of Argyle and other Chiefs and a peace agreement was signed between them to support Ranald Gallda and thus reduce the independent nature of Clanranald. As Lovat was about to return home, he was advised by his brother-in-law, the Chief of Mackintosh, that the MacDonalds were waiting in the Great Glen to ambush the Frasers and that he should take another route home. He was about to take this advice when another of his relatives, James Fraser of Foyers, a very headstrong man, dissuaded him, saying that it would be cowardice to run from the MacDonalds, particularly as he had enough men to match them. Fraser of Lovat agreed with his kinsman and advised he would not change his route home just to avoid the MacDonalds.

At the Water of Gloy the forces separated, Huntly and the Laird of Freuchie proceeded with the bulk of the army by Brae-Lochaber and Badenoch to Strathspey, while Lord lovat and Ranald Gallda, with the Frasers and the Grants of Glenmoriston and Urquhart, took the direct route to their own lands, along the Great Glen.

John Moydartach and his clansmen were indeed waiting for the Frasers and Grants. John had guessed the route they were likely to take on their way home and marched his men down behind the range of mountains to the north of Loch Lochy, and encamped on the night previous to the battle in a glen among the hills, immediately behind the farm of Kilfinnan. There was a small loch, afterwards called the 'Loch of Staves' or Lochan-nam-bata in Gaelic. It was here that the Clanranald men left their staves on the morning of the battle, so that by the number of unclaimed ones after the battle would give an indication of their losses.

John then hid his men behind a hill and waited for the enemy. The Frasers had around three hundred warriors, of which there were around one hundred Glenmoriston Grants. The MacDonalds had around five hundred men. But before they met, Lord Fraser sent fifty of his bowmen to reconnoitre ahead on the lookout for MacDonalds, and this reduced his number to around two hundred and fifty. Just as Lovat's force arrived at the east end of Loch Lochy, John Moydartach and the MacDonalds descended in a charge from the hills opposite. Retreat was impossible and the Frasers and Grants had no choice but to fight the **Battle of Blarleine (Blar-nan-leine) or Battle of the Shirts** on 15 July 1544.

North End of Loch Lochy, where the Battle of the Shirts took place.

Copyright: Eileen Sinclair 2020.

"Accordingly he [Lord Lovat] made the best disposition of his forces by placing the gentlemen of his little army, who were well armed, in front, and the others to the rear. The day was unusually hot. To ease themselves as much as possible, they prepared for the conflict by stripping themselves of their upper raimes – all but their shirts and kilts."(88)

The battle began with an exchange of arrows and when they were finished the fighting continued hand to hand with swords and battle-axes. In some instances fire-arms may also have been used by some of the wealthier warriors. The battle was fought from mid-day till late in the afternoon, and consisted latterly of isolated single combats. Both sides fought with determined courage, neither side yielding until, of the Frasers and Grants, only four remained unwounded, and of the Clanranalds eight. The others were dead or disabled. The records of Grant deaths are not known but it must also have been considerable.

Ranald Galldha fought bravely and distinguished himself in the battle and he killed many of his former Clanranald kinsmen until he himself was mortally wounded. "two noted Moydart warriors, father and son, fought under the banner of their chief. The son, known by the soubriquet of 'An Gille maol dubh', while performing deeds of valour himself, had his eye upon his aged sire, marking how, as foe after foe fell beneath the weapon of Ranald Galldha, that warrior came nearer and nearer to his father. The two at length joined in deadly strife. The older combatant gave ground before his more vigorous rival – on observing which, the 'Gille maol dudh' exclaimed, ... 'I like not the backward step of an old man'. The father replied, ... 'Are you there, if so be here'; whereupon the son stepped forward and took his father's place at the moment the latter had fallen mortally wounded. For a while the contest was doubtful, but finding himself overmatched by the skill and prowess of his opponent, the 'Gille maol dubh' exclaimed. 'I won't take advantage of you, look behind'. Apprehending treachery, Ranald instinctively turned round, and in the act of doing so the Moydart man felled him to the ground. This ended the fray. With Ranald Galldha dead, as it was thought, John Moydartach had nothing to fear from him, nor the Frasers anything further to contend for; and the few that survived unscathed on either side sullenly withdrew from what may be called a drawn battle."(88)

Lord Lovat, despite his age, also fought bravely, hacking down many MacDonalds with his battle-axe and sword. So many did he kill that afterwards the MacDonalds gave him the name, 'Cruoy Choskir', which translates into English as 'Hardy Cutter'. The burn leading into Loch Lochy, where they fought, ran red with blood. Eventually, however, both he and his eldest son were overcome by the MacDonalds and died side by side. Of the Frasers, only Fraser of Foyers and another 4 men survived and they, with their surviving Grants allies returned home bearing tidings of the disaster and carrying the bodies of Lord lovat, his eldest son, and Ranald Gallda.

"The young and accomplished Master [of Lovat] owed his death …. to the taunts of his stepmother. He did not at first accompany his father in the expedition, but after her insinuation of his cowardice prompted him to follow, and he joined his friends in time to share their fate. His stepmother's end was attained in the succession of her own son to the title."(89)

Patrick Og Grant of Glenmoriston was one of the few who survived and was able to return home, although he had a battle axe wound on his shoulder and three dagger wounds on his arms and legs.

But Donald Galldha was not quite dead, only severely wounded. Near the battlefield was a hostelry and adjoining barn called afterwards 'Cnocan-oich-oich. 'Oich' in Gaelic is an expression of pain. Hence the name 'hill of pain'. The MacDonalds who survived, including the wounded, were carried here after the battle to get what little medical attention was available. Unbeknown to them, Ranald Galldha, severely wounded, was carried with many others to the barn. Regaining consciousness he listened to the MacDonald survivors boasting of their battle prowess during the night, fuelled by large amounts of whisky.

At last he could take it no longer and shouted out that there was one MacDonald on the battlefield who, if not wounded, could slay them all. They were startled by this and soon discovered that this was Donald Galldha and then put the severely wounded brave man to death with a surgeons pin pushed into his brain.

With the death of so many Frasers the whole future of the Clan was threatened. However, folklore states that the wives of every one of the eighty Fraser Lairds killed were left pregnant at home and each one bore a son, thereby ensuring the continuation of the Lovat Fraser Clan. Fraser of Foyers was the only Fraser Laird to survive. He was badly wounded and he owed his life to his foster brother who helped him escape. He rewarded the man's family by giving them a gift of the croft they rented from him.

"The result of the Battle of Blarleine cleared the way from active opposition to John Moydartach, and left him in undisputed possession as Captain and actual Chief of Clanranald of Moydart."(90) He continued in a bitter dispute with the clans who had opposed him, particularly the Grants and the Frasers. In this fight, John was supported by all the other MacDonald branches, particularly those of Keppoch and Glengarry.

"The Laird of Freuchie, no doubt on account of the part he acted in marching with the Earl of Huntly, suffered considerably from the retaliations of the Clan Ranald and the other insurgent chiefs. His lands of Urquhart and those of the Laird of Glenmoriston, were overrun by MacDonald of Glengarry and by Cameron of Lochiel, and a large booty carried off."(91)

Indeed after the Battle of the Shirts the Grant lands at Glenmoriston and Urquhart were looted by Clan Ranald and Clan Cameron in what is termed 'The Great Raid'. It was at this time that James Grant became known as 'James of the Foray's, for his retribution on those who had raided his lands.

Ewan Cameron, 13th Captain and Chief of Clan Cameron, along with John Moydartach of Clan Ranald, made two raids in October 1544 and April 1545, into the Grant lands of Glenmoriston and Glen Urquhart, commonly known as the **'Raid of Urquhart'**. He was accompanied by his grandson and heir, Ewan (Eoghainn Beag), the son of his son, Donald, who had died a few years before, and Agnes or Anne Grant, daughter of Sir James Grant. It appears that Ewan Cameron had little feeling or love for his Grant relatives. The Treaty of Alliance between the Grants and Camerons, which had been signed in 1520, was disregarded and the two clans, once so friendly, were now at feud.

The plunder taken was huge. Among the goods, cattle and horses taken from the Laird's house and farm were 200 bolls of oats, with the fodder, 100 bolls of 'bere', 100 calves, 40 young cows, 10 one year old 'stirks', 8 horses and 4 mares, 140 ewes, 60 gimmers and dinmounts and 100 lambs.

From Castle Urquhart, which was captured, the raiders carried away, 12 feather beds, with bolsters, blankets and sheets, 5 pots, 6 pans, 1 basket, 1 cheat containing £300 pounds in coins, 2 brewing cauldrons, 12 pieces of artillery, 10 harnesses, and several other items including doors, bedstands, chairs and 3 large boats. Much plunder was also taken from the tenants of the Glen and their houses were burned to the ground.

After this raid the Dowager Queen, Mary of Guise, was trying to bring law and order back to the Highlands. The Laird of Freuchie was given a Commission as Justiciar of the Crown over all his lands in Strathspey and Urquhart and Glenmoriston. This meant that he was personally responsible for all unlawfulness in his lands and was directly responsible for punishment of all crimes committed in his lands. At one point he captured John Roy Grant, a notorious thief and murderer, along with all his men. James Grant had them all beheaded and presented the heads to the Dowager Queen at Inverness. The Early of Huntly and James Grant later apprehended Ranald MacDonald Glas of Keppoch and Ewan Cameron of Locheil, who had led the destruction of the Grant lands and had then beheaded after a trail for High Treason.

There is little recorded of how the 'Great Raids' on Urquhart and Glenmoriston affected the ordinary Grants but they must have suffered terribly. Many were killed during the raids but many more starved during the following winters. What we do know comes from highland legend, particularly the legends of the Grant Smith of Polmaily.

However, the first legend concerns a woman of the district, who seeing her only cow being driven away by the Camerons, seized the animal by one of its hind legs and held it fast: and how Locheil, amazed at the woman's strength, ordered the men to leave the cow with her.

The other legends tell the story of 'An Gobha Mor', the Big Smith, or Armourer of Polmaily. This Grant and his seven sons were famous for their great strength, and their skill in the art of armoury, being said to be the most skilful in the whole of Scotland. The Big Smith also excelled at husbandry and he had the best herd of cattle in the Highlands. But then suddenly one night the cattle lost their good condition and became lean and famished. Feed them as he might the Big Smith could do nothing to improve their appearance.

"At the time the fairies of Urquhart had their favourite retreat at Tor-na-sidhe (Tornashee), near Polmaily. The smith had one of them for his 'leannan-sidhe', or fairy-love, and, as he rumbled with her one day in the woods, she informed him that her fellow-fairies had stolen his beautiful cows, and that the lean kine which gave him so much concern were 'croth-sidhe', or fairy cattle. Furious with rage, he hastened home, and, armed with an axe, rushed into the byre to slay the unearthly herd."(92)

But before he could strike a blow the cattle rushed out of the barn and escaped. The Big Smith seized the last to flee by the tail and was carried with them to Carn-an-Rath, in Ben-a-Gharbhlaich, near Achnababan. As they neared the cairn an opening appeared and the cattle rushed in, carrying the Smith with them.

He eventually reached a spacious chamber which was covered with jewels and precious stones and other things of the greatest value. In the blink of an eye the cattle turned into ordinary fairies, who then asked the astonished Smith to choose

126

what he pleased for his own. In the corner of the chamber he saw a 'little shaggy pony' of whom he had heard from his fairy lover to have extraordinary power and he replied he would take it as his prize. However, they made him promise to only use the pony for pulling the plough. She then became a marvel in the Glen for many years.

But, one day, the Smith, forgetting his promise to the fairies, put the pony on a cart for the purpose of removing manure. He had broken his promise to the fairies, and her wonderful power left her for ever.

Prior to the 'Great Raid' of Urquhart and Glenmoriston one of Cameron of Lochiel's followers killed a man in Lochaber, and fled to Urquhart, where he found shelter and employment with the Smith at Polmaily. Cameron of Locheil learned that the man was in the Glen and sent his clansmen to bring him back. But the man had cut his hair and changed his appearance and although they saw him working at the Smith's anvil, they did not recognise him and went home without him. But it soon came to Lochiel's attention that the Gille Moal – the Bald Young Man – whom they had seen at the Smithy was the man they were seeking, and he became angry with the Smith and the population of Urquhart and swore revenge on them.

Soon after the Camerons agreed to take part in the Great Raid of Urquhart and Glenmoriston and they seized the Castle and plundered the land. "But not daring to meet the Big Smith and his sons in a fair fight, he sent for Gille Phadruig Gobha, the Smith's son-in-law, and promised to give him the lands of Polmaily as his own if he brought him the Smith and his sons, dead or alive.

'Chose out for me two score of your bravest and boldest men', replied Gille Phadruig Gobha, yielding to the temptation, 'and I shall be their guide tonight'. The Smiths sons slept in a barn which stood on the hillock at Polmaily which is still known as Torran nan Gillean – the Young Men's Knoll – and at midnight the traitor and a party of Camerons quietly left the Castle, and proceeded to Polmaily, with the intention of killing the sons and then overcoming the father. Some of the Camerons remained at the door of the barn while the rest entered and attacked the sleepers, who, being without their swords, were all slain, except the youngest, whose back was broken, and who afterwards bore the name of An Gobha Crom, or the Hump-Backed Smith."(93)

While this treachery was going on the Smith's wife woke from a nightmare that the foundations of the barn were falling down. She implored the Big Smith to go and see that all was well with their sons. He grabbed his great sword and proceeded to the barn, and rushed at the Camerons. They fled for the Castle and he followed, cutting them down at every stroke. He then tried to grab his treacherous son-in-law, whereupon the traitor cried, 'It is I, It is I'. The Smith shouted back, 'I know it is you' and with a swing of his great sword, cut off his ear and shouted, 'tell Locheil I will breakfast with him at break of day.' But on hearing that the Big Smith was coming the Chief of Cameron fled the castle before sunrise and returned to his lands in Lochaber.

The Smith returned to the Barn and found all his sons dead, except the Gobha Crom. The Smith's heart and soul were broken and he soon left the Glen and no one heard from him again. A few months later, however, the half-eaten body of his treacherous son-in-law was found tied to a tree, where it had been gorged by wild animals.

This legend is interwoven with the tale of the Great Raid as the list of dead from Polmaily shows, which included: William, son of the Smith, Fair John, son of Donald, son of the Smith, and Baak (Beathay), daughter of Gowry, or the Red Smith.

In calmer times the Great Raid would have been avenged by Fire and Sword by the King but at this time the country was in turmoil, with the Regent Arran, governing in the name of the infant, Mary, Queen of Scots. He had his own troubles in the south of the country so had to let the Highlands look out for itself. The Grants tried to get recompense through the Courts but the Camerons and the MacDonalds stayed in their vast lands in the west and refused to attend their summons to appear for trial in Edinburgh. They were officially forfeited and James Grant was awarded much of their territory but taking possession was another matter and he ruled these lands in name only.

The Grants of the Trough. A brother-in-law of James Grant, Gordon of Brackley, was murdered by some Farquharson's of Deeside, probably in retaliation for James Grant's raiding of their lands. The Earl of Huntly and James Grant then combined forces and killed most of the Farquharson's of Deeside. "A year later James, when visiting Huntly for dinner, was invited by Huntly to come outside after dinner, and see something he had never seen before. In the courtyard was a large trough and the remains of dinner was emptied into this. A whistle was blown, and immediately a horde of children burst into the yard fighting to get at the contents of the trough. Huntly told James that they were the orphan whelps of the Farquharson's, and that he was hard put to feed them. James, as may be imagined, was horrified by this, and he said that as he had helped to make them orphans, he should share the burdensome responsibility by taking half the children,"(94).

He led the children back to his lands and then divided them among his clansfolk and they were brought up as Grants. Thus the Grants of the Trough were created.

Back on the international scene, King Henry VIII died in January 1547 and Scotland thought it would have peace from English invasion. However, instead of decreasing, the pressure intensified under the Earl of Hertford, now Duke of Somerset and Lord Protector of England during the minority of King Edward VI. In September 1547, the English invaded Scotland again with an army of 18,000 men and with a fleet to accompany him up the east coast. He was still trying to force the Scots into a marriage between King Edward VI and the infant Mary Queen of Scots.

The Scots gathered their forces in Edinburgh to oppose them. An army of up to 30,000 men marched out of Edinburgh and headed south and drew up a defensive position along the banks of the River Esk, at a place called Pinkie Cleugh. The English army amount to around 17,000 men (with 30 warships in the Forth Estuary). With their overwhelming numbers the Scots were confident of success. However, the English won the battle and thousands of Scots were killed. Luckily the Grants were not part of the Scots army and missed out on the bloody carnage.

Although they had suffered a significant defeat, the Scottish Government refused to agree terms with the English. The young Mary, Queen of Scots, was escorted out of the country to France, where she was betrothed and later married to Francis, Dauphin of France, and heir to the French throne. Her mother, Mary of Guise, then became Regent of Scotland, but not without significant opposition.

Meanwhile in England, King Edward IV had been crowned in 1547 at the age of nine. However, in early 1553 at the age of fifteen, he fell ill and died of Tuberculosis in July the same year. He was succeeded by his older half-sister, Mary Tudor, known as 'Bloody Mary'. She was a strict Catholic and spent her five-year reign in a vicious battle to return England to Catholicism and away from the new Protestant religion.

Queen Mary of England died childless in 1558 aged forty-two and was succeeded by her half-sister, Queen Elizabeth I of England and Ireland. This famous monarch would rule England and Ireland from 1558 to her death in 1603 aged seventy. She never married, afraid that any husband would usurp her position, and this left, initially, Mary Queen of Scots, and then on her death at the hands of Queen Elizabeth, her son, King James VI of Scotland, as the only legitimate heirs to the Kingdom of England and Ireland.

Back up north, Iain (John) Mor Grant, 1st of Glenmoriston, died in 1548 and his brother, the Laird of Corrimony died some years earlier in 1533. Glenmoriston was succeeded by his eldest son, Patrick Og Grant. No sooner was the old laird dead than John Grant of Ballindalloch applied to the Queen Regent for the grant of Glenmoriston on the grounds that Patrick Og's father's marriage to Isobella of Lovat was 'irregular'. He was initially successful and in March 1549, Ballindalloch received possession in law of the Glenmoriston estates. This lasted of 7 years, although Patrick Og took no cognisance of the legal proceedings and retained physical possession of Glenmoriston. "But in 1556, through the influence of his uncle, Lord Lovat, and Campbell of Cawdor, Patrick recovered his rights, and got himself a new Crown Charter."(95) However, this was the start of a bitter feud between the Grants of Glenmoriston and the Grants of Ballindalloch.

The closing years of James Grant's life were relatively peaceful. He died on 26 August 1553 and was the first Grant of Freuchie to be buried at Duthil, where the old family mausoleum can still be seen and stands in front of the church.

He was married twice, first to Elizabeth Forbes, daughter of John, 6th Lord Forbes, then secondly to Christine Barclay. With his first wife James left 4 sons and a daughter:

- John Grant, who succeeded.
- William Grant of Muckrach and Finlarg.
- Duncan Grant of Easter Elchies. In 1568 he and James Grant of Wester Elchies were in dispute over land at their borders but this was settled amicably without violence. He sided with the Earl of Huntly in his rebellion. His son, James Grant of Easter Elchies was denounced a rebel in 1619, he died soon after this and his land reverted back to the Laird of Freuchie.
- Archibald Grant of Monymusk.
- Isobel Grant, who married Campbell of Cawdor.

John Grant , 4th of Freuchie, Chief of Clan Grant 'the Gentle'. He was Chief of Clan Grant from 1553 and 1583. He was born around 1520. There is no known marriage date for James Grant but his son and heir, John Grant, was himself married in 1539, so his father must have been married quite young.

His first wife was Margaret Stewart and his 2nd wife was Janet Leslie, daughter of the 4th Earl of Rothes. John Grant inherited his father's Speyside estates, and the Sheriffdom of Elgin and Forres, together with his father's land of Urquhart. John was served heir to his father's Urquhart estates in October 1553, but because the estates were still suffering from the effects of the Great Raid he was remitted from paying his rents to the Crown in 1554.

In 1549 prior to him becoming Chief, and in compensation for MacDonald raids on Glen Urquhart the Grants was given the forfeited MacDonald lands in Loch Broom, Loch Carron, Strome Castle, Lochalsh and Glengarry. These lands were a poison chalice to the Grants. John could not effectively rule these vast lands on the west coast of the highlands so far away from his main base in Strathspey. They were full of MacDonalds who refused to pay their rents to him and continued to support their attainted leaders. So much so that John Grant found it difficult to pay his feu duties to the King. Luckily the Crown rescinded these duties owing to the difficulty of controlling this part of the Highlands. The resistance of the MacDonalds and Camerons was illustrated a few years later in 1553 when they led a raid on Castle Strome and threw out the Grant Garrison.

John was then made Baillie of Kinloss Abbey and he also acquired additional land at Rothes from the Earl of Rothes. "On 9 July 1552, he received from Queen Mary [Dowager] a remission for joining Matthew, Earl of Lennox on Glasgow Moor in May 1544."(49) This was in connection with the **Battle of Glasgow** which was fought on 16 March 1544, between Matthew Stewart, 4th Earl of Lennox and the Scottish Regent James Hamilton, 2nd Earl of Arran. John Grant had fought for the Earl of Lennox but their force was defeated by the Regent and the Grants had to retreat from Glasgow. When the remainder of Lennox's garrison surrendered many of the captured men were hung at the Tolbooth of Glasgow.

In 1555 Clan Ranald of Clan MacDonald and Clan Cameron were again making trouble and John Grant was given a Commission to act as Justiciar of the Crown by the Regent Arran and the Queen Dowager, Mary of Guise, in order to secure peace in his extensive land holdings. As part of this writ he was ordered to apprehend one of his own clan, James Grant, a notorious cattle raider. John eventually found his hide out and surrounded it. James Grant and his men refused to surrender knowing that they would probably be hanged. John Grant's men attacked and after a fierce fight all of the cattle thieves were killed. John had their heads presented to the Queen Dowager Mary of Guise when she travelled north to Inverness to help secure peace in the Highlands.

These were troubled times for Scotland with the first great divide between those who remained true to the Catholic religion and those who now adopted the new Protestant religion. The former also generally supported continued close ties with France while the Protestants generally favoured closer ties with England.

During this period the Grants generally stayed loyal to the Government of the day. "The Grants lands as a whole were much better agriculturally than those held by other clans, so it is easy to understand how it was nearly always possible for the Grants to be on the side of law and order, as presumably they did not have to face the alternatives of stealing or starving."(97)

In 1560 the Scottish Parliament at Edinburgh abolished the Catholic Religion and enacted the 'Confession of Faith'. This is generally referred to as the 'Reformation'. John Grant was quick to grab as much of the Church lands as he could and in both Speyside and Urquhart he 'appropriated' much property. He was joined by Patrick Og Grant who did the same at Glenmoriston.

In 1561 Mary Queen of Scots returned from France after the death of her husband. For a short while she had been Queen of France and Scotland. Mary came back to Scotland determined to be a good and true Queen of all her people, no matter their religion and had she not been caught up in the religious division within the country it is likely that she would have been a great Queen and a just ruler. But when she landed she was still a girl of less than 20 and at the mercy of the bickering nobles. "During her five years on the throne she worked hard to win the respect of her people and to be accepted as Queen of all Scots, whatever their religion."(98) However, the country was largely controlled by Protestant leaning nobles, including her illegitimate half-brother, Robert Stewart, Earl of Moray. He would eventually become her arch-enemy.

As part of her attempt to reconcile the differing factions of the nation she spent much of her time travelling the country to get close to her subjects, particularly her Lords. However, Mary soon fell out with the Gordon, Earl of Huntly, and gathered a small army to march north to quell the rebellion of the Gordons, who were most powerful Catholic family in Scotland.

Previously friendly with the Earls of Huntly, the Grants backed the Queen this time. Five hundred men of Clan Grant and Clan Fraser met the Queen at Blair Atholl to escort her to Inverness. When the Queen arrived safely at Inverness, the commander of the Castle, by the Earl of Huntly's order, shut the gates of the town against her. Mary refused to leave and set up lodgings in a house near the old

132

bridge. The Grants and Frasers surrounded the house to protect her against assault from the Castle garrison. During the night more loyal clans, such as the Munros, Mackenzies and Rosses, arrived to support her.

Mary Queen of Scots.

Francis Clouet.

With a small army now under her command she laid siege to Inverness Castle and it eventually fell after three days. For his treasonable action against the Queen, the commander of the Castle was hanged at the gate where he had refused to give the Queen entry. The Grants were in a difficult position, they remained loyal to the Queen but for years had been on good terms with the Gordon, Earl's of Huntly.

Mary then gathered her army and occupied Aberdeen with the objective of attacking Huntly in his own castle. The Grants formed part of this force. Huntly did not wait for her and gathered his clansmen and vassals and marched to Aberdeen but his army melted away on route and he only had around 500 men, who were met by the Queen's army of 2,000 men under the Earl of Moray, 12 miles outside of Aberdeen. Here the **Battle of Corrichie** was fought on 28 October 1562.

The Earl of Huntly and his small army was utterly defeated. The Earl was captured alive and was mounted on a horse to be taken to Aberdeen as a captive but before leaving he, seemingly, had a heart attack or stroke and instantly died. After the battle, Huntly's eldest son, Sir John Gordon, was taken to Aberdeen and was executed three days later. A younger brother, Adam Gordon of Auchindoun, also captured at Corrichie, was spared. In 1565 the Queen restored the Earldom of Huntly and those of the name Gordon who had been forfeited.

John Grant was in a difficult position. Huntly was his friend and the Grants also held many of their estates in feu from him, essentially making them his vassals. It appears that John reluctantly joined the Royal forces but was able to keep himself and his clansmen out of the direct battle. Soon after the battle, however, he was ordered to take Drummin Castle, near Aberdeen, which belonged to Huntly and garrison it for the Queen. He did this on 3 December 1562. When they arrived they found the Castle empty and boarded up and they gained entry by using a ladder to scale the walls of the deserted fortress.

"On 3 December 1562, acting on an order …. of Queen Mary, he demanded and took possession of Drummin Castle, the keepers having fled. This Order of the Queen is the first authoritative document in which the Laird of Freuchie is denominated Laird of Grant."(99) For his loyal service to the Queen, the Chief of Grant was given the official title of Laird of Grant from this time.

The downfall of Mary, Queen of Scots, was her marriage to her first cousin, Henry Stewart, Lord Darnley in 1565. When the Queen decided to marry Darnley, a Catholic, a number of the Protestant Lords were hostile to him and feared for their own positions if he came to power beside the Queen.

The Queen's half-brother, the Earl of Moray, rebelled in August 1565 with the Earl of Arran. They did not get much support from the other Lords and the Queen's army chased the rebels all over Central Scotland in what became known as the **Chaseabout Raid**. Eventually the rebels had to flee to England.

Mary Queen of Scots was at the height of her power but the love match with Lord Darnley soon turned sour and he became more and more estranged from the Queen, particularly when Mary refused to give him joint sovereignty. He also continued to alienate many of the important nobles.

Then came the murder of the Queen's favourite, David Rizzio, when Mary was six months pregnant. Rizzio was an Italian who had risen to become the Queen's

Secretary and was accused by the Protestant Lords of being a Popish spy. They persuaded the gullible Darnley that Rizzio, his former friend, was having an affair with the Queen. This was clearly a lie but it turned Darnley into the arms of the conspirators.

George Gordon, Huntly's eldest surviving son was, unlike his father, a supporter of Mary, Queen of Scots and John Grant was with him at Holyrood Palace in 1566 when David Rizzio was murdered. On the evening of 9 March 1566 the conspirators surrounded the approaches to Holyrood Palace and occupied the building with 150 men. Then Lord Darnley and Lord Lyndsay entered the Queens Chamber with their armour on under their cloaks and daggers in their hands and demanded that Rizzio come with them out of the Queen's presence. "Five others now came bursting in. Rizzio clung to the Queens skirts, screaming for mercy. While Mary pleaded with Darnley, with a pistol pressed to her belly, Rizzio was dragged from the room .... to the head of the main staircase, where he was done to death with more than fifty stab-wounds; Darnley's dagger, deliberately used by one of the murderers, was left protruding from his body."(100)

With the Earls of Huntly, Atholl and Bothwell, John Grant tried to prevent the conspirators taking possession of the Queen and the Palace. They fought with the murderers but eventually had to retreat. A truce was entered into but Huntly and Bothwell feared for their own safety and escaped through a 1st floor window. Eventually John Grant, with the Earls of Sutherland and Caithness, were later allowed to leave on guarantee that the Queen was safe.

Two days later the Queen, together with the Lords Huntly, Bothwell, Caithness and others, of whom John Grant was possibly one, removed to Dunbar Castle some miles east of Edinburgh. She then marched on Edinburgh and the conspirators fled, with the Earl of Moray and Earl of Morton fleeing to England. The Queen declared them rebels and they remained exiled in England for nearly a year.

Meanwhile, on 19 June 1566 at Edinburgh Castle, Mary Queen of Scots gave birth to a son, the future King James VI of Scotland and James I of England and Ireland. Scotland rejoiced that an heir to the throne had been produced and for a short time Mary's enemies had to remain quiet and show their support.

Darnley soon returned to his old ways and started plotting against the Queen. He had lost the favour of the Queen but also the Protestant nobles, the Earls of Morton and Moray. Rumours abounded that he was plotting to murder the Queen and seize power as Regent for his son James. On the evening of Sunday 9 February

1567 Lord Darnley was murdered. The Edinburgh building he was staying in, Kirk o' Field, was blown up by a huge explosion. It appears that he survived and struggled out to the gardens where he was strangled to death.

The murder of Lord Darnley, 'King of Scotland', and father to the future King James VI remains one of the greatest unsolved mysteries of Scottish history. Within a few days, however, suspicion fell on the Earl of Bothwell and then the Queen herself.

The Queen eventually allowed Darnley's father, the Earl of Lennox, to put Bothwell on trial for the murder. However, Bothwell packed Edinburgh with his supporters and he was acquitted. Lennox left for England in disgust. But although he was declared innocent the common people and Church of Scotland continued to suspect Bothwell and the tide of public opinion turned against him. Then the Queen of Scots made a fatal error and married him, some say he forced himself on her, but no matter what, it would eventually lead to her downfall. They were married on 15 May 1567 at Holyrood Palace in a Protestant ceremony.

Mary believed that many nobles supported her marriage, but relations quickly soured between the newly elevated Bothwell (who was created Duke of Orkney after the marriage ceremony) and his former peers and the marriage proved to be deeply unpopular. Catholics considered the marriage unlawful, since they did not recognise Bothwell's divorce or the validity of the Protestant service. Both Protestants and Catholics were shocked that Mary should marry the man accused of murdering her husband.

Civil war then broke out with the Protestant nobles gathering a large army to confront the Queen and Bothwell and their small number of supporters. The majority of the Queens supporters, such as the Gordons and the Grants, were still in the north and could not help their Queen.

The two forces faced each other at Carberry Hill, about three miles south east of Musselborough, in June 1567. The Queen could see that she was badly outnumbered and surrendered. The Earl of Bothwell fled to Orkney and Shetland, and from there escaped to Norway, where he was imprisoned until he died insane.

Mary, Queen of Scots, was then taken to Edinburgh. The common people had turned against her and lined the streets to call her adulteress and murderer. The next day she was taken to Lochleven Castle, where she was imprisoned. As soon as she got there she miscarried twins. On 24 July she was forced to abdicate in favour of her one year old son, James.

After the arrest of the Queen, John Grant returned home to his estates in Speyside to secure them. There was then formed a Northern Bond to support Mary Queen of Scots. "The Laird of Freuchie was the first after the Earl of Huntly to sign this bond, and he eventually acted with the Earl in support of the Queens party...".(101) For his support the Earl of Huntly gave John Grant a Charter for the lands of Rothiemurchas.

Also in 1567, with the Queen in captivity, despite being a strong supporter of her cause, the Chief of Grant lost no time in seeking the aid of the Government of the young King James VI when he heard rumours that the Camerons and MacDonalds were preparing for another raid into Urquhart again. The King was the feudal superior of these lands and the Regent Moray, on behalf of the King, sent letters to the Chiefs of Mackintosh and Mackenzie ordering them to assist the Chief of Grant in defending his lands. This was issued on 1st March 1567.

Both of these clans were at feud with the MacDonalds and Camerons and they were only too happy to assist. This made the raiders think again and the raid was abandoned. The friendship between the Clans of Grant and Mackenzie was sealed in 1570 when the Chief of Mackenzie received in marriage the Laird of Grant's daughter and her dowry was the territory of Loch Broom which the Grants had been given but had never occupied, as it was fiercely defended by the MacDonalds and Camerons.

Despite this aid from the Regent Moray, most of the Highland Clans were still loyal to Mary, Queen of Scots.

The Queen escaped her imprisonment in Lochleven in May 1568. She fled to Lanarkshire and with the help of the Hamiltons and Campbells, raised an army of over 6,000 men. Mary still did not want an open battle and decided to head for Dumbarton Castle which was under the command of one of her supporters. From there she hoped the Highland Clans would flock to her cause and she could then regain her throne and the charge of her young son.

The King's Party, as the former rebels were now known, were anxious to stop the Queen reaching Dumbarton and formed up their force at the village of Langside (now a suburb of Glasgow) on 13 May 1568, where the **Battle of Langside** was fought and the Queens forces were destroyed. The Queen managed to escape but was forced to flee into exile in England where she was arrested and imprisoned by her cousin, Queen Elizabeth I of England. She would never return to Scotland and, after a long captivity, she was beheaded on 7 February 1587.

After the Queens escape to England John Grant was one of the Lords who signed another Bond binding them to support the Queen and not to acknowledge any other.

After Langside, "... Huntly still held out for her [Mary Queen of Scots], and with an army in which were the Laird of Grant, Patrick Grant of Glenmoriston, John Grant of Corrimony, William Grant in Borlum, John Grant in Cartaly, and Alexander alias Alasdair Grant in Urquhart, followed doubtless by the youth and valour of our Parish [Urquhart and Glenmoriston], went through the country with 'displayit banners' – now marching through the streets of Inverness, now disturbing the sober citizens of Aberdeen, or creating terror among the peaceable inhabitants of Fetteresso and the Haugh of Meiklour."(192)

During his short tenure as Queens Lieutenant of the North, Huntly acted as an arbiter in a dispute between the Laird of Freuchie and James Mackintosh of Gask regarding the lands of Laggan. In addition, Mackintosh was also charged with the murder of William M'Inchrutter, a tenant or servant of the Laird of Freuchie, as well as the 'violent occupation of Laggan' for five years. Huntly's verdict was that the murder was unpremeditated and that Mackintosh should seek the pardon of the Laird of Grant and make a money payment to the deceased family. He was also to remove himself from Laggan and return all the goods and property taken. This agreement was signed 30 September 1568.

But soon after the Earl of Moray became Regent of Scotland on behalf of King James VI, and in June 1569 he persuaded John Grant to sign a 'bond' supporting the new King at Aberdeen. It was obvious that the Queen, in captivity in England, was not going to reclaim her throne and the Earl of Huntly had, himself, surrendered to the Regent in May 1569. On 9 July the whole Grant Clan was pardoned in the name of young King James VI.

Soon after this Patrick Og Grant, the young Laird of Glenmoriston, married Beatrice, daughter of Archibald Campbell of Cawdor. "Tradition tells that the father, visiting the young couple at 'Tom-an-t-Sabhail [Barnhill, a knoll on the south side of the river Moriston, opposite Duldreggan] was so affected with the meanness of the wicker dwelling that he offered to build them a house at Invermoriston, more befitting the daughter of the Thane of Cawdor. The offer was accepted, skilled workmen were imported from the Thane's country; and Patrick and his wife removed to Invermoriston, which has ever since been the family seat."(103)

Out with national politics John Grant was continually involved in the feuds and turmoil of the Highlands. The Laird of Freuchie assisted his son-in-law, Mackenzie, in his dispute with the Munros in respect to the possession of the castle and lands of the Canonry of Ross.

"Munro of Milntown had received from the Regent Murray [Moray] a grant of the fortress, but his title was not completed at the Regent's death. The Mackenzies were jealous of the possession of the castle by the Munro's, and laid siege to the place. The Munro's held out three years, but one day, getting short of provisions, they made a sortie to the Ness of Fortrose, in the hope of securing fish from the salmon still there. They were immediately discovered and followed by the Mackenzies, who killed their commander and twenty-four others. The garrison of the castle then surrendered, and the Mackenzies took possession."(104)

Also in 1569, a band of 'free-booters raided Rothiemurchas and Glencarnie and stole away with many cattle and killed a servant of Duncan Grant, son of Chief John Grant. With his father, Duncan captured the raiders and hung them all.

Ballindalloch Castle.

Copyright: Redsonje

Ballindalloch Castle. The lands of Ballindalloch and Glencarnie were granted to John Grant of Freuchie by King James IV in 1498. John's grandson, also John Grant, began construction of the Castle in 1542. "Constructed at a time when the highlands were rife with clan feuds and prey to the avarice of monarchs, both English and Scottish, Ballindalloch Castle was once a fortress as well as a family home. The original castle was formed in the shape of a 'z' plan, with the living quarters a three-storey square block of stone, flanked to north and south by two high circular towers, each protecting two sides of the rectangle. The River Spey and Avon formed a natural moat to north and west, and the entrance to the castle was guarded by an apparatus designed to drop stones and sewage upon unwanted visitors."(105)

In the 18th century two additional wings were added to form the original Rose Garden. The first was added by Colonel William Grant in 1718 and then, in 1770, General James Grant built a further wing to the north to accommodate his French Chef who had returned with him from his time as Governor of Florida.

Two Mausolea of Duthil Churchyard.

Copyright: GentryGraves

Duthil Church and Graveyard is a historic site in the centre of the Parish of Duthil, near Carrbridge in Inverness-shire and is now maintained as a Clan Grant Heritage Centre. The first recorded church on the site was built around 1400, probably on the site of an earlier one. The Old Duthil Church was closed in 1967 and much of the interior moveable's were taken to the Carrbridge United Free Church. In addition a number of memorial plagues were removed and rehung in the vestry of Carrbridge Church, including one for Field Marshall Sir Patrick Grant.

Many of the Chiefs of Grant and other prominent members of the Clan are buried in the Old Parish Churchyard. There are 2 Mausolea for the Grant of Grant family. The Mausoleum adjacent to the church serves as the resting place of the Earls of Seafield. Members of the Grant family buried in the Mausoleum before it was sealed up in 1913 include:

- Lewis Alexander Ogilvy-Grant, 5th Earl of Seafield (1767-1840)
- Francis William Ogilvy-Grant, 6th Earl of Seafield (1778- 1853)
- John Charles Ogilvy- Grant, 7th Earl of Seafield (1815- 1881)
- Caroline Stuart, Countess Dowager of Seafield (1844- 1911).

The Chiefs of Grant had their burial place at Duthil from the late 1500's and the first Chief to be interred here was James Grant, 3rd of Freuchie and his grandson John Grant of Freuchie was also buried here in 1585.

CHAPTER 8. KING JAMES VI AND THE UNION OF THE CROWNS.

King James VI was crowned in an austere Protestant ceremony in Stirling on 29 July 1567. For the next 18 years he became a pawn in the battle for power of the magnates of Scotland, both Protestant and Catholic. During this time there were four Regents (most of whom were assassinated and one beheaded) and they took their eyes off the Highlands and allowed the Clan Chiefs, including the Grants, to govern themselves.

In 1571 John Grant gave the MacDonalds and Camerons back their lands in the West Highlands, ridding himself of a troublesome burden and unprofitable estates. He swapped these lands for others closer to his Speyside base. He then married his daughter Barbara to Colin Mackenzie, younger of Kintail and then his other daughter, Helen, to Donald MacDonnell, younger of Glengarry. These were good political moves as it tied him to two powerful (and potentially troublesome) Highland Clans.

Patrick Og Grant, Laird of Glenmoriston, died in 1581. From him his successors took the patronymic Mac Phadruig, or Mac 'Ic Phadruig. He was succeeded by his son John, who soon became one of the most prominent men of his time in the Highlands of Scotland.

In 1582, John, the Laird of Freuchie's eldest son, Duncan Grant of Abernethy and Master of Freuchie, died. He had married Margaret Mackintosh of Mackintosh and they had five sons and two daughters. John Grant's second grandson, James of Logie, was the ancestor of the Grants of Moyness, near Auldearn, Nairnshire. He was bequeathed Arndilly Castle near Rothes. His third grandson, Patrick, received the lands of Strome and Easter Elchies and he became the ancestor of the Grants of Easter Elchies. His fourth grandson became the ancestor of the Grants of Lurgy and his fifth, Duncan, was given the estate of Dandaleith.

By 1584 John Grant was in poor health and he made most of his properties over to his eldest grandson, also John. He eventually died in June 1585 leaving much land and wealth. By his two marriages he had two sons and seven daughters:

1). Duncan Grant, who predeceased his father and his eldest son, John, succeeded.

2). Patrick Grant of Rothiemurchas. He may have been illegitimate.

3). Elizabeth Grant (Elspet or Isobel), who married John Leslie of Balquhain in 1564.

4). Grissel Grant, who married Patrick Grant of Ballindalloch.

5). Margaret Grant, who married Alexander Gordon, son of George Gordon of Beldornie.

6). Katherine Grant, who died in 1561.

7). Marjory Grant.

8). Barbara Grant, who married Colin Mackenzie of Kintail.

9). Helen Grant, who married Donald MacAngus Vic Alestir, younger of Glengarry. This marriage was originally a 'hand-fasting', although John Grant tried to formalise this marriage through the Church. The marriage allowed him to grant the lands of Glengarry MacDonalds back to them. It seems Helen continued to reside at Strome Castle with Glengarry and they had a son, who if he had lived would have become the Chief of the MacDonalds of Glengarry. However, later he seems to have taken a mistress, the daughter of the Captain of Glengarry and then put away the Laird of Grants daughter, and later married his mistress.

Duncan Grant, Master of Freuchie predeceased his father. He was initially given the lands of Abernethy around 1563. Duncan died at Abernethy in spring 1582 and was buried at Duthil. He had married Margaret Mackintosh in 1569 and they had five sons and two daughters:

1). John Grant, who succeeded his father and grand-father.

2). James of Grant of Ardneidlie, more commonly known as James Grant of Logie, who was the ancestor of the Grants of Moyness, Nairn. He died in July 1623.

3). Patrick Og Grant of Easter Elchies. On the death of his brother he was designated as Tutor to the children of Sir John Grant of Freuchie. He married Margaret, daughter of Sir Robert Innes of Balvenie.

4). Robert Grant of Lurgie, ancestor of the Grants of Lurgie. In 1613 he was fined, along with other members of the Clan, for aiding the outlawed members of Clan MacGregor. He died in 1634. Robert married Catherine Stewart, daughter of Stewart of Kilcoay.

5). Duncan Grant of Dandaleith.

6). Elizabeth Grant, who married Alexander Cumming of Altyre.

&). A daughter, name unknown.

John Grant, 5th Laird of Freuchie from 1585 until 1622. He married Lilias Murray of Tullibardine. He was the first Grant to own all the lands of Freuchie. During his long Chieftainship he fell out with the Gordon, Earl of Huntly, formally an ally of the Grants. The Gordon Chief was known as 'the Cock of the North' because he was the King's Lieutenant of the North.

Prior to becoming Chief, John was a formidable knight in the jousting tournaments all over Europe. In 1580 he defeated an English champion at a jousting tournament while on an embassy to England.

Although his official minority ended in 1578, King James VI did not take up full control of his Government until 1583. But he was too pre-occupied in plots against him in the South to worry much about the North. He was also taken up with keeping good relations with England in the hope that he would one day be its King when Queen Elizabeth eventually died.

In 1586 the Earl of Huntly allied himself with Clan MacDonald and Clan Cameron both of whom had a history of raiding Grants lands. The Grants responded bringing in their allies Clan MacGregor but they came off worse in a skirmish with Huntly and his new allies at Ballindalloch. This had much to do with the Grants now being Protestant and Huntly being Catholic.

In 1588 the Spanish Armada threatened England. Although this invasion was against England, the Protestant Scottish King and his Government were alarmed by the potential Spanish takeover of England and therefore by default, having a Catholic takeover of Scotland. After the Spanish fleet arrived in the English Channel, a 'Convention of the Estates' was quickly brought together in Edinburgh to decide what to do. The Laird of Freuchie attended. "The chief act of the Convention was to appoint Commissioners with justiciary powers, and very extensive authority. To apprehend and try Jesuits, rebels, and similar offenders."(106) John Grant of Freuchie was one of the Commissioners appointed for Elgin and Forres.

He was soon drawn into the struggle between the Earls of Sutherland and Caithness which lasted from 1587 until 1591.

The Mackintoshes and the Grants both claimed Rothiemurchas as their own but it was occupied by the Grants. Eventually they came to an agreement. Mackintosh resigned their rights to the estate to the Grants with the Grants binding themselves to guard the Glens of Urquhart and Morriston against raids from the Camerons and Clan Ranald in the west. This secured peace with Clan Mackintosh, at least for a time. Then in 1589, the Grants signed a bond with Cameron of Lochiel for mutual assistance, but this failed to ensure more friendly relations as within a year the Camerons were again raiding Grant lands.

"He [John] signed three bonds, one along with the King in person, John, Master of Forbes, George (Abernethy) Lord Saultoun, Ogilvie of Findlater, Lachlan Mackintosh of Dunachton, and other northern barons, dated at Aberdeen 30 April, 1589, in defence of the true religion and His Majesty's Government, against the Roman Catholic Conspiracy, and the Earls of Huntly and Errol in particular."[107]

Soon after this in late 1590 the Earl of Huntly got the support of Spain and with other Catholic Scottish noblemen, rebelled against the King James VI. John Grant was a Protestant and he stayed loyal to the King and fought against Huntly. On 5 November the Earl of Huntly attacked the Grant House of Ballindalloch. John Grant collected his men and with the Earls of Atholl and Moray, the Frasers, the Campbells of Cawdor and Lachlan Mackintosh joined up to fight the Earl of Huntly and his supporters.

Huntly advanced towards them and they retreated to Darnaway Castle. Huntly then marched to Darnaway and all the King's supporters fled, including the Grants, except the Earl of Moray. The Castle was well furnished to resist a siege and Huntly soon gave up and disbanded his forces on 24 November 1590. The rebellion failed and Huntly was taken prisoner but was soon released.

Also 1590 John was ordered to assist Campbell of Glenorchy against Clan MacGregor and raise the whole of Clan Grant against them. This caused John a problem as he was in dispute with the Government at the time as it was alleged he has harbouring outlaws (mainly MacGregors) in Strathspey. For this he had been fined £10,000, although he was refusing to pay it.

Then John Grant and the, now released, Earl of Huntly, quarrelled again. "All of this arose because Grant of Ballindalloch's widow, Margaret Gordon, married John Gordon, the son of Thomas Gordon of Cluny. Margaret Gordon took offence over some money matters, and called in some Gordon friends to maintain her rights. The Grants objected to these Gordons in Speyside, and one of them was killed. Huntly then besieged Ballindalloch Castle, but John Grant of Ballindalloch escaped."[108] He was the former' Tutor' of Ballindalloch and administrator of the estate. The Grant Chief was highly incensed by Gordon's action, but matters were eventually settled by arbitration. Nevertheless the Grants and Mackintoshes maintained a quarrel with Huntly for a number of years and in this they were helped by other allies, such as Campbell of Cawdor, the 'Bonnie' Earl of Moray and the Earl of Athol. There were a number of raids and counter raids as well as legal battles in the courts.

In the end the disputes ended with the Earl of Huntly murdering the 'Bonnie' Earl of Moray at Donibristle, Fife in February 1592. For this deed Huntly was imprisoned in Blackness Castle on the southern shore of the Firth of Forth but he was soon freed and he returned north. The Grants and Mackintoshes were itching for revenge against Huntly but before they could achieve this the Camerons and MacDonalds again raided their estates and 18 Grants were killed and the Laird of Ballindalloch was wounded. John Grant then "entered into a bond of mutual assistance with the proscribed Clan MacGregor, who had been allied to the 'Bonnie Earl'. Then King James VI ordered the Earl of Angus to proceed north to try and regulate matters, and this seems to have been accomplished by the end of 1592."(109)

The MacDonalds and Camerons fled west again into their homelands in Lochaber, chased all the way by a force which included John Grant of Freuchie and the Grant lairds of Ballindalloch, Rothiemurchas and Glenmoriston. They were accompanied by the MacGregors. Shortly after this and still in 1592, the Earls of Angus, Huntly and Errol fell into disgrace because of their part in the 'Spanish Blanks' conspiracy and King James personally led an army against the traitors. The Grants joined the King's force and the traitors were forced to flee. The lands of the three Earls were forfeited and in 1594 they were declared traitors.

Huntly and Errol then gathered their forces in arms and supported by the Earl of Bothwell, openly rebelled in the North. Clan Grant accompanied the King's army led by the young Campbell Earl of Argyll. "men gathered to his standard from all quarters under various leaders, and as it [Argyll's army] reached the neighbourhood of Badenoch and Strathspey it was joined by the Laird of Mackintosh and the Laird of Freuchie."(110) The first thing the King's army did was besiege the Castle of Ruthven in Badenoch, which was being held for Huntly by Clan MacPherson. The castle was stoutly defended and the army soon abandoned the siege. This did not bode well for the forthcoming campaign.

They were then met by Huntly's small force of 2,000 men near Glenlivet and the **Battle of Glenlivet** took place on 3rd October 1594. Although Huntly's force was small it was full of experienced warriors. They were mostly horsemen who were well armed and they had at least six pieces of artillery.

The King's army was nearly 10,000 strong and full of confidence that they would easily win the forthcoming battle. "The right wing of the army consisted of the Macleans and Mackintoshes, the left wing of the Grants, MacNeils and MacGregors, the centre being composed of Campbells."(111) The Campbells themselves amounted to over 4,000 men.

Huntly brought his cannon forward and the battle commenced when he started to fire on the Campbell centre, killing hundreds. One of the Campbell leaders, Campbell of Lochnell was killed at the very start and this was said to throw the Campbells into confusion. Huntly took advantage and his horsemen immediately charged and routed the Campbells in the centre. It was a complete victory for the rebels and the young Archibald Campbell was led away from the defeat in tears. The battle of Glenlivet was the young Earl of Argyll's first battle and he lost. Indeed the whole campaign went so poorly that King James VI, before he departed to London, called a halt and gave Archibald Campbell a 'cooling-off' period in prison in Edinburgh Castle.

However, there is much more speculation and intrigue as to the real events of the day and treachery may have played a major part. Campbell of Lochnell had ambitions to become the Earl of Argyll and tried on a number of occasions to kill the young Archibald. His last attempt was at Glenlivet. Prior to the Battle, Lochnell communicated with the enemy, telling them exactly where young Archibald Campbell would be standing on the day of the battle and where a sniper could kill him. But the treachery backfired on Lochnell. He stood to close to Archibald and it was he who was shot and killed by the sniper instead of the young Earl.

It is also said that the Chief of Clan Grant ordered his men to retreat as soon as the battle began and that this treacherous move led to the defeat of the mighty Clan Campbell. However, this is clearly a slur on Clan Grant made up by others later as the King took no action against John Grant or any of his clansmen after the defeat. Indeed, the Chief of Grant was probably not even at the battle and the Clan that day was led by John Grant of Gartenbery. It is more likely that seeing the Campbell centre routed by the horsemen of Huntly, the Grants and other clans on the wings decided to retire, knowing the battle had been lost.

Whatever the cause of the rebel victory, the Earls of Huntly and Errol's victory was short lived. The King them came north in command of his own army and demolished their castles and in the end forced Huntly and Errol to flee abroad. However, they were both pardoned in June 1597 and their titles and estates restored. Indeed two years later the Earl of Huntly was created a Marquis and the Grants again submitted to his authority in the North.

Around this time a further non-aggression bond was signed by Cameron of Locheil, Glengarry and John Grant at the latter's residence at Balmacaan in Glen Urquhart in the late 1590's.

In 1602, John Grant was given a commission to put down witchcraft in the Highlands. "Beside the main road in Forres, there is a commemorative stone which states that formerly witches were put into barrels studded with nails and rolled down the hill at this point. Few must have survived this terrible ordeal, and presumably if any did, they were judged 'not guilty' of witchcraft."(112) It may be that John Grant used this very place to make good on his commission.

Down in Edinburgh at the court of King James VI another John Grant (or Iain Mor), by this time the 3rd Laird of Glenmoriston, was ingratiating himself with the court of the King. "This Laird was distinguished for his stature, his prowess, and his skill in the use of the sword. When on a visit to King James at Holyrood, he was induced to accept a challenge from one of the champions of those days, who went from place to place parading their strength, and defying the lieges to fight them. This man was so formidable and so invariably successful in his duels, that no one was disposed to accept his challenge. But Laird John soon decided the contest in a rather unique way. One of the preliminaries on these occasions was to shake hands, to show, we suppose, there was no personal animosity between parties, but so mighty was Laird John's grasp, that he crushed his opponents sword hand so effectively as if it had been caught in a blacksmiths vice. So this formidable champion had to confess himself utterly discomforted, without drawing his sword."(89)

Iain Mor was to became a prominent and well respected Highland Laird but in 1602 he committed a foul murder. A merchant named Donald Vic Norssiche, was passing through Glenmoriston on his way to Kintail. With two other men, Iain Mor Grant waylaid the humble merchant, for what reason it is not known. They bound his hands behind his back and carried him into a nearby wood where they hanged him from the branch of a tree until he was dead. They then cut the dead man down and placed him beneath the overhanging bank of a stream and pressing down the earth upon it, buried him out of sight.

Tidings of the evil deed soon reached the ears of the dead man's brother who tried to get legal proceedings against Iain Mor and the other two men. But the law was slow to move and it took twenty years before writs were served on the murderers to appear for trial in Edinburgh on 2 July 1623. The accused men failed to appear and after their surety, Patrick Grant of Carron, paid a fine of 700 merks, the matter was dropped and Iain Mor was free to go about his business.

The dead man's brother was distraught and summed up the situation by his Gaelic Proverb:

Is cam 's is direach an lagh'

Crooked as well as straight is the law.

Many years later the Laird of Glenmoriston was in London in either 1631 or 1632, when a sneering English noble scoffed at the 'fir-candles' from his Glen. "The Laird retorted by defying the scoffer to produce in London a more elegant candlestick, or more brilliant lights, than he could bring from his Highland estate. A wager followed, and Iain Mor despatched a servant to the North with a message for the stalwart Iain Eobhain Bhain – a Glenmoriston bard distinguished alike for keen wit and manly beauty. At the appointed time Iain Mor's opponent appeared with a magnificent silver candelabrum furnished with the finest of wax candles. Glenmoriston had no such work of art to show; but on a given signal the bard stepped into the chamber, dresses in his Highland garb, and holding aloft blazing torches of the richest pines of Corri—Dho. The effect on the astonished spectators was even greater than the proud Glenmoriston had ventured to hope, and he was declared the victor with acclamation."(114)

Iain Mor's reputation and character suited the troubled times in which he lived and he was often called on to be a judge in disputes between other Clans. The Laird of Grant was also impressed with his kinsman and appointed him Chamberlain and Baillie of Urquhart.

Meanwhile, as all this was going on in the North, probably the most important event in British history took place in 1603, when on the death of Queen Elizabeth I of England, James VI of Scotland became King James I of England and Ireland, uniting the three kingdoms under one monarch for the first time in history. After this he based himself in London and only once returned to Scotland in 1617. He was the first monarch to style himself King of Great Britain and Ireland. This was to have the most profound impact on Scotland, the Highlands and the Grants.

Although he never achieved it, he was a great advocate of a single Parliament for Scotland and England. He also began the Plantation system in Ulster, which saw thousands of largely Protestant Scottish and English settlers emigrating to the North of Ireland. He also began the Colonisation of the Americas.

Despite concentrating his efforts in consolidating his position in England, James continued to control Government policy in Scotland and one of his key objectives was the pacification and 'civilising' of the Highlands. In 1608, in a bid to pacify the Highlands, the King sent Lord Ochiltree to the Western Isles as his Lieutenant of the North. Ochiltree ordered all the Clan Chiefs to attend a meeting with him at Aros in Mull. After several days bickering the Chiefs could not agree to make peace and Lord Ochiltree therefore stopped the meeting but invited them all to attend a dinner on his ship, 'The Moon'. That evening after the fine meal was finished Lord Ochiltree had all the Chiefs arrested and sent off south as prisoners. As loyal subjects of the King the Grants were not arrested as part of this move.

All the Chiefs were eventually set free after they agreed to sign the 'Statute of Iona' in 1609 when all the Highland and Island Chiefs agreed to sign a pact of friendship and non-hostility. A new set of rules were established which the King hoped would bring the Highlands into a state of lawfulness. These rules were as follows:

1. War between the clans was forbidden and all disputes were to be settled by the Courts of Law.
2. Each Chief must send some of his kinsmen to reside in the south, as hostages for his good conduct.
3. Each Chief was to be held responsible for the malpractices of his clansmen.
4. Each Chief must appear annually before the Government each July to answer for any indiscretions during the previous year. This was relaxed to every two years in 1623.
5. The household of the Chiefs was to be restricted. Most Chiefs were only to be allowed six warriors in their retinue, and they were only allowed to have one birlinn or galley.
6. Old churches were to be repaired and new ones built. The number of clergy was to be increased and the Chiefs were to pay for this.
7. The Chiefs and all owners of sixty cattle or more, were to send their children to be educated in the south. No heir who had not been educated in the south would be allowed to succeed. Luckily for the Grants the south also meant Aberdeen and Perth and most of the sons of the Chiefs and Lairds of Grant went to one of these two cities to be educated.

8. The consumption of liquor was to be curtailed. This was not adhered to very successfully.
9. Sorning was to be put down with a strong hand. Criminals, masterless men had found a refuge in the Highlands. These turbulent spirits were called sorners. The Chief was glad to welcome them because they added to the fighting strength of the clan, but they lived at free quarters on the people to whom they were great burdens, and they were a cause of endless strife in the country; for this reason a Chief was forbidden to receive sorners in his territory.
10. 'Handfasting' was to be outlawed. This custom, then common in the Highlands, allowed a man to take a wife for a year, with the ability to send her back within a year and a day, if she had not produced a son.

These agreements were kept and slowly clan feuds came largely to an end. With this the Highlands prospered.

"In 1610 the king had wished to elevate the Laird of Freuchie to Lord Strathspey, but John refused this title with the words, 'wha'll be Laird of Grant?".(115)

After the Battle of Glenfruin in 1603, Clan MacGregor had been proscribed and outlawed. To harbour or shelter them was a crime. Because of their friendship through Clan Alpin, many Grants, including the Laird of Grant, gave shelter to them, despite it being a criminal offence, in the Glens of Strathspey, Urquhart and Glenmoriston. Eventually the Government appointed Commissioners to discover and punish those who were sheltering the MacGregors.

In 1613 John Grant was accused of harbouring the outlawed MacGregors. Prior to this, in 1606, a number of the outlawed Clan MacGregor had been compelled to change their name to Grant in order to avoid persecution. The Earl of Argyll charged that he had been hiding them and that the only MacGregor outlaws left were those on the Grant estates.

Those fined along with the Laird of Grant were Archibald Grant, brother of the Laird of Glenmoriston, James Grant in Pitterrald, Patrick Grant, son of the Laird of Corrimony, Alisdair Roy Grant in Shewglie as well as many others of Clan Grant. The law at the time made Clan Chiefs responsible for the conduct of their people and Argyll called upon the Laird of Grant to pay not only his own fine but also that of his clansmen and dependants. The Laird admitted his liability, but disputed the amount.

John had to do something to prove his 'innocence'. He therefore arrested Alistair MacGregor, a notorious highland thief. This secured the Grants a temporary remission of the fines and penalties which were going to be imposed on them. But these were soon renewed and fines had to be paid by a number of Grants. The Chief of Grant himself was fined £16,000 merks for protecting the MacGregors. The original fine had been £40,000 merks. Alistair MacGregor died in the custody of the Laird of Grant. Despite this he seems to have done his best to aid the persecuted MacGregors.

It was not only the MacGregors who fell foul of the law. Also in 1614 there was an infamous Grant reiver by the name of Dugald Grant, sarcastically called Doule Shee or Dugald of Peace. He made a raid, with a gang of other men of Urquhart, on Colin Campbell of Clunes, near Nairn, burning his house, barns, sheep-cot and slaying three men and a horse. Dugald Grant and his associates were summoned to trial but failed to appear and were 'put to the horn'. A Royal Commission was issued for their arrest. But Dugald Grant could not be caught and he remained at large and was found later in the company of the even more famous outlaw, James Grant of Carron.

In February 1615, John Grant of Freuchie was one of the jury who found Patrick Stewart, 2nd Earl of Orkney guilty of treason. He and his son had tried to raise a rebellion on Orkney which had been put down by the Earl of Caithness. His son was also found guilty and both were beheaded. In 1617, James VI, now also King James I of England, visited Scotland, and John Grant "was asked to provide capercaillies and ptarmigan – forest and hill game birds- for the kings entertainment. They had to be sent down to Newcastle to greet the king."(116)

John Grant died on 20 September 1622 and was interred at Duthil. His wife, Lilias Murray, survived him by 21 years. The King and Queen had attended his wedding in 1591. The couple had one son and four daughters:

1). Sir John Grant, who succeeded. He was born on 17 August 1596. He was knighted by King James VI, and during his father's life-time was known as Sir John Grant of Mulben.

2). Agnes Grant, who married Lachlan Mackintosh of Dunachton and lived at Moy. The Laird of Grant paid a dowry of £10,000 merks. She was born in 1594.

3). Jean Grant, who married Sutherland of Duffus. Her father paid a dowry of £9,500 merks as her dowry. She was born in 1597.

4). Lilias Grant, born in 1599 and who married Sir Walter Innes of Balveny; and

5). Katherine Grant, born in 1624 and who married Alexander Ogilvie of Kempcairn.

John Grant also had an illegitimate son, Duncan Grant of Clurie who was legitimised in 1615. He married Muriel Ross, the widow of Duncan Grant of Rothiemurchas, and became the ancestor of the Grants of Clurie. Clurie House still exists between Aviemore and Carrbridge.

CHAPTER 9. THE SCOTTISH RELIGIOUS WARS.

Sir John Grant of Mulben, 6th of Freuchie, Chief of Clan Grant between 1622 until 1637. He married Mary Ogilvie of Deskford, daughter of Sir Walter Ogilvie of Findlater, afterwards Lord Ogilvie of Deskford. Born in Edinburgh in 1596, Sir John Grant lived mainly in Edinburgh, where he frequently attended the Scottish Court. He lived an extravagant lifestyle through his relatively short life.

Early in his tenure he had to sell the Grant estate of Lethan to Alexander Brodie in order to pay off his debts. Then in 1622 his fortunes must have changed as he was able to purchase the lands of a number of Speyside churches and he also acquired the estate of Pitcroy in the parish of Knockando. He then introduced forestry into his estates and sold much timber to the south.

DIAGRAM 4. THE CHIEFS OF CLAN GRANT.

Name	Chief Number	Title	From	Until
Sir John Grant of Mulben	17	6th of Freuchie	1622	1637
James Grant	18	7th of Freuchie	1637	1663
Ludovick Grant	19	8th of Freuchie, 1st of Grant	1663	1716
Brigadier-General Alexander Grant	20	2nd of Grant	1716	1719
Sir James Grant of Pluscardine	21	3rd of Grant	1719	1747
Sir Ludovick Grant	22	4th of Grant	1747	1773
Sir James Grant 'The Good'	23	5th of Grant	1773	1811
Sir Lewis Alexander Grant-Ogilvy	24	6th of Grant, 6th Earl of Seafield	1811	1840

A local Gaelic Bard and cattle rustler, Domhnall Dubh, fell in love with the Laird of Grants daughter Mary. The Laird did not approve of this suitor and he had him arrested and imprisoned in Urquhart Castle where he was beheaded. Mary would have to find another husband.

In 1622 Sir John Grant also received the forfeited lands of Allan MacDonald of Lundie (Ailean dubh Mac Raonuill) who had been forfeited after his murderous raid of 'Cilliechriost'.

The massacre of 'Cilliechriost' illustrates the vengeful nature of the Highlands at this time. Allan MacDonald undertook a terrible and murderous raid into Brae Ross, Mackenzie country, his mortal enemies. It took place on a Sunday and all of the people of Cilliechriost were at the church service. MacDonald "without a moments delay, without a single pang of remorse, and while the song of praise ascended to heaven from fathers, mothers, and children, he surrounded the church with his band, and with lighted torches set fire to the roof. The building was thatched, and while a gentle breeze from the east fanned the fire, the song of praise mingled with the crackling of the flames, until the imprisoned congregation becoming conscious of their situation, rushed to the doors and windows, where they were met by a double row of bristling swords. Now, indeed, arose the wild wail of despair, the shrieks of women, the infuriated cries of men and the helpless screaming of children; these mingled with the roaring of the flames appalled even the MacDonalds, not so Allan Dubh.

'Thrust them back into the flames', cried he, 'for he that suffers aught to escape alive from Gilliechriost shall be branded as a traitor to his clan'; and they were thrust back or mercilessly cut down within the narrow porch, until the dead bodies, piled upon each other, posed an insurmountable barrier to the living. Anxious for the preservation of their young children, the scorching mothers threw them from the windows in a vain hope that the feelings of parents awakened in the breasts of the MacDonald's would induce them to spare them, but not so. At the command of Allan of Lundi; they were received on the points of the broadswords of men in whose breasts mercy had no place."(117)

Soon all were dead and the raid over, the MacDonalds split into two groups and headed west for home. But they would not be allowed to escape and the Mackenzies soon found out about the massacre of their kinsfolk and sought revenge. A large number of Mackenzie warriors gathered together and they were assisted by the Grants from Glen Urquhart and Glenmoriston. One group of the MacDonalds headed towards Inverness and then headed west along the southern shore of Loch Ness. These men were soon surprised in a public house near Tobreck, three miles west of Inverness. In a poignant act of revenge the house was set on fire and all 37 raiders suffered the same fate as they had so recently inflicted on the inhabitants of Cilliechriost.

Meanwhile the other chasing group, led by Mackenzie of Coul but assisted by the Grants of Urquhart and Glenmoriston, caught up with the other MacDonalds as they rested near the Aultsigh Burn. They were seen by the MacDonalds and they fled. Some were caught before they made the ford on the Aultsign Burn and were killed. The rest escaped and were pursued throughout the night. By dawn Allan Dubh and his remaining men were ascending the southern ridge of Glen Urquhart with the Mackenzies and Grants close behind. Seeing that the enemy were getting closer, Allan Dubh commanded his men to disperse, trying to divert the chase from himself. However, after continuing to flee for some time he took a rest and scanned behind him, only to see that all the avenging Mackenzies and Grants were still following him and his now small band of warriors.

Again, he split his remaining men up and he headed towards Loch Ness, but still saw that all his enemies were following him. He split up the last of his men and proceeded alone. Allan, to show his rank as a leader of the Glengarry MacDonalds, always wore a bright red jacket and thus was easily recognisable from the rest of his men. It was this jacket which the Mackenzies and Grants had followed, knowing that it belonged to Allan.

Sensing he would soon be caught if he did not take drastic action, Allan resolved to do just that. He ran towards the Aultsigh ravine, a fearfully high precipice. On reaching this chasm he pulled off his plaid and buckler and then turned to his pursuers, who were close to catching up with him, beckoning them to follow. Then he took a run and flung himself over the chasm, a feat never before undertaken successfully. Being of a strong and athletic nature, he made it over the abyss. One of the young lairds of Grant, on whose land they were now on, decided to follow and attempted the jump. Although his shoes touched the other side, it was not enough, and he fell but managed to grab the branch of a slender hazel which had grown over the abyss. By this time Allan Dubh had regained his feet and his composure and calmly walked over to the chasm and "hoarsely whispered, 'I have *given much to your race today, I shall give them this also; surely now the debt is paid*'; then cutting the hazel twig with his sword, the intrepid youth was dashed from crag to crag until he reached the stream below, a bloody and misshapen mass."(118)

Alan Dubh then turned to flee again but one of the Mackenzies had brought a musket and firing, wounded Allan Dubh. After this he had to slacken his pace but as no-one else tried to jump the chasm, he was able to increase the distance between himself and his Mackenzie and Grant pursuers.

Eventually, however, his pace got slower and slower, the loss of blood taking its effect and the Mackenzies and Grants were soon getting closer to him again. By this time, he was on the banks of Loch Ness, in the heart land of the Grants and, like a wounded animal, chose to dive into the Loch's cold waters rather than face the oncoming Mackenzies and Grants. He soon swam beyond the range of the

Mackenzie and Grant muskets. However, being desperately weak from his wound there was no way he could have swum the full width of the loch to escape and reconciled himself to ending his days, drowned in the great loch.

However, the shouts of the Mackenzies and Grants on the opposite bank alerted Fraser of Foyers and seeing a large body of men on the shore and a single swimmer in the Loch, he got out his rowing boat and rescued the wounded man, much to the annoyance of the Mackenzies and Grants. He was, however, the only MacDonald who survived their murderous raid.

The ridge where Allan Dubh made his leap between the Glens of Urquhart and Aultsigh was thereafter named 'Monadh-an-Leumanaich' or the Moor of the Leaper. The MacDonalds suffered for this raid as soon afterwards they were forfeited their lands which were then given to the Mackenzies and Grants.

A few years later, however, the Laird of Grant befriended Allan Dubh MacDonald , thinking it was better to have such a fierce warrior on his side rather than his enemy. He got his kinsman, the Grant Laird of Lundie, to sign a Bond of Friendship with him, and when Allan Dubh was forfeited, the Laird of Grant allowed him to remain in his estate. Allan Dubh MacDonald died an old man, never having been brought to the law for his massacre at Cilliechriost.

King James VI and I died in 1625 and was succeeded by his eldest surviving son, King Charles I. "After his succession in 1625, Charles quarrelled with the Parliament of England, which sought to curb his royal prerogative. Charles believed in the divine right of kings and was determined to govern according to his own conscience. Many of his subjects opposed his policies, in particular the levying of taxes without parliamentary consent, and perceived his actions as those of a tyrannical absolute monarch. His religious policies, coupled with his marriage to a Roman Catholic, generated antipathy and mistrust from Reformed religious groups such as the English Puritans and Scottish Covenanters, who thought his views were too Catholic."(119)

In 1627 the Protestants of France, the Huguenots, were at war with King Louis XIII of France. The French Protestants were besieged in the Fortress of La Rochelle and King Charles I, despite his Catholic leanings, decided to relieve the siege.

"When King Charles I was investing La Rochelle in France for the relief of the Protestant inhabitants, he wrote to John [Grant], as to many other gentlemen, asking him to send soldiers to reinforce his Scottish regiment. John put this in train, but as it took time to get them to Leith Harbour, Charles's army was repulsed in the meantime, and the Grant contingent did not go to La Rochelle. John's soldiers were, however, recruited into a force to go to Sweden."(120) The Grants were commanded by John Grant of Auchterblair and were sent to serve in Colonel Hamilton's Scottish contingent serving the Swedish King Gustavus Adolphus.

At home John was having trouble with his own clan. James Grant of Carron, also known as Seumas 'an Tuim' (of the hill) was a notorious cattle raider. He was a descendant of John Mor of Glenmoriston, the illegitimate son of the 2nd Laird of Freuchie. For years he and his family had been at feud with the Grants of Ballindalloch and several killing had taken place. The feud was sparked again when Seumas killed a son of Patrick Grant, Laird of Ballindalloch.

This all reignited in 1615 when Thomas Grant, a son of Grant of Carron, was met at an Elgin Fair by one of the Grants of Ballindalloch, and was savagely assaulted. James Grant, another son of the Laird of Carron, rushed to his brothers aid and killed the assailant. "Summoned before a court on a charge of murder, James refused to appear and was outlawed".(121) He took up the challenge of being an outlaw with vigour and concentrated on attacking the possessions of Ballindalloch. Iain Mor Grant of Glenmoriston continued his friendship with James Grant and helped to hide him. Glenmoriston was not friend of the Ballindalloch's who had tried to disinherit his father decades earlier. The outlaw 'Doule Shee' and his sons Donald, John and Ewan Grant joined the outlaws under James of Carron.

Chief John Grant made efforts to reconcile the Carrons and the Ballindallochs, but in 1628 there was a fight between the two parties at Abernethy. "... John Grant of Ballindalloch attacked John Grant of Carron, the nephew of the outlaw Sheumas an Tuin, who had proceeded to the wood of Abernethy, accompanied by several of his friends, to cut timber. Carron was slain, and so also were several of Ballindalloch's friends, including Thomas Grant of Dalvy. Young Ballindalloch was afterwards charged, at the insistence of the widow of John Grant of Carron, with the murder of her husband, but he procured a remission from Charles I for himself, his brother Patrick, William Grant of Cardells, and Archibald Grant of Dalvey."(122)

The feud even reached the ears of the King and in 1630 the Chief of Grant visited him in London to discuss it. The Laird of Ballindalloch had written to the King complaining that Sir John Grant "to the further contempt of justice, he associate into himself a number of broken Hieland men of the Clanranald, Clangregor, and some others out of Strathspey and Strathdoun, and with unlawful lymmars, armed with unlawful weapons he goes athort the cuntrie community opin stoutes, heirships, sorning and depredations', Ballindalloch also added that James Grant, 'wes the cheefe instrument of the troubles fallin out betuix the hous of Carron and the compleaner, and of the slaughters unhappily committed hinc inde'."(123) He further stated that this was being done at the instigation of Sir John Grant of Freuchie. The complaint was dismissed.

James Grant of Carron (Seumas an Tuin) carried on the feud and "in December 1630, burned Ballindallochs corn yard, stables, byres and barns, and drove away as many of his cattle as escaped the flames. The Ballindallochs sought the protection of the Earl of Murray, who employed a party of 'broken MacGregors' to capture James, and succeeded in taking him in a house in Strathavon after a desperate fight, in which nearly all his men were killed and he himself severely wounded. When sufficiently recovered, he was despatched under a strong escort to Edinburgh Castle...."(124) He remained a prisoner for two years, until his wife secretly sent him a rope concealed in a cask of butter, which he used to escape from his prison cell window in October 1632. Those of his men who had been captured were not so lucky and were tried, convicted and executed at the Tolbooth in Edinburgh.

On his escape, Seumas (James) immediately returned north and renewed his attacks on Ballindalloch who again employed the MacGregors to hunt him. But this time he successfully alluded them. Seumas then killed one of his hunters, Patrick Gar MacGregor, the leader of the group hunting him. "The death of Gar appears to have been a relief to the people of Strathspey, and James Grant rose in their esteem on account of this deed."(125) Indeed the Laird of Ballindalloch appears to have been frequently betrayed by his own people as even those he sent to find Seumas would send information to Seumas to warn him.

Then Seumas, with a party of his own men, went to Ballindallochs House at night and sent a message to him that a friend wanted to meet him in secret with interesting news. Ballindalloch agreed and when he approached Seumas and his men seized him, and wrapped him in their plaids and bore him away to Elgin, where he was imprisoned for 21 days, until the prisoner bribed one of his guards and escaped.

After this Seumas got even bolder. He captured Thomas Grant of Culquoich and his brother, both friends of Ballindalloch. After keeping them captive for a short time he murdered them, cut off their heads and sent them to Ballindalloch.

Chief John Grant again attended the Privy Council meeting in Edinburgh in 1636 and was given a Commission of Fire and Sword to capture the outlaws. He hired four Bounty Hunters but they had no success. Once he also sent out three dozen of his own men who returned with only two of 'an Tuim's' men. Then Ballindalloch hired Thomas Grant of Speyside, a renowned warrior, to capture or kill Seumas. When Seumas heard of this he immediately went to the home of Thomas grant, killed or drove away all of his cattle and then despatched Thomas Grant with his dagger.

After this the Chief, John Grant, eventually took action and wanting peace within his Clan he brokered a peace agreement between Seumas and Ballindalloch which was signed on 9 August 1635. Seumas was eventually pardoned by the King in 1639 and he fought for King Charles II at the Battle of Worcester. Despite his eventful and dangerous life, Seumas Grant died at a very old age in his own bed.

In 1636, an Allan Grant, son of the tenant of Wester Tulloch was executed for harbouring Gilderoy MacGregor and a number of his MacGregor outlaws. His lands were then forfeited. Then in 1637 two Grants, alias McJochie in Tulloch and his son, Patrick Grant McJochie were arrested for aiding and abetting members of Clan Gregor, assisting then to evade capture and the slaying of two of the King's officers.

The Scottish Privy Council did not believe that Sir John Grant had tried very hard to arrest James Grant and the outlawed MacGregors and he was ordered again to appear before the Privy Council in Edinburgh. Here he was found guilty and placed in custody for not apprehending the outlawed Clan MacGregor. Due to his ill health he was soon set free but he supposedly died the same day as he was released on 1 April 1637. He was buried in Holyrood Abbey. His kinsmen Iain Mor Grant, Laird of Glenmoriston, had also died one month before the Laird of Grant.

John Grant, Chief of Clan Grant, left 7 sons and 3 daughters, among whom were:

- James Grant, who succeeded.
- Patrick Grant of Cluniemore and Cluniebeg, but better known as the 'Tutor of Grant', which he became on the death of his brother James in 1663. In 1651, his brother appointed him Lieutenant-Colonel of the 1400 Grant levies which were raised to support King Charles II and which took part in the **Battle of Worcester**, 3 September 1651.
- Alexander Grant, who did not get on with his elder brother and took legal action against him regarding his inheritance.

- Major George Grant, who in 1668 was appointed Governor of Dumbarton Castle and held this post for some time. "He is probably the Captain Grant who, on his own petition, was, on 11 October 1666, granted a warrant to uplift and free the county of beggars, gypsies, and idle persons who cannot give an account of their ways of living, by apprehending them and carrying them beyond the sea to the plantations."(126) Obviously not one of the nicer Grants.

- Mary Grant, who married first, Lord Lewis Gordon, who became 3rd Marquis of Huntly. "According to tradition, Lord Lewis Gordon was concealed for some time in a cave in the rocky glen about two miles from Castle Grant. To that hiding-place the Laird of Grant's sister Mary carried suppliers to the fugitive, and her attentions led to their marriage. The cave is called 'Huntly's cave'."(127) The marriage took place in November 1644. Her dowry was £20,000 merks. Her husband died in December 1653 and their son became 1st Duke of Gordon. Secondly she married James Ogilvie, 2nd Earl of Airlie. For some reason she had been excommunicated by the Church so the arrangements of her 2nd wedding were done with some difficulty. But eventually the marriage did take place in October 1640.

James Grant, 7th of Freuchie, Chief of Clan Grant from 1637 and 1663. Born in 1616 he married Lady Mary Stewart, daughter of the 2nd Earl of Moray on 25 April 1640. He lived through Charles I, the Civil War, the Cromwell Protectorate and the return of Charles II. His father left the Grant estates with a large debt. He was young when he inherited and his uncle, Patrick, became Tutor.

He had initially been engaged to marry Lady Jane Fleming, daughter of John, 1st Earl of Wigtown. His friends seem to have opposed the match, and he broke it off. Possibly broken hearted, she died in December 1637.

He became Chief at the same time as the Covenanting religious struggle began in Scotland and he was a keen supporter of the Covenant, being one of the first Northern lords to sign the Bond adhering to it. For a time he was in the army, serving under General Leslie, the commander of the Scots Covenanting Army. The new and also young Laird of Glenmoriston, Patrick Grant, also became a keen supporter of the Covenant as was his Tutor, John Grant of Coineachan. Many other Grants did not feel the same way, particularly the Laird of Grants mother, Dame Mary Ogilvy.

In 1638 King Charles attempted to reform the Scottish Protestant Church and this caused a fierce reaction from the Scottish Lords who formed the Scottish National Covenant to oppose the Kings reforms. The National Covenant was a charter emphasising the independence of the Scottish Parliament, renounced the Catholic faith and upheld Presbyterianism. Essentially it was a declaration to radically reduce the power of the King.

This eventually led to direct rebellion of the Scots against their Monarch in what is called the 'The Bishop's Wars'. Determined to assert his authority against his Scottish rebels the King began to organise a military campaign to defeat them. He began to muster an army at Berwick-on-Tweed in preparation of marching onto Edinburgh and smashing the Scots. However, this is not how it turned out. With little money the army he was able to assemble was untrained and ill-equipped and was no match for the Scottish Covenant Army which was full of experienced Scots soldiers who had been fighting for years as mercenaries in Europe. The King quickly realised the forces were inadequate to beat the Scots and he negotiated a truce, known as the 'Pacification of Berwick'.

The Grants did not form part of the Scottish army which opposed the King. James Grant was given the task, in 1638, of enforcing the Covenant in Invernesshire. His mother, the Dowager Lady Grant was of a much different persuasion. After she was widowed she retired to Urquhart Castle. "She did not sympathise with the Covenanters by whom she was badly treated and driven out of Urquhart."(128) She was alive in 1646 but died soon after. His wife also had problems with the 'Covenant' and a sentence of excommunication was pronounced against her in the Parish Church of Duffus on 17 October 1658 for her adherence to 'Poperie'. These two ladies were probably Episcopalian in their religious beliefs.

In August 1640 the King again attempted to crush the Scottish rebels and assembled a new army of about 20,000 poorly equipped and poorly fed soldiers. The Scots again took the initiative and its army crossed into England. After scattering the King's English army, they captured Newcastle upon Tyne. Again, King Charles saw he could not win against the Scots and signed another peace treaty in September 1640. As part of the agreement the King had to pay £300,000 compensation to the Scots to fund the provisioning of the army in Northern England. At this time the Scots had the support of many of the English Lords who were beginning to hate the rule of King Charles I.

James Grant and his clan joined the Covenanting Army and he was given the rank of Lieutenant Colonel. They wore blue ribbons and the King's supporters wore red ribbons. James spent £7 12s 6d on blue ribbons. He was, however, soon at loggerheads with his mother, who refused to allow him to recruit the Grants of Urquhart into his Covenanter Regiment.

Meanwhile the Earl of Huntly had refused to sign the Covenant and raised his forces to support King Charles I. James Grant and his clansmen joined the Covenanting Army which then marched to and entered Aberdeen to confront the Earl of Huntly, who soon capitulated and he and his eldest son were made prisoners. This Covenanting force was then under the command of the Earl of Montrose, before he abandoned the Covenanter cause and joined the side of King Charles I.

While Huntly and his eldest son were taken captive to prison in Edinburgh, his second son, Lord Aboyne, took up the cause of opposition to the Covenant in the North East. While the main Covenanter Army was marching to Berwick to take on the King's army, the Grants, Frasers, Mackenzies, Munro's and others gathered their forces to stop the Gordons marching south to support the King. However, before the forces came to blows the 'Pacification of Berwick' was signed by the King and an uneasy peace ensued for a short while.

The English Civil War began in 1642 between the Parliamentarians (Roundheads) and the Royalist (supporters of King Charles I). The Parliamentarians sought to curb the power of the Monarch and strengthen the power of Parliament. "On 22 August 1642 King Charles raised the royal standard at Nottingham as a symbol of armed opposition to the powers claimed by the English Parliament."(129) Both the King and the English Parliamentarians appealed to the Scots for help. "None was immediately given to either, for while it had taken a constitutional shape, Scotland's quarrel with Charles was religious not political. The intransigent Covenanters were already bigots, the Presbyterian Church was the only true faith and should be established throughout Great Britain, ….. the abolition of English episcopacy was the price of Scots help. This the King was told at Oxford and Parliament informed in London, and since the latter was as anxious to reform the Church of England as it was to secure a supply of Scots coal, it struck the bargain."(130). The Scots would support the Parliamentarians.

Initially the Royalist forces were triumphant and won victory after victory, securing the West Country, Wales and the North of England. Then the Parliamentarians won the Battle of Newbury, Berkshire in September 1643 and a few weeks later they were joined by a Scottish Covenanting Army of 21,000 who invaded the North of England. In overall command of the Scottish Army was Alexander Leslie, Earl of Leven and the Scots would make the difference in the English Civil War. The Scots and English Parliamentarian joined forces and fought and won the Battle of Marston Moor, near York, on 22 July 1644, which effectively gave victory to the Parliamentarians.

Before this, however, a month after the Scottish army had crossed the border, King Charles I appointed James Graham, Earl of Montrose, his Lord Lieutenant of Scotland and raised him to Marquis of Montrose. James Graham had been a reluctant or moderate Covenanter but he had fallen out with the Covenant leaders and pledged his support to the Royalist cause.

Montrose was joined by Alistair MacColla MacDonald (Colkitto). Originally from Colonsay, he, his father and brothers had been exiled to Ireland by the Campbells. They had, however, continued to be a thorn in the side of the Campbells and intermittent warfare had continued between the two clans for years with many atrocities and killing by each side. Although in his early twenties, Colkitto was an experienced and seasoned warrior and commander of men, having fought as a mercenary in Ireland for many years.

At the outbreak of the Civil War, Colkitto proclaimed his support for King Charles I and with 1,600 men he landed on the west coast of Scotland and soon took revenge on the Campbells `by taking two of their castles and killing all the garrisons. The huge MacDonald Clan supported the King, not out of loyalty, but because the Campbells supported the other side and they saw the cause of King Charles I as a way of getting back their lands and titles which the Campbells had 'stolen'. Eventually nearly all of the MacDonald Clans joined Colkitto and his force marched to Blair Athol where they were joined by the Marquis of Montrose, who at this time had few men of his own.

Colkitto MacDonald is given much of the credit for developing the famous 'Highland Charge'. The novelty of this method of attack lay in the fact that the combatants no longer wore heavy armour and used a single-handed rather than a two-handed sword, leaving the other hand free to carry a target or buckler (small shield). This light weaponry gave them a huge speed advantage. When they had fired one musket volley they dropped their guns and ran forward with blood curdling yells in a wedge formation. This tactic proved able to break any but the most determined enemy.

Montrose and Colkitto decided to join together and they made a strong team, Montrose with his experience in the Continental Wars and Colkitto with his undoubted personal courage and opportunistic flair. Moreover, the Clans who were reluctant to join the half-Irish Colkitto were prepared to join Montrose and this widened the appeal of the Royalist cause.

Early in the campaign Colkitto sent a demand to the Grants of Glenmoriston to supply his men with cattle to feed them in the name of the King. The Tutor of Glenmoriston, John Grant of Coineachan, "…. unwilling to grant the request, and still more unwilling to incur his displeasure, forwarded a large supply from the untamed herds of Corrie-Dho. On approaching the camp and seeing the soldiers and their tents and banners, these denizens of the remote glens broke away in a wild stampede, and with a speed that defied the winds made their way back to their native pastures. A good joke was never lost on Alasdair Mac Colla [Colkitto], and he sent a message to 'Toitear Ghlinne- Moircastium' – the grey tutor of Glenmoriston, complementing him on the success of his trick."(131)

Montrose then sent out letters seeking the support of the other Highland Clans. Initially Montrose wrote to James Grant of Freuchie, appointing him the King's Lieutenant in Morayshire, all directed to get him not to obey or acknowledge the Covenanter Government, without the King's authority. But Grant was not prepared to forsake the Covenant at this time. To counter this the Covenanters appointed him a Lieutenant-Colonel in the Covenanting Army in fear of a Gordon rising in the North East. Grant raised 1,000 men of his clan and stationed them at Elgin to counter the threat from the Gordons.

"The Laird continued to maintain a steady adherence to the covenanting cause, although, in doing so, he acted against the wishes of several of his relatives, including his own mother, who was at that time living on her liferent lands of Urquhart."(132) Relations with his mother were therefore strained.

From Blair Athol, Montrose and Colkitto made a rapid march south towards Perth. With all the best Scottish troops with the Covenanting army in England, fighting against King Charles I, the Government hastily assembled an inexperienced force to defend Perth under Lord Elcho and James Murray, Earl of Tullibardine. Montrose's force was around 2,000 men, of which almost 1,500 were from Clan Donald. The Government force could have been up to 7,000 infantry and 800 cavalry, but they were mainly inexperienced troops and local levies. The Chief of Grant sent around 200 of his Clansmen south, led by Captain David Grant, to join the main Covenanter army.

The two armies met at the **Battle of Tippermuir** on 1 September 1644. After an initial cavalry charge by the Covenanters was repulsed, Montrose then gave the order to charge and the experienced Highland warriors soon routed the inexperienced Government troops. As usual in these types of battles, the majority of the casualties occurred during the rout which turned into a bloodbath. A group of townspeople had come to watch the battle, confident that the Government force would be victorious, and they too got caught up in the rout and many were killed, both men and women. It was said that you could walk from Tippermuir to Perth on the bodies of the dead. The Government force lost around 2,000 men and although Montrose was reported to have lost only one, this is likely to be Royalist propaganda. His losses were, however, minimal. The Grants lost around 30 men killed and another 30 wounded, including their commander Captain David Grant who suffered a wound from a musket ball to his shoulder.

The Highland army then surrounded Perth and it immediately surrendered. It was then sacked for two days by the Highlanders. After this Montrose decided to try and take the City of Dundee, but it was well defended and refused to surrender. He then moved onto Aberdeen. At this time, many of the Clansmen left to take their spoils home. Colkitto remained with his warriors. By this time the army of Montrose amounted to around 1,500 men.

Aberdeen had a large Covenanter force defending it and refused to surrender. Unfortunately, during the negotiations a soldier from the Covenanter garrison shot and killed a young drummer boy from the Royalist army, who was accompanying Montrose's negotiators. This infuriated the Royalist troops who would soon seek vengeance. The Aberdeen Covenanter garrison were so confident that they came out of the City and prepared to attack the Royalists. Colkitto's Highland Charge was again used and this quickly overwhelmed the Covenanter force who fled back into the City. They were pursued by the Highlanders and were slaughtered in the streets.

The Burgh of Aberdeen was subjected to a three-day orgy of murder, pillage and rape which Montrose made no attempt to stop. He may have wanted to make an example of Aberdeen for resisting him, but the atrocities committed there greatly damaged his cause. On hearing that the Marquis of Argyll's pursuing army was advancing from Brechin, Montrose withdrew towards the Highlands, heading directly towards the Grants.

Montrose directed his progress to Strathbogie and Strathspey. On his arrival at the Spey, he found that all the boats had been withdrawn to the opposite bank, and that the men of Grant were prepared to dispute their crossing. Montrose decided not to risk a battle with the Grants at this time and retired to camp at Abernethy Woods.

By this time the Earl of Argyll was marching from the south to attack Montrose, but with Montrose in a strong position Argyll moved on to Aberdeen. After this Montrose moved to Rothiemurchas Woods and then moved further south to Athol. He looked as if he was preparing to march into Central Scotland and Argyll was forced to act and eventually marched north with a large Covenanter army of 4,000 men to face him. They fought an indecisive skirmish near Fyvie Castle in November 1644, when Montrose's army had been depleted by Colkitto's departure west to gather more MacDonalds and men from other clans. The Grants continued to protect the River Spey and stop the Jacobite Army from attempting a crossing.

Indeed the Laird of Grant also gave orders to his men not to allow any army across the Spey, be it Jacobite or Covenanter. The boats were again removed and the Grants guarded the Fords across the river. It seems the Grants at this time were more concerned about their own property than loyalty to either the Covenanter cause or that of King Charles. Although they stopped both armies crossing the Spey it did not stop looting and raiding by both armies on their property and much of Speyside suffered severely.

After this the Campbell force retired south again for the winter and Archibald Campbell returned to Inveraray. Colkitto brought 5,000 reinforcements, mainly more MacDonalds, MacLeans from Mull and Morven, Stewarts from Appin and the Farquharsons from Braemar, all intent on revenge against the Campbells in particular. At this time the Grants were the only effective Covenanter Army left in the Highlands and if they had to face Montrose's much larger force they, in all likelihood, they would be destroyed.

Luckily for the Grants, despite the onset of winter, Montrose and Colkitto decided to undertake a surprise attack on Argyllshire, the heartland of Clan Campbell. Initially Montrose wanted to march into Central Scotland but the MacDonalds preferred to attack Campbell territory and revenge themselves on their hated clan rivals. They managed to persuade Montrose that the Campbells needed to be destroyed before they marched into Central Scotland.

In early December 1644, "Montrose's men struck first through the Breadalbane country, wading the snowdrifts and driving through weather in which no army could be expected to be abroad, killing every Campbell of fighting age they encountered, burning houses and driving off cattle."(133) and then launched an attack on Inveraray.

At Inverary, Archibald Campbell had no force of warriors with which to resist and the Royalists totally routed the Campbells and the Earl of Argyll prudently slipped away to safety down Loch Fyne in his galley to his castle of Roseneath, leaving Inveraray and his remaining Campbell clansmen to their fate. In his defence, if Archibald had been captured he would, undoubtedly, have been executed by the MacDonalds. From 13 December 1644 until the end of January 1645 the MacDonalds plundered and burned Campbell properties slaughtering Campbells of arms-bearing age. Inverary was burned to the ground. A total of 895 Campbells were reported to have been killed and 18 parishes are said to have been destroyed.

Passage of Montrose's Army Through Glencoe.

Sir George Reid, 1876.

Eventually, when the killing spree had finished, Montrose and his army marched up the West Coast of the Highlands, then through Glencoe until they arrived at the fortress of Inverlochy, now Fort William, where they rested. From here they then marched up the Great Glen till they reached Kilcumin (now Fort Augustus). From here they made raids on the Grant estates of Glenmoriston and Urquhart. Eventually, when the killing spree had finished, Montrose and his army marched up the West Coast of the Highlands, then through Glencoe until they arrived at the fortress of Inverlochy, now Fort William, where they rested. From here they then marched up the Great Glen till they reached Kilcumin (now Fort Augustus). From here they made raids on the Grant estates of Glenmoriston and Urquhart.

At around the same time James Grant's sister married Lord Lewis Gordon, 3rd son of the Marquis of Huntly, a staunch Royalist. Initially this was against the wishes of the Chief of Grant but they were later reconciled by the actions of his mother, another strong Royalist. Later Lord Lewis Gordon would succeed his father as 3rd Marquis of Huntly. His son by Mary Grant was George, 4th Marquis of Huntly and was created Duke of Gordon.

Meanwhile Mackenzie, Earl of Seaforth, had gathered an army of around 5,000 men at Inverness to fight against Montrose. James Grant and around 400 of his men formed part of this Covenanting force. James was very concerned that the Grant lands along Loch Ness would be devastated by the army of Montrose if it were allowed to proceed any further east than Fort Augustus. Montrose at this time had been reduced to around 1,500 men because the MacDonalds of Glengarry and the men of Athol had returned home with their spoils of victory so far.

Mackenzie, with the Grants, marched down the side of Loch Ness ready to fight. Despite his significantly fewer numbers, Montrose decided to attack, knowing that many of the 'soldiers' pitted against him were raw recruits with no military experience. However, before the forces met Montrose got the news that the Earl of Argyll had reached Lochaber with a great army of Campbells, intent on revenge for Montrose's attack on his lands in Argyll. He therefore changed his plans and headed back west, to Inverlochy (Fort William) to take on Argyll.

On 31 January 1645, Montrose and Colkitto led their 1,500 men on a bold flanking march over the mountains. The Highlanders and Irishmen covered thirty miles of extremely rough mountainous terrain in under thirty-six hours to descend on the Campbells at Inverlochy at the foot of Ben Nevis during the early hours of 2 February.

Montrose deployed his 600 Highlanders in the centre with the Irishmen on the flanks: Colkitto on the right and Manus O'Cahan with his regiment on the left.

MacDonnell's regiment and Sir Thomas Ogilvy's troop of horse were kept in reserve.

The Marquis of Argyll, suffering from a dislocated shoulder, retired to his galley on Loch Linnhe leaving Sir Duncan Campbell of Auchinbreck in command of the opposing army. Auchinbreck drew up his forces in front of Inverlochy Castle. In the centre were 1,000 Campbell levies and the 500 men of the Marquis's own regiment, which had been recalled from Ireland. Regulars recalled from the Covenanter army were placed on each wing under the command of Lieutenant-Colonel Roughe of the Earl of Tullibarne's regiment and Lieutenant-Colonel Cockburn of the Earl of Moray's regiment.

Montrose struck at dawn with a swift ferocious charge before Auchinbreck could assess the position in daylight. Under fire from the Covenanters on the flanks the advancing Irish and MacDonalds held their own fire until they were almost in contact with the enemy. After delivering a single devastating volley, the Irishmen threw down their muskets and charged home with swords and dirks. The Covenanters broke and ran. Meanwhile, the Highlanders clashed violently with the Campbells in the centre. Ogilvy's cavalry worked around to outflank the Campbells and block their retreat to the castle. Attacked on all sides, the Campbells were slaughtered by their bitter enemies and hundreds of Campbells were killed, including Auchinbreck who was beheaded personally by Colkitto.

Campbell of Auchinbreck had previously been responsible for the massacre of hundreds of MacDonald men, women and children of the island of Rathlin, off the northern coast of Ireland. He was not killed in the battle but after being surrounded he surrendered. This did not save him from MacDonald vengeance. "According to the bards, the General [Auchinbreck] was offered a choice of methods of execution by Alasdair MacColla, perhaps a sign that there was a particular grudge between them, and when he made his choice Alistair cut him down in cold blood"(134)

Ian Lom MacDonald, the Keppoch MacDonald bard, whom Argyll had offered a large reward for his head, wrote in Gaelic:

"Though the braes of Lochaber a desert be made

And Glen Roy may be lost to the plough and the spade

Though the bows of my kindred unhonoured, unurned,

Mark the desolate place where the Campbells have burned

Be it so. From the foray they never returned."(135)

The power of the Campbell's in the Highlands was shattered. Having witnessed the massacre of his clansmen, the Marquis of Argyll escaped from the scene in his galley and fled to Edinburgh.

The victory at Inverlochy boosted Montrose's reputation in the Highlands and brought in large numbers of recruits. He was also joined by George, Lord Gordon, son of the Marquis of Huntly, who brought with him his regular regiment of horse, which in combination with Ogilvy's dragoons gave Montrose an effective force of cavalry for the first time.

MAP 13. BATTLES OF MONTROSE.

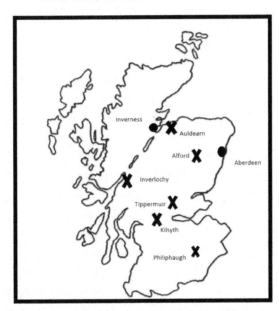

After the battle Montrose returned to Moray, by Badenoch, intending to march again on Elgin, when he was met by Thomas Mackenzie of Pluscardine, brother of the Earl of Seaforth, who had been sent by Seaforth and the Covenanters as Commissioners to treat with him. The Marquis of Montrose refused to negotiate and offered again to accept the services of those (including the Mackenzies) who had only so recently sworn allegiance to King Charles I.

Meanwhile the Covenanter Government in Edinburgh were becoming mightily afraid of the Royalists in the north and that some of their supporters might change sides. In February 1645 they appointed James Grant of Freuchie a Commissioner for Invernesshire to 'suppress the rebellion'.

But Montrose was determined to consolidate his powerful position in the North and to put pressure on those Clan Chiefs who were remaining loyal to the Covenanting Government. He carried Fire and Sword into the territories of his opponents, including burning the Grant Laird of Ballindalloch's three houses of Ballindalloch, Pitchaish and Foyness, as well as other houses in the district.

"In 1645 Montrose's forces were gaining ascendency, and James, together with other Highland lairds, submitted to him. Elgin was badly pillaged by Montrose's forces, which then included 300 men supplied by James; these were, in fact, some of the worst offenders "(136) "The Grants evidently thought it was better to be the plunderers than the plundered, and they took a leading part in pillaging Elgin, and left nothing portable uncarried away."(137)

They then marched with Montrose towards the Bog of Gight in the beginning of March, but they were sent back by Montrose to guard their own estates. The threat was from the Covenanters who were holding Inverness. No sooner had Montrose marched south than raiding parties from the Covenanting regiments stationed in Inverness came to the 'Place of Elchies', which was then the home of the Laird of Grant, and plundered his home, sparing neither his ladies clothes or jewellery. But at least he was reconciled with his mother, who supported Montrose and King Charles. At the time she even wrote a letter of encouragement to her son. Her happiness was short lived, however, as the Covenanters then invaded Urquhart and robbed her and her household of all their personal effects and drove her out of her home and the general area. She found shelter at the Gordon stronghold of Lesmoir Castle in Aberdeenshire where she now wrote again to her son to, "Dispense with your goods, by way of care for the loss of them, as I have done with mine; for, in conscience, there is not left with me worth one servit [serviette] to eat my meat on. Yet think me upon a way of reparation, and, ere long, you joining him [Lord Lewis Gordon, her son-in-law] who is coming in purpose to aid you, I believe in God that the Christmas pie which you have unwillingly swallowed shall be paid at Easter [referring to his loses at Elchies and a Royalist victory by Easter]. How soon I either see my son-in-law or hear word from the camp, I shall not fail to advise you. Meanwhile, be courageous, and remember still how both your mother and yourself have suffered."(138)

When Montrose left he appointed James Grant the King's Commander in Moray and the Laird soon afterwards sent a force of his clansmen to join up with Montrose's army. It seems, however, that many of them did not want to march south to fight for the King and soon deserted. So much so that Montrose had to write to James Grant again asking him to send more men who would not desert. He also wrote, alluding to the theft of Lady Grant's clothes and jewellery, "Remember my service to your lady, and show her that in a few days we shall repair her wrong".(139)

The Royal Army then attacked the City of Dundee and the Grant Brigade was again commanded by Captain David Grant. But Montrose had to retreat quickly as a Covenanter army under General Ballie had advanced to relieve the city. Montrose and Colkitto eventually halted at the village of Auldearn in Aberdeenshire, where another Covenanter Army, under General Urry, caught up with them and they fought the **Battle of Auldearn** on 9 May 1645.

Montrose left Colkitto and his five hundred men in the village with the royal flag flying, to convince Urry that this was the main Royalist force. Meantime, he hid his main force in a hollow a mile from Auldearn. The Covenant army attacked the village with their full force, believing that the entire Royalist army was defending it.

As they were doing this Montrose and his remaining thousand men, including the Grants, emerged from the hollow and attacked the Covenanters in the rear. The Covenanters soon broke and fled. Some fifteen hundred Covenanters were killed in the battle and it was a complete victory for the Royalists.

The only part of the Covenanter Army to make a stand was a detachment of Clan MacLennan, who were the standard bearers to the Chief of MacKenzie. They became isolated during the battle but refused to retreat and to give up the 'Cabar Feidh': the standard of the Mackenzies. Despite being offered quarter by the Chief of Gordon, they continued to refuse and Ruairdh MacGille Fhinnein, Chief of MacLennan, his clansmen, with some MacRaes and Mathesons, were all cut down. It is estimated that around 2,000 Government troops were killed. The Royalist casualties amounted to around 200, mainly the MacDonalds who had taken the brunt of the original Government assault. Fewer than 10 Grants were killed or wounded, although one of these was Robert Grant, son of the Laird of Shewglie.

Eventually, the defeated Covenanters returned to Inverness, and the Laird of Drummond, who commanded the Covenanter cavalry, and who fled first, was blamed for the defeat. A Council of War sentenced him to death and he was immediately shot. General Urry eventually joined the army of Montrose and many years later suffered his same fate: death by execution.

The Royalists army had won another great victory against the Covenanter forces and this was consolidated two months later at the **Battle of Alford**, Aberdeenshire, in July 1645.

After the victory against Urry, Montrose now wanted to attack the remaining Government force left in the field, under Lieutenant General William Baillie. If he did this he would be one step closer to taking control of the whole of Scotland. Although Baillie was in command he was also under the direction of the Committee of Estates, the religious Covenanting body who now controlled the Government in Scotland.

Unfortunate for Baillie, the Committee of Estates decided to take half of Baillie's experienced men away from him and create a second army under Lord Lindsay. Many of his experienced regiments were taken from him and were replaced by inexperienced men who had never fought in a pitched battle before.

Initially Baillie sought to avoid Montrose, happy to keep him wandering about the Northeast looking for him. But Montrose eventually caught up with him on 24 June 1645 near the village of Alford. By this time, however, Baillie thought Montrose's forces had been depleted considerably with the Highland Clans leaving the army with their booty and heading to their home glens. He was very wrong, although many of the clansmen, including a number of Grants. had returned home with their loot many still remained. The only one missing was Colkitto and some of his men who had been sent away to recruit more men.

Baillie now decided to fight and drew his forces in a defensive position, inviting the Royalists to attack. But Montrose did not take up the bait and the two forces stood off watching each other for a number of days. On 1 July 1645, Montrose decided to try and dislodge Baillie's army by crossing the River Don, threatening to advance south to Central Scotland. This Baillie had to avoid at all costs and he was forced to pursue him.

The Government force consisted of two cavalry regiments and six infantry regiments. Unfortunately, many of these regiments were under strength and had inexperienced men. The total army was around 2,100 men. Montrose, for once, had about an equal number of men.

The battle took place the next day, on 2 July 1645. Montrose hid the bulk of his men behind Gallow Hill, including the remaining Grants under Captain David Grant. This persuaded Baillie to fight and he advanced to meet the enemy. Montrose then led his main force over the hill to face a surprised Baillie. As usual the cavalry was on the flanks with the infantry in the centre.

Initially the Government forces got the upper hand. Lord Gordon's Royalist cavalry charged against the cavalry of the Government commander, Lord Balcarres. But the Government cavalry under Balcarres were experienced soldiers, many having fought in the English Civil War. They held against the charge of Lord Gordon and using their superior numbers, repulsed the rebels.

But, having retreated, the Royalist cavalry regrouped and aided by the Grant foot soldiers, attacked again and this time forced the Government cavalry to retreat. The left wing of Royalist cavalry then attacked and the remaining Government cavalry was broken and routed.

In order not to be outflanked Baillie stretched his infantry line until they were only 3 deep. Montrose sensed this weakness and ordered his 6 deep infantry to undertake another Highland charge downhill on the thin ranks of the largely inexperienced Government infantry. Clan Grant was on the left and undertook a full speed assault towards the enemy line. Within 20 feet of the enemy, they discharged their muskets at short range and then closed in with their hand-held weapons.

The Government troops broke again and were pushed back towards the river ford at Montgarrie, their only chance of escape. As this happened the Royalist cavalry again entered the fight and pursued the fleeing government troops, killing hundreds as they sought to escape. Over a 1,000 of them died.

For the Royalists, Lord Gordon was killed, depriving Montrose of a very powerful ally. But Montrose was now the undisputed master of Northern Scotland and his next step would be to march south into Central Scotland.

Apart from Lord Gordon, the royalists lost around 100 men. Again, we do not know if many Grants were killed but any casualties would have been light. Montrose now headed south. By this time Montrose had also been reinforced when Alistair MacColla returned to his side with a large amount of recruits from the Highlands, including many of the Clan Donald clansmen who had left to take their loot home. In addition, Lord Aboyne brought more cavalry from the Gordon and Ogilvy Clans. The Royalist army now amounted to around 3,500 men, many experienced soldiers.

Montrose now proceeded to invade Central Scotland, marching down the east coast through Dundee, Perth and Stirling. Baillie, however, was far from beaten yet, as he had received reinforcements from Fife, the Borders and Ayrshire, amounting to nearly 5,000 men.

Aware that more Government reinforcements were being drafted in the south, Montrose decided to try and bring Baillie to fight in one last battle. This he did at the **Battle of Kilsyth**.

The Highland Charge at Kilsyth.

The battle took place on 15 August 1645 near Banton Loch. By this time, however, the Grant contingent was down in numbers to around 100 as the rest had returned home with their plunder, not wanting to venture into the lowlands. Initially the two armies tried to outflank each other but eventually the two forces came together. The Highlanders under Colkitto attacked a regiment of government troops who were trying to reach the high summit of Auchinrivoch. Usually the Highlanders, with their famous charge, could rout any Government regiment, but bogged down by the terrain, they got into a pitched battle with much death on both sides. The Government cavalry then charged, trying to break the Highlanders. Lord Aboyne and his Gordon cavalry saw this happening and counter-attacked the Government horse. This saved the Highlanders.

The fleeing government cavalry brought panic to their own infantry as well as exposing their right flank to a Royalist cavalry attack. Seeing this the Government infantry started a full retreat towards the relative safety of Stirling Castle. The Royalists pursued them all the way killing and capturing hundreds. It is estimated that 3,000 government troops were killed.

Montrose was now in command of Scotland but his real intention was to take a Scottish Army south into England to assist King Charles I who was on the verge of defeat from the English Roundheads and the Scottish Covenanter Army. However, his Highland army was not prepared to march into England. They had done enough in their minds by delivering Scotland for the King and now wanted to return to their glens and islands with their plunder. All the remaining Grants returned home with their riches.

Colkitto, supported by his Irish MacDonnells and a large number of the Scottish MacDonalds, particularly those from Islay and Kintyre, left Montrose to pursue his main aim of killing Campbells. The Irishman, O'Cahan, a confederate of Colkitto, remained with Montrose to the end and with hundreds of Irishmen and their camp followers, were murdered in cold blood after the **Battle of Phillipshaugh**. This was fought in the Scottish Borders where Montrose's depleted force was destroyed by the experienced Scottish Covenanter Army which had been fighting in England but had been recalled to counter the threat from Montrose.

After the defeat of Montrose at Philliphaugh he returned north to try and raise another Royalist army and spent much of his time in Strathspey, staying at a variety of Grant houses. However, by this time the Laird of Grant, with other Highland Chiefs, was lukewarm to the prospects of a successful Royalist campaign and Montrose wrote to him expressing his concern about the lack of Grant men supplied to him.

Montrose's success had achieved the primary objective of King Charles I: to force the Scottish Covenanter Army back from England. The large battle-hardened Covenanter Army, under the seasoned commander, Major General Sir David Leslie, was sent back to Scotland to destroy the royalist army. However, by this time the English Royalists had been defeated and the King's cause was lost. All Montrose and his Highlanders had accomplished was for nothing and the executioner would soon take the King's head.

Montrose retired north again and sought to raise another army. Although the MacDonalds and the Mackenzies continued to support him, the Grants remained in Speyside and refused to join him on his siege of Inverness, which he soon had to abandon and retire to the hills of the Northern Highlands.

Around the same time, King Charles surrendered in England to the Scottish Covenanter Army. The Scottish leaders made the captured King command Montrose to disband which he duly did and went into exile in France. The Covenanters returned North and took control.

In March 1647 James Grant then obtained a remission for his part against the Covenanter General Middleton. However, at the same time James Grant did write to King Charles' wife, Henrietta Maria and Prince Charles in exile at the Palace of St. Germain in France, expressing his continued loyalty to the King and that he would be prepared to assist in the King's restoration when the time was right.

In the same year Clan Cameron raided the lands of Clan Grant and they took many cattle and sheep. The Grants were led by Allan Grant of Lurgie. The Grants gave chase and catching the raiders they fought the **Battle of the Braes of Strathdearn**, near Tomatin. Before battle commenced Grant of Lurgie sent forward a powerful man named Lawson, who requested that the Camerons leave them the cattle to avoid blood-shed. The Camerons shot him dead with an arrow and the battle took place between the two sides in which, although many died on both sides, the Grants eventually defeated the Camerons. 19 men from one branch of Clan Cameron alone were killed and many more seriously injured. The Grants recovered all their cattle and sheep. "As of October 18 [1645], as reported in a letter from Allan to James Grant, there were *'eight dead already and I have twelve or thirteen under cure, which I know not who shall die or who shall live of the same'*."(140) Afterwards Sir James Grant complained to Cameron of Lochiel who replied in writing that the Camerons did not know the lands belonged to the Grants, and if they had they would not have carried out the raid. The Grants had taken over the lands some time previously from the family of Dunbar.

Meanwhile the Scottish Covenanters had 'sold' King Charles I to the English Government now under the control of Oliver Cromwell and he was imprisoned in the Isle of Wight. Then in 1648 the Scottish Covenanters fell out with themselves and formed two separate factions. The moderates, called the 'Engagers', eventually took control of the Government and sought to mend their loyalties and friendship with King Charles I and restore him to his throne if he would agree to the extension

178

of the Protestant faith in both Scotland and England. King Charles gladly signed up to their demands as he was, at this time, being held prisoner in the South of England by the English Parliamentarian forces under Oliver Cromwell. The Scots were his last chance.

James Grant supported this faction but declined to take part in its invasion of England to free the King. His lands had been devasted by the Civil war and many of his clansmen killed and he decided that Clan Grant would hold fast in the Highlands at this time. In July 1648, a largely untrained and ill-equipped Scottish army of 20,000 men marched into England to free the King. Oliver Cromwell, now Dictator of England, and his professional 'New Model Army' destroyed the Scottish Army at the **Battle of Preston**. The Engagers were finished.

Oliver Cromwell then marched his army into Scotland and declared it part of the 'Commonwealth of Great Britain', effectively ending it as an independent nation. King Charles I was put on trial by Cromwell, found guilty of treason, and executed in London in January 1649. England and Scotland then became a Republic until the restoration of King Charles II in 1660. James Grant of Fruchie was suspected of being a Royalist sympathiser (which in fact he was).

Montrose The Day Before His Execution.

While all this was happening, in March 1650 Montrose, at the behest of the now exiled King Charles II, landed in Orkney where he gathered a small force of largely untrained troops. On 27 April his force was surprised and routed at the **Battle of Carbisdale** in Ross-shire, although he did manage to escape. After wandering for some time, he was betrayed by Neil MacLeod of Assynt and captured. He was brought as a prisoner to Edinburgh, and on 20 May 1650 sentenced to death by Parliament. He was hanged the very next day. His head was removed and placed on a spike at the Old Tolbooth outside St Giles Cathedral from 1650 until 1661. So died one of Scotland's greatest warriors by the hand of own people.

Shortly after Montrose's death the Scottish Government, led by Archibald Campbell, switched sides to support King Charles II in his attempt to regain the throne, providing he was willing to impose the Protestant religion in England. The Scottish negotiators travelled to Holland where Charles was in exile. After lengthy negotiations, the 17 year old King Charles II signed a draft Treaty. His real intention was to break his word when he came to the throne. He then agreed to return with the Scottish Commissioners and he set foot on Scottish soil in June 1650 when he was proclaimed King of Scots. This infuriated Oliver Cromwell and in July 1650 he invaded Scotland again with his New Model Army and destroyed the Scottish Government forces at the **Battle of Dunbar** in September 1650. The Scots army was largely composed of inexperienced troops from the lowlands and very few Highlanders. The Grants did not fight at this battle. Despite Cromwell's success and his takeover of half of Scotland, Charles was still at Scone Palace on New Years Day 1651, where the last coronation of a Monarch was held in Scotland.

The new King Charles II immediately began it form a new army at Perth to oppose Cromwell and this one was composed of many of the Highland clans. James Grant of Grant was made a Colonel of a troop of infantry from his clansmen. James quickly raised over 600 Grants and their vassals and appointed his brother Patrick Grant, Lieutenant Colonel of the Grant Regiment. The Regiment then marched south and joined the growing army of the new King at Perth.

Eventually the Royalist army moved south, with the King intent on invading England where he expected the general population to rally to his cause. But the English were sick of civil war. By-passing Cromwell, who had moved into Fife, the Royal Army marched south into England. On 23 August 1651 it reached Worchester where King Charles II was warmly welcomed by the city. The army then rested from their three-week march from Scotland. It has also been said that Cromwell let them slip by him, content to let them enter England where his main armies were waiting to stop them.

The King's army amounted to only 14,000 men, mainly Scots, as the English had not risen in any great numbers for their new King. At Worchester they were surrounded by 30,000 roundheads under Cromwell. These were experienced troops who had served in the English Civil War. In a two-pronged attack they eventually overwhelmed the significantly smaller Royalist army. 3,000 Scots were killed and 10,000 were captured. 2,000 of these prisoners were transported to the English Colonies in North America and the rest were put to work in the Durham mines and Fenland Drainage schemes in Norfolk. King Charles escaped abroad and waited for Cromwell to die in 1558 before being restored to the throne in 1660. Patrick Grant escaped and returned home, but with only around 100 men, the rest either dead or captured and transported as slaves.

MAP 14. THE BATTLE OF WORCESTER 1651.

Scotland was then occupied by General Monck on behalf of Oliver Cromwell and both the castles of Urquhart and Grant was garrisoned by Monck's troops.

However, this was not the end of the Royalist rebellions against Cromwell in Scotland. The most important one was the **Glencairn Uprising** between 1653 and 1654. In early 1652 Angus MacDonald of Glengarry was appointed as Acting Chief of the Royalist forces in Scotland by King Charles II. It appears that Angus

MacDonald continued to support the exiled King not only out of loyalty but also because he hoped to be made Earl of Ross when the King was restored to power.

In early 1652 Glengarry travelled around the North trying to gather support for an uprising. He met many of the Clan Chiefs in Inverness, including James Grant. "It appears that although Glengarry viewed this meeting as a failure in terms of attendance and enthusiasm but although most clan leaders were hesitant in offering open encouragement, they nevertheless did not prevent all members of their clan from joining the rebels … The main outcome of the rendezvous was the agreement to raise a 'flying army' of 1500 to 2000 men."(141) James Grant remained loyal to King Charles II but after the loss of nearly 500 clansmen and vassals at Worchester only the year before, he was in no position to officially support the new rebellion to Cromwell's rule. He did, however, make it known that he would not stop any of his clansmen supporting Glengarry if they so wished. Many of the Grants from Urquhart and Glenmoriston, whose lands bordered those of Glengarry, took up the call and agreed to join the rebellion.

Then in March 1653, William Cunningham, 9th Earl of Glencairn was appointed as the King's Commander in Scotland. He and Glengarry gathered their troops but it was slow and by July 1653 they had only just over 1300 men, including around 100 Grants, commanded by the sons of Grant Lairds. The Lairds themselves did not take part lest they be declared outlaws and their lands forfeited. Despite this the uprising started with a guerrilla campaign launched against the English forces in northern Scotland. The Royalists expected General Middleton to arrive in Scotland at any time from the Continent with a large army and funds to support them.

However, this army could not make the journey as the English navy had defeated the Dutch navy, and there was no transport available. This came as a major setback to the Rising, as they could not now expect any help from Europe in the near future. The Royalists then agreed to disperse but continued to undertake guerrilla war. The rebel Grants went with MacDonald of Glengarry who concentrated on raiding the English garrisons in or near Lochaber, where they attacked small parties of the enemy and engaged in sudden raids on the garrisons.

Unfortunately, the Royalist cause was hampered by internal conflict. Most of the Highlanders resented having Glencairn, a lowlander, as their Commander and many of the clans were still at feud with each other. Despite this the rebellion started to grow and there were skirmishes as far south as Galloway in Southwest Scotland. So much so that the gates of Edinburgh were shut at night to prevent rebels entering the city. Then the English army, based in the Lowlands, proceeded North and the Glengarry force, now supported by the Campbell, Lord of Lorne, with about 1000 men, retreated to Badenoch, just south of Inverness and close to the Grant lands in Strathspey.

At the beginning of 1654 the rebels raided English supporters in Moray and Nairn. Elsewhere, however, the English had more success and either captured or killed over 200 rebels at Kildrummy Castle and Dunkeld. Then in February 1654, Middleton landed in Scotland, but with only 80 men, not the thousands that had been promised. This did nothing to encourage the rebels or bring more of the clans out to support them. Despite this the rebel army did continue to grow as the English occupiers ravaged the lands that they passed through. Overall the Royalist army may have eventually had at its peak, 5000 men.

Despite having many of his clansmen in the Royalist army, James Grant raised his Clan to protect his Strathspey lands from pillaging from both the Royalist and the Cromwellian forces. Meanwhile the rebel leaders continued to quarrel and at dinner one evening, Glengarry had to be physically restrained by Glencairn from assaulting Munro, Middleton's second in command. But then Glencairn and Munro had a sword duel the next morning. Glencairn got the upper hand and wounded his opponent and was only prevented from killing him by the intervention of one of his servants.

Then on 20 April 1654, the experienced Cromwellian General Monck arrived at Dalkeith to take command of the English forces. He re-organised the army and got further reinforcements from England. He then systematically took control of southern and then central Scotland and then moved north to confront the main Royalist forces. He marched into the territory of Glengarry and destroyed everything he could find. The rebels retreated before him. Support among the rebels began to wane and Monck chased Middleton all over the Highlands.

Eventually on 19 July 1654 an English cavalry force under Thomas Morgan surprised General Middleton at Dalnaspidal, near the Drumochter Pass. The Royalist cavalry and foot had been separated and when Morgan attacked the royalist cavalry they fled. After this Morgan advanced on the Royalist infantry, mainly MacGregors and Robertsons, and they too turned and fled. Not many were killed but the **Battle of Dalnaspidal** effectively ended the rebellion. Angus MacDonell and his Glengarry clansmen were not involved in this battle as they were raiding English garrisons on the west coast at this time. Most of the rebel

Grants were with them. They quickly returned to Glenmoriston, Urquhart and Strathspey.

Middleton soon escaped to France and most of the other rebel leaders surrendered, apart from Glengarry, who refused their terms. Eventually, however, even he surrendered as one of the last leaders and was granted a pardon. This was the last rebellion against Cromwell and all the main clans retreated back into their glens waiting for the Dictator to die of natural causes.

After this it was a relatively quiet time and James Grant used the opportunity to put his estates and finances in order, and to make financial provision for his brothers. Monck's soldiers brought a measure of peace and security to this part of the Strathspey and Glen Urquhart and the Grants were even allowed to keep their arms and weapons.

Cromwell eventually died in 1658, and despite naming his son as his successor, his Commonwealth soon crumbled. King Charles II was restored to the throne in May 1660.

However, not all was well for the Laird of Freuchie. His younger brother, Alexander Grant, took offence at the inheritance he had been given and instigated legal proceedings against James Grant but the case was dismissed by the Scottish Courts. His other brothers were happy with their settlements.

In 1660 James Grant was given a Commission by the Scottish Government to secure the 'peace' of the country and the letter of commission contained a very significant postscript: "Sir, be pleased to take spetiall notice of Gavine Cirinn alias Halket Stirk, and use all possible means to apprehend his person and send him to the Committee."(142) Halket Stirk was a notorious highland thief. After a number of failed attempts the Laird of Grant managed to capture Halket Stirk but he then sent his Chamberlain, James Grant of Ackernack, to Edinburgh to advise the Government of likely reprisals by the MacDonalds of Clanranald. He then dispatched Halket, with a strong guard, to Aberdeen and from there they boarded a ship and he was taken to Edinburgh.

However, despite capturing the thief, the Laird of Grant then interceded on his behalf to the Scottish Government. This seems to have been successful as Halket was not put on trial but released on 'security'. But as soon as he got home Halket resumed his old ways. On one of his raids he was severely wounded in a fight at Ridaros, close to the Green Loch, in the Cairngorm mountains. Although he escaped, his men had to leave him behind in Glenmore in the 'Cave of the Stewarts'. Here he was cared for by Mrs Stewart who brought him food daily. On one of these trips she brought her young son and on seeing him Halket advised that the boy was of an age when he required schooling. Mrs Stewart replied that her son had gone to school at Ruthven where he had excelled. To which Halket Stirk responded, "It was not the school of White paper I was thinking of, but the school of the moon [i.e. the school of cattle raiding]."(143) He then offered to repay the woman's hospitality by taking the boy under his wing and teaching him the way of cattle raiding. We do not know if she took him up on this offer.

Many years later, just before his death, the raider made confession of his sins, his last words being that "he had never taken anything from the poor, that he had been kind to the widows and the fatherless, and that he had always gone far away for spoil."(144)

When Charles II became King in May 1660 there was much apprehension in Scotland generally, from fear of being indited for treason, because there was a delay in passing a Treaty of Indemnity. In fact, James Grant, with many others, was indicted by the Lord Advocate. It appears that Alexander, his brother, may have been behind this. James and his wife and children went to Edinburgh where he was successful in clearing his name and having all the charges dropped, although he did have to pay a fine of £18,000. The family then returned home in easy stages, as Lady Grant was unwell and had to travel in a sedan-chair, with a doctor in attendance. She did not get any better and died the next year in 1662.

Mary Grant had lived and died a Roman Catholic and she was a firm believer in witchcraft. "It is said that Lady Grant lost several of her children at the beginning of her married life. She thought they were bewitched, and sent for an Italian 'pricker' who pretended that he could distinguish witches by pricking the body with pointed iron sticks. Of Course, it did no good, and he caused a number of patients to die, probably from blood poisoning."(145).

As soon as the Cromwellian troops had left Strathspey and the wider highlands the old ways of cattle revieing began again and the MacDonalds from Glengarry carried away much cattle from the Laird of Grant's estates in Glen Urquhart. The new King also ordered the destruction of the Fortress of Inverness which had been built by Cromwell's forces and the Laird of Grant helped raze it to the ground. Crime and disorder followed.

In 1663 the King elevated James Grant to Earl of Strathspey and Lord Grant of Freuchie and Urquhart, in return for his services to the Crown. Unfortunately, James died before the patent could be completed, and it was not passed on to his son and heir, who was a minor. James died in Edinburgh in 1663 and was buried in Holyrood Abbey. He died in much debt, leaving the estate with debts of over £72,000 Scots.

He had married Lady Mary Stewart in Elgin in April 1640, only daughter of James, 2nd Earl of Moray. Her father and brother, 3rd Earl, had opposed the marriage and neither of them nor any of her friends had attended the wedding ceremony. She did, however, eventually become reconciled with her brother in May 1643, and he paid her dowry of £22,000 Scots.

The Laird of Grant and his wife had the following children:

1). Ludovick Grant , 8th of Freuchie.

2). Patrick Grant, who was granted the lands of Wester Elchies. He was a Lieutenant Colonel in the Grant Regiment.

3). Anna Grant, who in 1644 married Sir Patrick Ogilvy of Boyne, Banff.

4). Margaret Grant, who married Roderick Mackenzie of Redcastle.

5). Mary Grant , who in 1669 married Sir Alexander Hamilton of Haggs, Lanark. It seems that her brother, Ludovick, did not pay her dowry and she and her husband had to take him to court to recover it.

"It appears that this was the Mary, daughter of the Laird of Grant, who is connected with the romantic story of Domhnull Donn MacFhir Bohuntuinn. Donald was the son of MacDonald of Bohuntin, in Brae-Lochaber, of good family, but who looked upon revieing and cattle-lifting as the proper calling of a Highland gentleman. Domhnull Donn (Brown Donald) was also a Gaelic poet of no mean order. He died with the reputation of never having injured a poor man, or imbued his hands wantonly in human blood.

On one of his journeys he met and fell in love with Mary, daughter of the Laird of Grant, who resided at the time of Castle Urquhart. The lady reciprocated his tender feelings; but her father refused to have him for his son-in-law and forbade all intercourse between them. They, however, found opportunities of meeting on the wooded banks of Loch Ness. But then the Laird of Grant found out about their meetings.

Donald had to flee, as the Laird of Grant, incensed at his cattle-lifting propensities, had sworn *Bheir an Diabhal mise a mo bhrogan, mar teid, Domhnull Donn a Chrochadh'* – 'The Devil may take me out of my shoes if Donald Gorm is not hanged'. Donald found refuge in a most inaccessible cave, where for a time he was safe from his pursuers and their sleuth hounds – the 'black dogs of Italy' – but the hideout was eventually discovered, but the Grants knew he had a good defensible position in the cave."(146)

The Grants then sent him a letter, pretending to be from Mary proposing to meet at a nearby house of one of their trusted friends. He turned up and was welcomed by the supposed friend, who told him that Mary would arrive soon. He was then given whisky and he drunk quite a lot of it. Soon, however, over sixty Grants rushed in to capture him. Donald jumped to his feet and drew his pistol but it misfired. But using the butt end of his weapon he fought his way out of the house and tried to run for his life. He nearly escaped but slipped and fell and was captured and was then taken to the dungeon of Urquhart Castle, where he was tried and convicted of cattle stealing. His sentence was death.

"He begged that he should be beheaded like a gentleman, and not hanged. On being told his prayer was granted, he exclaimed, *'The Devil will take the Laird of Grant out of his shoes and Donald Donn shall not be hanged'*. To the last his thoughts were of his beloved; and the legend tells that as his head rolled from the block, his tongue uttered the appeal, *'Tog mo cheann, a Mhairi'* – 'Lift my head, O, Mary".(147)

He was executed at Craigmonie. The short period which passed between his sentence and his execution was occupied by him composing songs of exceeding sadness. Speaking of his hide-out he wrote in Gaelic:

> "If the summer would come,
>
> And the leaf would open,
>
> I would go to Ruiskich
>
> As light-hearted as any man;
>
> If evil news reached me,

187

I would make for the Cuilionn,

And the English-speaking folk ,could not find me –

The hat – wearing regiment!

It is I who is in the Castle

Which is the strongest on earth,

At the mouth of Allt-Saigh,

Where guests will gather;

And, although there come back the folk of the hats;

And the tight long coats,

And the bomb shells

Thy will never bring me to bay!"(148)

In reference to his capture he wrote:

"A thousand curses for ever

On the gun as a weapon of defence,

After the deception and disgrace

I have experienced.

Although I should get as my own

A fold full of cattle,

More dear to me would have been

a sword and shield in that hour!

There were sixty and three

Pursuing me among the bends

Until with their speed

They deprived me of my strength.

God! But it was I who was ashamed

When they sized me alive,

Without my bringing down one of them, fair-haired or red!"(149)

On his forthcoming execution he wrote:

"Tomorrow I shall be on a hill, without a head,

Have you no compassion on my sorrowful maiden –

My Mary, the fair and tender eyed!"(150)

Ludovick Grant 8th of Freuchie, 1st Grant of Grant and Chief of Clan Grant between 1663 and 1716, who was known as the 'Highland King'. He was a minor when he inherited and his mother had died the year before. Because of this his estates were put under a number of 'tutors' chosen by his father before his death. The main one was Colonel Patrick Grant, his uncle, who sent Ludovick to school in Elgin, and then to St Andrews University. Patrick managed the estates well for his nephew and paid all his debts off before Ludovick came of age.

Meanwhile, Hector MacLean, a fearsome highland raider went of the rampage through the Great Glen in early 1664 and a Commission of Fire and Sword was issued against him and his accomplices by the King. John Grant of Glenmoriston and John Grant of Corrimony, factor of Urquhart for Ludovick, were included in the summons 'to apprehend the rebels, and pursue them to the death', and were given immunity for any fire-raising, mutilation and slaughter that they had to undertake during this course of action. The lands of MacLean were attacked but despite this he managed to avoid capture and escaped.

In giving a Commission to John Grant of Glenmoriston (known in Gaelic as Iain Donn) the King had tried to use a thief to catch a thief. Twenty years earlier, Iain Donn's father, Patrick Grant of Glenmoriston, had been heavily in debt to John Robertson of Inshes when he died in 1642/43. Iain Donn was a minor at the time

189

and had his uncle as his Tutor as we have heard earlier. Prior to the death of Patrick, Robertson began legal proceedings for the recovery of his money and demanded the Baronies of Culcabrock and Glenmoriston, which were to remain in Robertson hands until the debt was paid. This was confirmed in law in 1645 and Robertson took possession of Culcabrock, near Inverness, which he let out to his own tenants. He was not, however, able to get possession of Glenmoriston. The Grants quickly retaliated and devastated the Robertson lands of Inshes. Robertson died in 1661 but his claims were taken up by his son, William.

By 1663 "... Iain Donn had now reached manhood, and the loss of his Inverness possessions, and the danger which threatened the estate of Glenmoriston, roused him to action. He began in the spirit of compromise. He proposed to relinquish all claims to Culcabrock if young Inshes would pay him eight or nine thousand merks, and discharge all claims upon Glenmoriston.(151)

Robertson declined the offer and in January 1644 the Grants raided Culcabrock and burned two barns full of corn. Although the arsonists escaped Iain Donn Grant was suspected and Robertson openly accused him of the crime. He then sought legal redress against Grant. Iain Donn retaliated with another attack on Culcabrock when three more barns full of corn were fired.

Robertson still refused Grants offer and Glenmoriston resolved to seize him and keep him a prisoner until he agreed to the terms offered. A meeting was organised between Grant and Robertson at Inverness on 23 August 1644. Robertson came with three friends but Glenmoriston had at least sixteen men which he concealed in an ale-house nearby until they were required. The meeting commenced but after no agreement was reached, Grant called his men and, capturing Robertson, carried him off to Glenmoriston.

Eventually, after many weeks incarceration, Robertson agreed to pay Iain Donn Grant 7,000 merks and was released. But the Government took a dim view of his actions and Iain Donn was himself captured by the Earl of Moray, Sheriff of Inverness-shire. Grant initially soon escaped but was again captured by Robertson of Straun, a friend and relative of Robertson of Inshes in March 1666. Friends of both parties now mediated for them and eventually an agreement was reached and Grant relinquished his title to Culcabrock for the sum of 7,000 merks and Robertson agreed to give up his claim to Glenmoriston.

In 1670, Ludovick Grant acquired the estate of Achmorie. It's owner Gillies MacKay had killed the Laird of Grants Chamberlain, who had been sent from Strathspey to

Glen Urquhart to collect rents. After business had been concluded the gentlemen, including Gillies MacKay, had all got very drunk together and in a state of intoxication the Chamberlain had insulted the tenants of Urquhart. All the men on both sides got to their feet and drew their dirks. At the same time the lights in the barn they were drinking in were extinguished and as the fight ensued the death cry of the Chamberlain was heard. This stopped the fighting but when a light was found the Chamberlain lay dead on the ground with a dirk in his heart. Later it was established that the knife belonged to Gillies MacKay.

Initially Ludovick took no action, but a few months later, Mackay was staying at Castle Grant when the Laird entered his bedchamber, told him of his guilt and advised him to yield his lands or his life. This was a gross betrayal of the Highland Hospitality traditions. "Mackay surrendered the estate on the understanding that it should be restored to him as a vassal of the Laird. The surrendered lands were, however, conferred by the Laird on William Grant, of the family of Glenmoriston who had possession of them in 1677. MacKay barely escaped with his life after all, as he was attacked on his way home at Slochd-Muic by an illegitimate son of the Laird, whose mother had married the murdered Chamberlain, and Achmonie [MacKay] and one follower alone escaped."(152)

In 1671 Ludovick married Janet Brodie of Leithen and in 1677 bought the estate of Pluscardine. He was not on friendly terms with James, Duke of York (the future King James VII) when he was put in command of Scotland in 1669. In Parliament he once demanded that his protests to James's policies be recorded. "On hearing this the Duke of York remarked that the wishes of his 'Highland Majesty' would be attended to."(153) After this Ludovick was mockingly known as the Highland King.

"In 1678, Ludovick was ordered by the Privy Council to provide Highlanders for the Marquis of Athole's army, called the 'Highland Host'. This force of 8,000 men gathered at Stirling to control Covenanters in the Lowlands. No one appears to have been killed, and after a few months the men returned home, taking with them much loot in the form of clothing and furnishings."(20) The Grants were quartered mainly in Ayrshire and Galloway where the Covenanters were strongest. On their march home, a Grant writer said, "when they passed Stirling Bridge every man drew his sword to show the world they had returned as conquerors from their enemies; but they might as well have shown the pots, pans, girdles, shoes taken off Country's men's feet, and other bodily and household furniture with which they were burdened."(154)

In 1681, Ludovick spoke out in Parliament against the Test Act. This act made obedience to the monarch a legal obligation, regardless of religion. In February 1685, despite his support for the Government, Ludovick was eventually fined a significant amount, £42,500 Scots for his sympathies to the Presbyterian faith and for his wife's reluctance to adopt Episcopacy.

CHAPTER 10. THE GLORIOUS REVOLUTION.

King Charles II died in 1685 and having no legitimate surviving children, although he did have a host of illegitimate ones, he was succeeded by his brother, James Duke of York who became **King James VII of Scotland and II of England and Ireland.** Almost immediately Archibald Campbell, Earl of Argyll supported a rebellion by Monmouth, the illegitimate son of King Charles II. This rebellion soon failed and in 1685, Archibald Campbell was beheaded for treason.

During the Earl of Argyll's rebellion Ludovick Grant was ordered to aid the Government with well-armed men, and assemble at Loch Ness to protect that part of the country. But before he had assembled all his men the rebellion was over and the Earl of Argyll captured. Because of his support for the King, he and his wife were given relief from a heavy fine that had been imposed on them over the religious practices of his wife.

Then in 1688 the Grants took part in the **Battle of Mulroy** near Keppoch between the Laird of Mackintosh and the MacDonalds of Keppoch. This was over a feud about the lands of Glenroy and Glenspean. MacDonald of Keppoch was known as 'Coll of the Cowes' for his proficiency at raiding cattle. The Mackintoshes were defeated by the MacDonalds and Mackintosh himself was captured. However, with the approach of the Grants to assist Mackintosh, Keppoch decided not to fight again and released his captive. The feud, however, would continue for many more years.

After the Campbell and Monmouth rebellion King James VII and II quickly moved towards getting rid of the penal sanctions which existed against Roman Catholics and this was initially approved by the Bishops of both the Scottish and English Churches. But by 1687, the King had become so frustrated by the lack of progress in allowing Catholics to again take public office, that he introduced his first 'Declaration of Indulgence'. However, he was unprepared for the fury it aroused. The 'Indulgence' was a significant change, as it permitted worship for all faiths, in houses or chapels. The Covenanters could go back indoors and start to construct their own churches. Bishops and clergy were given rights to the titles of their own churches and property and no one was to be debarred from public office because of their religious beliefs. Despite this 'reform' King James was despised by the Covenanters and all the other Protestants because he was a Catholic.

King James then tried to restore the absolute power of the Monarchy and widespread disorder broke out, particularly in England. This was further exacerbated with the birth of an heir, James Francis Edward Stuart, in June 1688. The thought of a Catholic dynasty sitting on the thrones of Scotland and England was too much for many of the leading lords.

The nobles rebelled and invited James's daughter Mary and her Protestant husband, William of Orange, to take the throne. William landed in England in November 1688 with a large army and James VII, without much support from his own nobles, fled into exile. The Protestants called it the 'Glorious Revolution' and William and Mary were crowned joint Monarchs of England in February 1689. The Scottish Convention of nobles also offered the throne of Scotland to William and Mary in April 1689 and almost immediately, Viscount Dundee (Bonny Dundee) raised the royal flag for King James at Dundee. Those who supported the deposed King James were known as **'Jacobites'**.

In March 1689 Ludovick Grant attended the Convention of Estates which was called to secure the Protestant Religion and recognise William and Mary as King and Queen of Scotland. They used that fact that James had fled into exile to state that he had voluntarily forfeited the crown. Ludovick was one of their main supporters. "On 19 April 1689, the Laird of Freuchie is named among those who offered to levy men for the public service, having volunteered to raise and equip them, and three days afterwards he was appointed colonel of his own regiment."(155) He was also appointed Sheriff-Principal of Inverness in the same month and ordered to guard Strathspey.

The Government sent a large army north under General MacKay and he counted on certain prominent Highlanders to give him support. "one such was Ludovick Grant, Sheriff of Inverness … but for the time being he was still in Edinburgh, and slow to return to his northern territory, a dereliction of duty which MacKay noted as being, 'without any design of prejudice to the service, though highly punishable, had he been a man of service'. "(156)

On 1 May, Mackay pressed on to the River Spey, when he got information that Dundee was heading to Elgin for provisions. It looked as if a battle would be fought there but General MacKay was not ready for battle. If he was defeated at this time he feared the whole north would come out for the Jacobites. Yet to retreat south would hand control of Elgin, Moray, Ross and Caithness over to the forces loyal to King James VII without a fight and a huge loss of face for the Government. "It was a difficult choice. MacKay believed he could rely on support from the Laird of Grant, who was now heading north and there was some promise of men from Lord Reay's Mackays in Sutherland, and Ross of Balnagowan in Ross-shire. But to fight a battle would be a gamble."(157)

He decided to take the risk and headed as fast as he could from Speyside to Elgin, a distance of 7 miles before nightfall on 2 May. When he arrived there was no sign of Montrose which allowed MacKay time to gather reinforcements. He probably breathed a sigh of relief. Not many highland recruits came forward, but Ludovick Grant had finally arrived in the north and he raised Clan Grant ready to fight for the Government. Mackay then learned that Dundee had marched south.

Ludovick had been ordered to raise and equip 600 men to join General MacKay to defend the River Spey against the rebel army. Ludovick became Colonel of this regiment which was called the Grant Fencible Regiment and he had to acquire the weapons for this regiment at his own expense. Dundee marched north again. Unfortunately, the men Ludovick Grant raised were inexperienced and ill-disciplined and they were unable to stop Dundee and his largely highland army crossing the Spey and marching towards Inverness unopposed.

Ludovick did, however, follow after Dundee and joined up with Mackay at Inverness. A number of marches and manoeuvres followed and General MacKay used the Grants as his scouts because of their knowledge of the countryside in the area. In May 1689 Ludovick was appointed to the Privy Council of Scotland.

However, not all the Grants were on the same side as their chief. John Grant, younger of Glenmoriston and James Grant of Shewglie, supported the exiled King against the orders of their Chief. "Young Glenmoriston, better known by the name Iain 'a Chragain [John of the Rock] brought 150 men into the field, while James Grant …. was followed by his tenants and by the MacDonalds and MacMillans of Urquhart."(158) Here they joined the regiment of Alasdair Dubh MacDonald of Glengarry on the 18 May 1689.

Despite now having a small army of MacDonalds and other highland clans, including the Grants of Glenmoriston, General Dundee was still counting on aid and men from King James in Ireland. But the exiled King was too busy besieging Londonderry, which would last for 3 months and have major consequences for the campaign in Scotland. Despite this, on 28 May, Dundee marched out of the clan assembly point at Dalcomera to the sound of bagpipes and bugles. The MacDonalds of Glengarry led the columns, accompanied by the Grants of

Glenmoriston, and the other clans followed in order of precedence. They crossed Glen Roy, the mountains of Garvamore, then forded the River Spey, heading east towards Raitt Castle, south of Nairn. Two days later they besieged Ruthven Barracks which was held by a company of Grants loyal to the Government under young Captain Forbes, brother of the Laird of Culloden. He refused to surrender and it looked like Grant was about to fight Grant.

"Dundee sent [MacDonald of Keppoch] forward to offer him a second opportunity, and when this was also refused, Keppoch began filling the moat with piles of wood, declaring that he intended to set the castle alight. Seeing his attackers were in earnest, Forbes announced that he was willing to surrender. He and his men were allowed to leave the castle unharmed ...., Keppoch then set alight to Ruthven and burned it to the ground."(159)

"In the end of May or beginning of June, about sixty of the Clan Grant, under their Captain, John Forbes of Culloden, marched into MacKay's camp, bringing the intelligence that the castle of Ruthven, in Badenoch, which they had lately garrisoned, was now a smoking ruin. On 29th May, Dundee had summoned the castle to surrender, and a few days later, after a sharp encounter, the defenders, weakened by want of provisions and succours, yielded to Keppoch."(160)

A few days later Dundee's army marched past Dunachton Castle, home of the Mackintoshes. He intended to leave it alone but MacDonald of Keppoch, ever on the lookout for destruction and plunder, veered off with his men and sacked it and then set it alight. When Dundee found out he turned on Keppoch in anger and rebuked him in front of the whole army, telling him 'he would rather serve as a common soldier amongst disciplined troops than command men like him'. He then ordered Keppoch to leave and take all his men with him.

For the first time in his life, Keppoch apologised publicly and said he had only attacked the castle because he thought Mackintosh was an enemy of the King. He promised to be obedient in future. Dundee reluctantly accepted his excuse and apology and the army moved towards Alvie, on the River Spey.

Meanwhile, General MacKay had moved all his forces to Castle Grant. After this Dundee moved towards MacKays position in Grant territory. On hearing this MacKay decided to leave his camp within Grant territory for a better defendable position. Before he departed he apologised to Ludovick Grant for leaving him and his clan exposed. The Laird of Grant replied, "Tho all his interests should be lost thereby, he would not wish the General to make one step to the prejudice of their

Majesties service."(161) In the middle of the night with the enemy only 3 miles away, Mackay retreated down the Spey, making a long night march until they reached Balveny.

Five days later MacKay returned when Dundee had marched away from the Grant lands. He then sent out of company of 200 horse to look for the enemy. Ludovick Grant acted a chief scout for this force. They soon encountered a group of Jacobite MacLeans on a march to join Dundee. The Jacobite force would have overpowered the Government scout force had not another body of Government troops arrived in the nick of time and they were able to force the enemy to retreat. The MacLeans did, however, kill a few of the dragoons and also captured a number of them.

The Grants were then left to protect the north while General MacKay proceeded south.

The Grants then captured a number of Cameron stragglers from Dundee's army who they found plundering the homes and cattle of Grant Lairds. They hung them all. The Camerons would not forget this and vowed revenge. Later they invaded Glen Urquhart, dispersed the Grants and raided their cattle.

When MacKay marched south, Dundee took the opportunity to gather more men and supplies and he returned to Lochaber in the west. The Camerons used this an opportunity to avenge their comrades. As many as 500 of them marched towards the Grant lands of Urquhart intent on retribution. The remaining Grants of Urquhart rallied their men to try and stop the Camerons. "Among the Grants, it was said, was one MacDonald of Glengarry's family, who imagined that the simple merit of his name and clan was sufficient to protect himself and the whole name of Grant from the revenge of the Camerons. This worthy came boldly up to the Camerons, and, 'acquainting them of his name and genealogy. Desired their peaceable departure. This they refused, but so far respected his name as to warn him to separate from the Grants, whom they meant to chastise. This kind advice he declined to take, and daring them to do their worst, departed in a huff, and the fray began with the onset of the Camerons. Their chronicler asserts that the Grants were defeated and dispersed, and their cattle carried in triumph to Dundee's rendezvous in Lochaber."(162)

But this did not end the matter as it nearly split Dundee's army. The MacDonald was killed in the conflict and his Chief, Glengarry, resented his death and demanded satisfaction from Lochiel, the Cameron Chief. Dundee had to intervene and make peace between the two Clan Chiefs.

Meanwhile, the Grants of Glenmoriston had again defied their Chief and under the Laird of Glenmoriston's eldest son, John Grant or, in Gaelic, Iain 'a Chragain (John of the Rock), joined the Jacobite army and fought alongside their age old enemies, the MacDonalds of Glengarry. "The shield and sword with which Ian-a-Chragain fought on this memorable occasion are still present at Invermoriston House."(163)

Young Glenmoriston is mentioned in the Memoirs of the Rebellion by Cameron of Lochiel who wrote :

'With them, also, from Glenmoriston, came as their companion in the war the valiant Grant; not that degenerate Grant who takes his name from Balachastle [Freuchie or Castle Grant], and who was following the party of the Batavian robber [King William of Orange], and was upholding the nefarious standard of the Dutch tyrant; but the bold Grant of Urquhart, bearing unstained honour in a faithful breast, and keen against the foes of the Cesar. He, following the ways of his great ancestors, took arms, and undeterred by the misfortunes of the time, contributed his help to his King. Through pathless tracts he climbs precipitous mountains with great equipment for the war. Tall in stature, he advances, leading his line; and there followed him into camp, as their chief, the children of Grant, all in good order'.

Having gathered more men, on 22 July 1698 the Royalist army marched out of Lochaber again with around 1,800 men, more than half of them MacDonalds, but including the Camerons, MacLeans and the Grants of Glenmoriston amongst others. They headed for Blair Castle in Atholl, by passing the Laird of Grants forces which were protecting Speyside. Mackay, who had returned to Edinburgh, immediately marched north with his 4,000 strong army to meet and destroy the Royalists once and for all. He occupied Perth on 25 July.

The Jacobites reached Blair Castle, which was held by a force loyal to King James, on 26 July. Here he held a council of War. His army at this time had risen to 2,000 men strong against the 4,000 of Mackay. The lowland officers advocated waiting until other Highland troops had joined them before confronting Mackay. The Highland Chiefs listened to this in silence. "But then Alasdair Dubh MacDonnell of Glengarry put into words what they really felt: 'Highlanders, he said, were different to other troops. Yes, they had suffered hardships, but did not affect them in the same way as ordinary soldiers, 'who are bred in an easier and more plentiful course of life'; they were ready to engage with the enemy and defeat him; they relished nothing more than 'hardy and adventurous exploits'; and it was his view that they should move immediately and attempt to prevent the enemy emerging from the pass [Killiecrankie], harrying then with 'quick sallies' and 'brisk skirmishes'."(164)

All the Chiefs agreed with him and when the experienced warrior, Cameron of Locheil, agreed, the course of action of the army was set. Fight it would be. The **Battle of Killiecrankie** was fought on 27 July 1689.

"The Government army consisted of Dutch, English and lowland Scottish troops. Most were regular infantry troops in established regiments, armed with the musket and the plug-bayonet. The soldiers were drilled to fire collectively in volleys to defuse and defeat a charging enemy. When hand-to-hand combat was inevitable, they would fit the plug bayonet, a relatively new invention (used for the first time in a British battle at Killiecrankie), which was slotted in the barrel of the musket. This enabled all the troops to carry muskets, rather than the traditional mix of musketeers and pikemen, greatly increasing the unit's firepower. The disadvantage was the troops could not fire with the bayonet in place and therefore only fitted it in the last moments before hand-to-hand combat ensued."(165)

On the morning of the battle Dundee sent his small cavalry force through the Pass of Killiecrankie to within site of the Government army. General Mackay thought they were a small force on their own and ordered his troops to follow their retreat through the Pass. Too late, he saw that the main Jacobite army was positioned on the high ground to his right (the north) and that he had been caught in a trap. If he retreated through the pass his rear would be open to attack from the rebel force. He quickly repositioned his troops in line to meet the inevitable highland charge, spacing his men out to cover more ground. Doing this he reduced his ranks from six deep to three, and this would prove his undoing. To his surprise there was no immediate charge by the Highlanders who continued to wait on top of the hill.

Meanwhile, Cameron of Lochiel was not just a great military leader but also had the power of divination, and just before the onset of the battle stated 'that the side will win that first spills blood'. Iain a' Chragain heard this as he was standing next to a Grant deer stalker from Glenmoriston and pointed to a Government officer on a white horse who had galloped out of MacKay's lines to survey the battlefield. The stalker immediately crouched down, took aim and killed the rider on the white horse, shot through the heart. The Jacobites therefore were the first to draw blood.

MAP 15. THE BATTLE OF KILLIECRANKIE 1689.

Still Dundee waited. The sun was in the eyes of his men and he was waiting until it had moved below the hills. Finally, when the sun began to drop below Beinn Dearg at 8pm, Dundee gave the order to charge. "Uttering a great roar, the clansmen set off down the slope, pouring over the ridge in a breaking wave of Highland fervour. They had thrown aside their plaids which left them for the most part dressed only in shirts. Many were bare-footed, as they ran over the springy turf, clutching their muskets, and screaming their battle cries. They came down the hill, holding their musket fire until the last moment. They were sustained, as they charged, by the momentum the ground gave them and the unleashing of their pent-up ferocity."(166)

Dundee "placed the MacLeans, under the chief, the nineteen-year-old Sir John MacLean of Duart, on the extreme right, opposite Balfour's battalion. Next to them were the Irish troops, commanded by Colonel James Purcell, and then the Clanranald MacDonalds under their student chief, with the Tutor of Clanranald in attendance. To their left, the tall dark Glengarry chief with his brother, Donald Gorm, formed up his MacDonald clansmen, alongside the smaller detachment of Glencoe men, under their formidable chief, Alasdair Maclain, and then came the Grants of Glenmoriston."(167)

Highlanders Charge At The Battle of Killiecrankie.

When the battle began the Grants of Urquhart and Glenmoriston charged with the MacDonalds of Glengarry. Almost immediately James Grant of Shewglie was brought down by a musket ball which struck his shield, but he got straight back up uninjured and continued the charge, exclaiming, *'Och, but the boddachs are in earnest'.*

The MacDonalds and Grants ran straight down to hit Kenmure's battalion. These lowland soldiers fired one volley which caused many casualties in the highland ranks, including Glengarry's brother, Donald and his son, Donald Gorm. But the clansmen continued their charge and when they hit the Government ranks, they caused much slaughter with their broadswords. Even then, the troops may have held their position a bit longer but the Government cavalry, trying to escape, ploughed straight into them, causing havoc and confusion.

"Many of General MacKays officers and soldiers were cut down through the skull and neck to the very breasts; others had skulls cut off above their ears like night-caps; some soldiers had both their bodies and cross-belts cut through at a blow; picks and small swords were cut like willows."(168)

General MacKay, seeing all this happen, called his closest cavalry and charged at the Highlanders. He passed through them unhurt although most of his men with him were unhorsed and many killed and when he eventually halted he was on the wrong side of the battle, almost alone.

On the far left of the Government line, Ramsay's regiment, which had taken the assault of Clanranald and the Irish regiment held its ground a little longer but then it too, broke and fled. Many ran in the direction of the village of Killiecrankie and they were followed hard by the MacDonalds and MacLeans, causing much slaughter at the mouth of the pass, where the fleeing troops were jammed together along the narrow pass. "one of them, finding himself trapped on a rock, leaped over a yawning chasm to escape, a seemingly impossible feat. Those who were not so lucky piled up, dead and wounded, in the roaring torrent of the [river] Garry."(169)

Meanwhile, General Dundee had waited on the hill while all this was happening. Before the battle the Chiefs had advised him not to participate as his death would effectively destroy the rebellion. However, near the end of the battle, he rode his horse downhill, heading straight for the centre of the Government force, where their remaining cavalry and cannon were still holding out. It was at this time that he was hit by a snipers bullet. The men with him had not seen this because of the battlefield smoke and continued to charge, driving away the remaining enemy cavalry and capturing the cannon. Dundee was then spotted on the ground being tended by one Jacobite soldier.

But the Government army were not totally defeated yet, because many of the Highlanders had continued to pursue the fleeing Government troops and left whole troops of Government soldiers intact on the battlefield. However, by this time General MacKay knew the day was lost and he gathered his remaining troops and made a tactical retreat. Viscount Dundee lay mortally wounded on the battlefield and he died that very evening. His body was taken to the Church of Blair and was interned the next day.

The death toll on both sides had been significant. The Government army had lost a third of its men, around 1,200 troops, although many thought that it was much more than this. In addition, around 500 prisoners were also taken. Despite this, however, only three senior officers had been killed: one being General MacKay's own brother. The same could not be said for the Jacobite force. Although their loses were fewer, with around 700 dead and 200 wounded, the Clan Chiefs and their leading officers suffered significant loss. The Camerons, in particular, lost half of their men who fought in the battle, and Lochiel himself was wounded.

"Those of the extreme left, the MacDonalds of Glengarry and Sleat, suffered worse. MacDonald of Largie was carried back to Blair, mortally wounded, and his Tutor too was killed ...., leaving no direct heirs to succeed him. Young Sir Donald MacDonald of Sleat, who had taken over command from his elderly father, was killed: 'You were young to be put to the test', said the [Glencoe] bard, 'and many a woman mourns you between Trotternish and Sleat'. Five of his relatives were also lost..."(170) Iain a' Chragain Grant survived although he had taken a musket ball in the arm and a bayonet thrush on his thigh. Many of his men were not so lucky and a significant number of Grants were wither killed or wounded.

However, despite the dead, it was a victory for the Highlanders and King James. News of the victory spread quickly and the remaining Government forces fully expected the Jacobite army to march south and take Perth. But as soon as the news of Dundee's death became known, the Government breathed a sigh of relief. Command of the remaining Jacobite force passed to General Cannon, an Irishman, who was not well respected by the Highland Chiefs. The spirit of the Highland Army vanished almost overnight with the death of Dundee. Within days of Killiecrankie there were disputes about tactics. The clans who had come in after the battle began to drift off home again, the Keppoch MacDonalds, under Coll of the Cows, were with the Jacobite army for little more than two weeks.

After the Battle, Alastair Dubh Grant, the Glenmoriston Chamberlain was returning home on his own, why we do not know. As evening approached he found a cottage in the Braes of Atholl and knocked on the door and asked for a night's shelter, as was the Highland Custom. Surprisingly, the woman of the cottage declined his request, giving as her excuse that her husband was not at home and had forbidden her to allow any strangers to be given shelter, given the troubled times currently affecting the country. Alastair responded that he only required shelter for one night and he would have it, and barged through the door and entered the house.

"By and by her husband arrived. She narrated her conversation with the stranger, and his reply. So the two get into grips – the Athole man to expel Alastair, and the latter determined not to be expelled. The struggle was a long one, but eventually the Athole man had the victory. Step by step, in spite of vigorous resistance, he drove his weary, way-worn, battle-worn opponent to the door, who in his desperation laid hold of the pot chain that was suspended over the hearth, yet he dragged him out, chair and all, and laid him on his back on the green sward at his door, adding, 'I did not believe any man could have so tried me. You are welcome to such hospitalities as my house can afford; and this chain you have in hand you will bring with you as a gift from me, to testify to your prowess'."(91) Many years later the very same chain was seen being used in a poor crofters house near Invermoriston House.

Alastair Grant is also prominent in another local legend of the Glenmoriston Grants. The Lairds of Glengarry and Glenmoriston were having a dispute regarding a boundary between their lands. Instead of going through the law courts they agreed to decide the dispute by each choosing a champion, who were then taken to the disputed land and here they were to wrestle for mastery. They were to push each other until they were exhausted and the spot where they ended the contest would be fixed upon as the boundary between the two estates. Alastair was the victorious champion and tradition states that he wore out a pair of new Highland brogues (shoes) in pushing his opponent that day. So the dispute was resolved.

The Government supporting Grant Regiment was always well spoken of by the leaders of the Government forces, even though it had never properly been provisioned with arms and uniforms. "At a later date (12 October 1689) General Mackay writes to Lord Melvill his belief that 'Strathnavar and Grant has as good men as any of the rest'. Ten days later he expresses an opinion that they are the 'best and completest'."(172) Eventually around December they got their arms and ammunition.

Meanwhile, Major-General Buchan took command of the Jacobite Army after Dundee was killed. Eventually, after raiding Aberdeenshire, Cannon decided to attack Dunkeld, just north of Perth, in August 1689. The town was defended by the Cameronian Regiment, consisting of Covenanter zealots from Lanarkshire and Dumfriesshire in the far south of Scotland. They had only 800 men against what they thought was going to be 3,000 Highland rebels. The Jacobites attacked on 21 August but in the narrow streets and well defended houses of a town the famous Highland charge was useless. The Cameronians fought well, inspired by religious fever but eventually retreated to defend the Cathedral and Dunkeld House as the dead piled up outside. The Covenanters even melted the lead off the roofs to make bullets when they started to run out.

The Highlanders eventually ran out of ammunition and when the Cameronians were on the verge of defeat, the Jacobites, with no ammunition left and demoralised by their losses, retreated. Cannon claimed it as a victory but it was anything but: the Cameronians remained in control of the town. After this the clans, including the remaining Grants of Glenmoriston, dispersed to go home and bring in the harvest.

Some Royalists remained at arms under Sir Ewan Cameron of Lochiel, one of the last great highland chiefs. He had left the Royalist army in disgust at not being given command before the Battle of Dunkeld and returned home with his men. A meeting was then held at Keppoch House, a MacDonald residence. Iain a' Chragain attended for the Grants of Glenmoriston and the leaders resolved to continue the struggle under the command of General Buchan, who had recently been sent over from Ireland by King James.

James Grant of Glenmoriston and his son Iain a' Chragain, after he returned home from the meeting, constructed a rude fortification on the Cragain Darroch (oak rock) of Blairie, where their friends and allies gathered around them. Meanwhile, the Castle of Urquhart was garrisoned by Captain Grant, won of the Laird of Grant's men, with three companies of Lord Strathnavar's Highland troops and those of the Laird of Grant. However, they were poorly armed, having neither sword nor bayonets, and only a few muskets between them.

Before the end of 1689 Castle Urquhart was besieged by the Jacobites with 500 men under Glengarry, including James and Iain a' Chragain Grant and their men. The garrison courageously held out and the Laird of Grant tried to reinforce the garrison up Loch Ness by boat but it sprang a leak and only around a dozen additional men and no provisions were able to make it there to strengthen the garrison.

The Camerons and the Jacobite Frasers and Mackenzies were expected to join the siege at Urquhart Castle. Then the Laird of Grant, after the leak in his boat was fixed, landed at the Castle water gate, which was beyond the range of fire from the Jacobites and was able to off load more men, food and ammunition. The Jacobites, without sufficient men, cannon and without effective leadership withdrew. But despite this, Iain a' Chragain and his father, James Grant of Glenmoriston, continued to support the Jacobite cause.

In April 1690 General Buchan took the field again with a small force of around 1200 men in total. He was not well liked by the Jacobite Chiefs and proved an ineffective leader. Had they a good general the Jacobites stood a good chance of easily taking the whole of the north for King James.

Buchan marched through Lochaber and Badenoch and on 1 May 1690 he was at the Haughs of Cromdale with 800 rebel troops. He was on his way to Aberdeenshire to try and link up with the Gordons. This was on Ludovick Grants land, a little east of Grantown-on-Spey. With Buchanan were 200 Grants of Glenmoriston, Iain a' Chagrain.

Castle Grant was being garrisoned by Government troops, under General Sir Thomas Livingstone, who himself was 8 miles away with 300 men of his own regiment and 300 Grants. He also had a troop of cavalry and other infantry totalling 1,200 men in all. Livingstone marched towards Castle Grant, and precautions were taken to prevent news of these troops movements getting to Buchan, who was with his own forces at Cromdale.

"Livingstone arrived at Ballachastell [Castle Grant] at 2am on 1 May, and Captain Grant of Easter Elchies, who was O.C. [Officer Commanding] Troops at Ballachastell, pointed out Buchan's camp fires from the top of Babetts Tower, and advised that he immediately attack, even though his men were pretty exhausted having had little or no rest after their march."(173)

They then marched down to a ford of the River Spey below Dalchapple but they found this guarded by around 100 of the enemy. They left a small number of men to occupy their attention while Captain Grant and Alexander Grant of Burnside guided the remaining force to another ford a quarter of a mile further down the river which they found unguarded. Here they crossed and Buchan's army was taken by surprise in the early hours and the **Battle of Cromdale** was fought. 400 Jacobites were killed or captured but the rest escaped over the hills. It was the end of the Rebellion.

The event was celebrated in a song. 'The Haughs of Cromdale':

"As I came in by Auchindoun,

A little wee bit frae the town,

When to the Highlanders I was bound,

To view the haughs of Cromdale,

I met a man in tartan trews,

I speer'd at him what was the news;

Quo' he, the Highland army rues

That e'er we came to Cromdale.

We were in bed, Sir, every man,

When th' English host upon us came,

A bloody battle then began

Upon the haughs of Cromdale.

The English horse they were so rude,

They bathed their hoofs in Highland blood.

But our brave clans, they boldly stood,

Upon the haughs of Cromdale.

But alas! We could no longer stay,

For o'er the hills we came away,

And sore we do lament the day

That e'er we came to Cromdale."(174)

There were no English at this battle but Highlanders were of the habit of calling Lowland Scots, English.

Ludovick himself was not present at Battle of Cromdale as he had returned to Edinburgh on his parliamentary duties. But after this victory Ludovick's star was on the rise and he increased his lands and estates. He then became a Member of Parliament for Inverness until the Act of Union in 1707. After the rebellion was over MacKay built a new Fort at Fort William (previously Inverlochy) and it was garrisoned by part of the Grant Regiment who received praise for their good behaviour from the locals.

The Grants of Glenmoriston still held out with the MacDonalds of Glengarry but the rebellion was effectively over and then totally extinguished after the defeat of King

James at the **Battle of the Boyne** in Ireland one month later. Eventually Grant of Glenmoriston and Glengarry surrendered and gave up their rebellion. The Government garrisoned Urquhart Castle from 1690 until 1692 with around 300 to 400 men. On leaving they blew up the keep and entrance towers and virtually destroyed it as a place of strength.

Castle Urquhart and Loch Ness.

Eileen Sinclair 2020

Meanwhile, despite all the fighting in connection with the rebellion, the Grants were still involved in local disagreements and in 1690 one such dispute concerned Patrick Grant, Laird of Rothiemurchas. He was a flamboyant character "... who went about the Rothiemurchas area with a band of two dozen desperadoes executing summary and often quite unsubstantiated sentences on supposed wrongdoers. He was dressed in fine velvets, satins, his shoes lined with down and his cap adorned with great tail feathers of eagles. His table was furnished with choice meats and imported wines.."(175) Despite all his dandiness, he was a man of violence and in 1690 he fell out with the MacIntoshes over the supply of water to his mill. MacIntosh built another mill further up the burn from Patrick Grant's and was diverting the water for his own use. Patrick Grant demanded that he stop diverting the water, but MacIntosh refused and threatened to burn his barn down.

Patrick immediately called on the old alliance with Clan MacGregor and sent word to Rob Roy MacGregor, asking for his assistance. In the meantime Mackintosh gathered his men and sent scouts to the top of all the adjacent hills to warn him if the infamous MacGregor warrior appeared with his men. Eventually Rob Roy appeared but only accompanied with a single piper. *"On being querulously asked by Grant where his 'tail' of the Clan MacGregor was, Rob slapped him on the back and said, 'Cheer up; what though the purse be light in the morning, who can say how heavy it may be by nightfall?'.* He bade the piper blow a pibroch, 'The Rout of Glen Fruin', and as the notes swelled, bands of MacGregors sprang from the rocks and bushes, fully armed. As they appeared, the Mackintoshes disappeared in inverse ratio. The force of Grants and MacGregors then set fire to Mackintosh's mill, while the piper composed a new air to fit in with the roar and crackle. It was named 'The Burning of the Black Mill' and is still given as a set piece in piping competitions."(269)

The Grants of Speyside, although part of the Government and clear supporters of law and order, were not above a bit of raiding on their neighbours. In 1691 a party of Clan Grant raided the lands of Dallas, Pluscarden and Duffus which belonged to Sir Robert Gordon of Gordonstoun. On hearing of the raid, Gordon gathered a number of men and overtook the Grants on their way home. He approached the raiders and demanded by what authority they were robbing and plundering his tenants. The Grants replied, 'By order of the Laird of Grant'. Gordon refused to believe this and demanded to see something in writing. The Grant leader produced a letter from the Laird of Grant and Gordon immediately grabbed it and turned his horse and rode all the way straight to Edinburgh, produced the letter before the Privy Council and obtained a writ against the Laird of Grant for the whole amount of his losses.

In the Highlands it was one thing to obtain a writ but another to enforce it and a Gordon messenger to Grant was ambushed and harshly treated when he tried to serve the writ on the Laird and barely escaped with his life. He was seized near Craigmuir by a party of Grants who hit him violently with the butts of their guns and stabbed him in the shoulder with a dirk. They then robbed him of all his money, clothes, sword and horse. After this they then kept him captive for 3 or 4 days before releasing him.

This was all about Highland pride, the treatment of the messenger was not to avoid payment but more to show the Grants displeasure at the means employed.

Ludovick and his heir, Brigadier Alexander Grant, then invited Gordon of Gordonstoun to come in person to Castle Grant and receive the full amount of his claim. Sir Robert, on entering the castle, was received with every mark of respect. On receiving the money he immediately handed it back to the Brigadier, saying *'this is a present from Robert of Gordonstoun, and I will see my tenants righted myself'*.

Ludovick Grant was zealous in his adherence to the Protestant religion. He even shut down the churches of Cromdale, Duthil and Abernethy between 1690 and 1691 until 'properly qualified' Ministers were found to occupy them.

In 1694, King William and Queen Mary erected Ludovick's land of Freuchie into a 'Regality of Grant', and directed that his castle should henceforth be known as 'Castle Grant'. From then on Ludovick and his successors were known as Lairds of Grant. In 1699 Ludovick handed over his Loch Ness estates to his eldest son, Alexander Grant, on his marriage to Elizabeth Stewart.

Ludovick's lands had suffered badly from looting by the Jacobite rebels. "It is estimated that he and his people had lost £76,000 Scots on Speyside, and in Urquhart £44,000 Scots. In addition, a further £30,000 Scots was claimed for rent losses over five years. Parliament agreed to give him £12,000 sterling, but, sad to relate, these large sums of money were never repaid, even though succeeding Lairds continued to press their claim."(177)

Part of being a Chief was to sometimes give out severe punishment. "In 1703, three women were charged with the crime of conveying aquavite [whisky] clandestinely to prisoners in ward at Castle Grant, who drank to such excess that they died. So unique and peculiar was the charge that the ablest lawyers in the nation were consulted by the judge, who was on this occasion Brigadier Alexander Grant. He was advised that the charge could not be made a capital one, and as it could not be construed as poisoning, the ends of justice might be served by the infliction of an arbitrary punishment with banishment upon the confession of the prisoners. The three woman were condemned to be taken to the Regality Cross at Grantown and tied there to, their bodies made bare from the belt upwards, and scourged with cords by the hangman, each receiving thirty stripes. They were then to be banished from the Regality. At the same sederunt the court adjudged another woman to be similarly scourged and banished, and one of her ears cut off, for haunting with a notorious freebooter called Hakit Steir and other outlaws."(178)

In another trial, a boy of 17 was sentenced, for stealing a plough, to have his ear nailed to a post and he had to stand there for one hour without moving. He then had to pull his ear off the nail himself. Sometimes the Chief of Grant had to meet out capital punishment. On one occasion two men convicted of housebreaking and stealing cheese were condemned to be hanged at the Gallow Hill in Belintome by the Chief of Grant.

Not all the Grant judges were tolerant men. Notorious was Robert Grant of Abernethy who hanged people for merely 'disobliging' him. He rarely called a jury and on one occasion hanged two brothers from a tree and then buried them on a single grave by the roadside. Another judge, called 'Baillie Roy' was known for handing out 'Jeddart Justice', by hanging men before they were tried and then finding them guilty afterwards. "On another occasion he is said to have hanged two notorious thieves and after par boiling their heads, set them up on poles; and at another time to have placed two men in sacks and drowned them in a river."(179) Ludovick Grant put an end to these acts. He would not tolerate this abuse of power. In any event, the Heritable Jurisdiction Act took jurisdiction away from the Chiefs and legal administration by Sheriffs was introduced.

As part of his duty as Sheriff of Inverness-shire, he apprehended a notorious 'free-booter' MacGregor, who was then imprisoned in Inverness. MacGregor had many friends and Lord Strathallan, Glengyle and others, wrote to Ludovick Grant, pleading for his release but declaring that if he was hanged, "they would have a Grants head for every finger in the MacGregors hands. The Laird's reply was that if the prisoner on trial was clearly proved to be guilty, hanged he should be, 'though a hundred heads should be lost on both sides'. MacGregor was duly convicted and condemned. On the way to execution, accompanied by the Sheriff, the condemned man was met by an express bearing a reprieve, which, without opening, the Sheriff placed, 'between the criminal's neck and the rope wherewith he was fastened, and thereby hanged both at the same time."(180) Through the help of his friend Lord Forbes, Ludovick Grant escaped censure for ignoring the reprieve.

Another story is told in the later years of Ludovick's life. At dinner with the Earl of Mar in Edinburgh, the Earl complained that his vassals, the Farquharsons of Braemar and the Forbes's of Strathdon, were disobedient to him, cutting his timber from his forests, killing his deer and refusing to pay their rents to his bailies and factors. The Earl of Mar was the Secretary of State for Scotland at this time but he still refused to ask for military assistance to make them see reason.

Ludovick Grant thought for a moment and then replied that if the Earl would do for him the first favour he asked, he would act as his bailie and bring his vassals into order. Mar eagerly accepted this offer and Ludovick soon went north to raise his clansmen. When the Grants heard the news of the agreement they were 'greatly affronted', thinking that their Chief acting as a Bailie was derogatory to his and their station. However, the Laird of Grant was determined to fulfil his promise and raised about 500 of his men and with about 40 greyhounds he pretended to go hunting in the Earl of Mar's forest, where he killed a number of deer.

He then invited all the gentlemen vassals of the Earl's to a feast at the old Castletown of Braemar, where the Bailie Courts were usually held. All Mar's vassals attended and were duly wined and dined. After dinner Grant's men surrounded the guests and he informed them that they were required 'on their honour' to promise to be faithful and honest to the Earl of Mar and refrain from all their illegal activities and to pay their rents. Those that refused would be hung. To emphasise the point he arrested the two worst offenders and had then strung up. After this all the vassals readily agreed and the Earl of Mar was greatly pleased and was forever after the Laird's strongest friend.

The Arms of Ludovic Grant, 8th Laird of Freuchie.

He was also involved in the trial of James MacPherson and others at Banff in 1700 which was made famous by a poem by Robert Burns. MacPherson was the leader of a gang of gypsies who roamed the north and they were renowned for their raiding and plundering. Some of MacPherson's gang were tenants of the Laird of Grant and he gave the gang a certain amount of protection. Prominent members of the gang were Peter and Donald Brown, tenants of Grant with whom he was on friendly terms.

Alexander Duff, Laird of Braco had long wished to arrest the gang but was afraid of offending the Laird of Grant. But eventually Braco ambushed the gang and MacPherson and Peter Brown were arrested. The Laird of Grant sent some of his men and helped them escape but they were soon recaptured, along with Donald Brown. Braco took them to Banff, outwith Grant's jurisdiction as Sheriff, where they were tried and convicted on 7 November 1700. Ludovick Grant claimed that the Browns, as his vassals, should be tried by him, but this was rejected.

They were all found guilty and sentenced to be hanged. MacPherson was executed but it seems that the Laird of Grant was able to procure a pardon for the Browns, on condition that they leave the country. The incident gave rise to a song:

"The Laird of Grant, that

Highland Saint,

Of mighty majesty,

Did plead the cause of Peter Brown

And let Macpherson die."(181)

Peter Brown was sent to John Campbell, Duke of Argyll (Red John of the Battles) and he followed him to fight in the Continental Wars, where he was killed at the Battle of Malplaquet. What happened to his brother is not recorded.

Meanwhile back in the Grant Glens of Urquhart and Glenmoriston during the last decade of the 17th century and the first years of the eighteenth, the inhabitants of Urquhart and Glenmoriston were freely plundered, and the Grants of these Glens freely plundered freely in return. A few of the many raids in which they were implicated may be mentioned.

In 1690, William Grant of Achmonie stole 2 horses from Murdo McCurdy and was fined. In July 1693, Archibald Grant of Coineachain carried away much spoil from

James Dunbar of Dalcross, a Baillie of Inverness. In May 1698, the same Archibald Grant and his brother, Patrick Grant, along with John Grant of Invermoriston stole a herd of cattle from William Chisholm. They all again fined.

The Grants also suffered from Reiving. "Patrick Grant of Craskie, who himself was known as a reiver was himself …. spoiled of a number of cattle by a party of MacMillans from Loch-Arkaig-side. Pursuing the reivers, with his brother and his friends, he overtook them at Corn-nam-Bronag, between Glen Loyne and Tomdoun in Glengarry. When he demanded restitution of the cattle, he got the reply, 'You may take them, if you can'. He tried and succeeded; but in the struggle several fell on both sides. The MacMillans still lie in the Corrie, where twelve cairns mark their grave. The Glenmoriston slain were brought home, and buried with their kindred in Clachan Mherchaierd."(182)

But the most notable event during this time of trouble was the 'Raid of Inchbrine' which occurred in 1691 or 1692. Twenty years before the raid a vagrant woman arrived at the home of Grant of Shewglie. She was provided with food and shelter but before morning she gave birth to a boy, whom the Lady of Shewglie offered to keep and rear. The mother agreed and went on her way. The boy grew up unchristened and as he tended Shewglie's cattle, he was known by the name of Gille Dubh nam Mart.

Because of his parentage the poor boy's life was made miserable by the youth of the estate and he eventually left Shewglie and made his way to Lochaber where he was welcomed. The men of Lochaber gave him protection and he agreed to guide them in a raid on Glenmoriston and Urquhart.

Crossing the mountains, they passed by Shewglie, and came suddenly to Inchbrine, while the people were absent cutting peat in the distant moss. While they were gone the Lochaber men lifted their cattle and headed slowly home at the pace of the slowest beast. The Grants became aware of the theft and quickly assembled and gathered at the house of James Grant of Shewglie, and requested that he should lead them against the invaders.

"Shewglie, whom we have seen distinguishing himself at Killiecrankie, had not a drop of coward's blood in his veins; but the followers of the Gille Dubh were more numerous than the Urquhart men who had hastily met, and he advised delay until more were got together. 'I will follow the Lochabermen', exclaimed his impulsive wife, Hannah Fraser, 'and you may stay at home and ply the distaff'. Smarting under the taunt, he bade his men to follow him, and set out after the raiders, whom he overtook on a small rocky plateau, lying to the south of the burn of Corribuy, ever since known as Carn Mharbh Dhaoine – the Rock of the Dead Men.

The Gille Dubh stepped out to meet his late master. 'I did not expect', said the latter, 'that you would be the one to lift cattle in Glen Urquhart'. 'Nor I', replied the young man, ' that you would be the one to follow me, seeing I have taken none of yours'. On Shewglie's account the spoil was at once given up, and the men of Urquhart turned their faces towards their Glen. They had proceeded but a few paces when a hare started from among the heather and ran across the moor between the two parties. Kenneth MacDonald [from Urquhart] .... raised his gun and fired at it. The shot had no effect on the hare, which was believed to be a witch, but it brought disaster on Kenneth and his companions. The Lochabermen thought it was intended for themselves, and returned the fire. A desperate fight followed. For a time the Urquhart men kept their ground, and several of their opponents fell; but in the end they were forced to fly, leaving eight of their number, including Shewglie, dead in the heather. The Lochabermen not only took possession of the cattle again, but they also returned to Shewglie and took every hoof belonging to that township. Hannah Fraser, weeping over the result of her rashness, approached Gille Dubh and appealed for mercy, 'Remember', said she, 'that I long befriended you, and that I am now a widow, and about to become the mother of a fatherless child.' There was no mercy in his reply; - 'Ma tha thu trom, beir searrach' – ' If you are with child, bear a foal'."(183) The place where the Glen Urquhart men died still contains cairns to their memories, with the largest one marking the place where Shewglie fell.

James Grant of Shewglie's son eventually reached manhood and he swore revenge on Gille Dubh. He rode to Lochaber and coming to Gille Dubh's house late in the evening requested shelter for the night. In accordance with the Highland rules of hospitality this was given without asking who the stranger was or where he had come from.

As evening progressed the two men talked of events in the highlands and the deeds of former days. Grant eventually alluded to the Raid of Inchbrine and induced his host to retell the whole story. As Gille Dubh finished his tale, the young man sprang to his feet and exclaimed, ' The hour of vengeance has now arrived'. 'Who are you'! angrily demanded the Gille Dubh. 'I' replied Grant, 'am the foal which the goodwife Shewglie carried on the day of the Raid of Inchbrine', and, with these words he plunged his dirk into the man's heart. Rushing out of the house, he leapt into the saddle, and was far on his way to Urquhart ere the morning light fell on the lifeless body of Gille Dubh nam Mart."(184)

Back on the National scene, in 1705 as an M.P. Ludovick Grant objected to the Union of the Kingdoms.

"In 1710 Ludovick formally resigned his leadership of the Clan to his son, Colonel Alexander Grant of Grant. He did this before a gathering of the gentlemen and others of the Clan at Ballintome. He had them all dressed in plaids and tartans of red and green, all wearing whiskers. (This I believe, is the first recorded instance of a Highland Clan wearing a standard tartan, instead of whatever colour the wearer happened to own)."(185)

At the ceremony he addressed his son as follows, "My dear Sandy, I make you this day a very great present, viz., the honour of commanding the Clan Grant, who, while I conducted them, though in troublesome times, yet they never misbehaved, so that you have them this day without spot or blemish. I hope and beg you will use them as well as I did in supporting their public and private interests agreeable to the laws of liberty and probity as are now happily established in our lands. God bless you all!"(186)

Ludovick died in Edinburgh 1716 and was buried in Holyrood Abbey. His wife, Janet, had died in 1697 and Ludovick married Jean Houston in 1701. He and Janet had 5 sons and 4 daughters. Their eldest son, John died young and the 2nd son, Alexander succeeded. Their 3rd son James, succeeded Alexander. The 4th son, George became Major General Grant of Culbin, "and was for a time Governor of the Castle of Inverness, or Fort-George, as it was then called. For surrendering it in the 45' he was tried by court martial and was dismissed from the army."(187)

Their youngest son, Lewis, became a regular army Colonel, who bought the estate of Dunphail, which passed on his death in Jamacia to his nephew, Sir Ludovick Grant of Grant. Their eldest daughter married Hugh Rose of Kilravock. His 2nd daughter married Grant of Ballindalloch and she was the ancestor of the Macpherson Grants of Ballindalloch. Their 3rd daughter married Sir Robert Mackenzie and their youngest daughter married Lord Lovat.

CHAPTER 11. 1715: A DIVIDED CLAN.

Brigadier-General Alexander Grant of Grant, Chief of Clan Grant was Chief from 1710 until 1719, although he did not officially succeed his father until his death in 1716. He married first, Elizabeth Stewart in 1699 and then on her death, Anne Smith in 1709. Although he had been in charge of the clan since 1710, he was only formally Clan Chief for 3 years (1716 to 1719). He was, however, one of the most important Chiefs of Clan Grant.

Brigadier General Alexander Grant of Grant.

In 1706 Alexander was one of the Commissioners who negotiated the Union with England. He was one of the signatories of the Act of Union and in 1708 he sat as an MP in the first British Parliament. Also in 1706 Alexander was commissioned into the army of Queen Anne, as Colonel of the Foot Regiment raised by the Earl of Mar and also as MP for Invernesshire. He was very young for this appointment and it appears to be a political decision to keep the Grants supporting Queen Anne rather than the Jacobite cause. With fears of a French Invasion and another Jacobite Rebellion at this time, Alexander recruited 800 Grants into this regiment. They marched to Newcastle, sailed to London and then onto the Continent to serve in the Duke of Marlborough's Army. In 1708 the regiment fought at the Siege of Lille.

Alexander got home on leave in 1709 when he married Anne Smith. He then returned to his regiment which was quartered at Ghent, Antwerp and Tournai (in modern day Belgium). Alexander then commanded the Regiment in September 1709 when he took part in the Siege of Mons. Here he personally mounted the breached walls with his regiment and only had one man killed and three wounded. The Regiment stayed in Europe until 1711.

Ann Smith 2nd Wife of Brigadier General Alexander Grant.

Anne Smith, the daughter of the Chancellor of the Exchequer, was Maid of Honour to Queen Anne. Shortly after their wedding he became ill with fever and rheumatism but after he recovered he went back over to Flanders (Belgium) to join his regiment and then he took part in the Siege of Mons. Then "in 1710 Alexander was captured by a French ship whilst proceeding home on leave. He was, however, soon released on parole, and returned home as part of a general exchange of prisoners from both sides."(188) In 1711 he was promoted Brigadier-General and his regiment returned from Flanders. Some of the regiment, including many Grants, went to North America to help capture Quebec from the French. The remainder of the regiment was disbanded. Alexander again took up his parliamentary duties.

Brigadier General Grant went back to Scotland in September 1713 and was elected as MP for Elgin and Forres. In early 1715, King George I made Alexander the Governor of Sheerness Castle.

The exiled King James VII and II died in 1701 and he was succeeded in exile by his son, James Francis Edward Stuart, known as the 'Old Pretender'. Then in 1703, King William III died and Queen Anne succeeded to the throne of Great Britain and Ireland. She was the Protestant daughter of King James VII and II and the sister of the Old Pretender. In 1707, Scotland and England had been joined in political union. It was deeply unpopular in large parts of Scotland and the Jacobites were able to gather not just those who wished to return the House of Stuart to the thrones of Scotland and England, but also those who wished to see the Union dissolved.

Then in 1714, Queen Anne died childless and the throne of Great Britain and Ireland became vacant again. She was the last Stuart Monarch, being the daughter of King James VII and II. Under British law, the Monarch had to be a Protestant and George of Hanover, a second cousin of Queen Anne, was the closest Protestant relative. He was actually 86th in line to the throne as all the rest were Catholics. He became King George I of Great Britain and Ireland.

John Erskine, Earl of Mar, had initially been on the Government side and in 1713 was made Secretary of State for Scotland. However, he was unceremoniously sacked from office by King George I in early 1715 and vowed revenge. After his dismissal he travelled back to Scotland and dispatched letters to all the principal Jacobite leaning Chiefs, inviting them to attend a 'grand hunting match' at his principal home in Braemar on 27 August 1715. The hunting party was attended by Iain a' Chragain Grant, now Laird of Glenmoriston.

This was a ruse meant to cover Mar's intention to raise the standard of rebellion. "Mar made a stirring address, expressing regret for his past conduct in favouring the Union, and, now that his eyes were opened, promising to do all in his power to retrieve the past and make his countrymen again a free people. He produced a commission from James appointing him Lieutenant-General and Commander of all the Jacobite forces in Scotland."(189)

He further advised them that he had money to pay the forces that were to be raised. Nearly all the Chiefs and Lairds agreed to join the rebellion, including Iain a' Chagrain Grant of Glenmoriston. They all then went home to raise their men and await the call from the Earl of Mar. They did not have to wait long, as only a matter of days later the Earl of Mar raised the Stuart flag at Braemar on 6 September 1715 in front of 2,000 men. However, "when, in the course of erection, the ball at the top of the pole fell off. This, which was regarded by the highlanders as a bad omen, cast a gloom over the proceedings of the day."(190)

Meanwhile, as all this was happening, in July 1715 hints of a possible rebellion had made it to the ears of the Government in London and they quickly called out their loyal supporters. Alexander Grant was ordered by King George to raise a regiment of 400 men and he was then ordered to march to Glasgow to assist the Earl of Argyll to quell the rebellion.

In September 1715 Brigadier General Grant was appointed Governor of Edinburgh Castle and he was ordered to reinforce the garrison with 2 companies of Grants. Prior to this the Jacobites had attempted to capture Edinburgh Castle by stealth and they nearly succeeded and the former Governor, Lieutenant Governor Stewart was not trusted and dismissed. Very shortly after taking command Alexander Grant was ordered by the Duke of Argyll to seize all boats and vessels on the Firth of Forth and to bring them to Leith, to ensure that they did not fall into the hands of the rebels.

By the end of September 1715, the Jacobite Army at Braemar totalled over 5,000 men and included the Grants of Glenmoriston under Laird Iain a' Chagrain with 300 men. As in the previous Jacobite rebellion the Grants of Glenmoriston joined the regiment of the MacDonalds of Glengarry commanded by Iain's old comrade in arms, Alistair Dubh, Chief of the Glengarry MacDonalds.

"Under the banner of Glengarry were found Iain a' Chagrain, as well as a company from Glen Urquhart, under the command of MacDonald of Aughtera, near Fort Augustus with William Grant, a son of Corrimony, as one of his Lieutenants. Alexander Grant of Shewglie, son of Shewglie who fell at Corribuy, privately exercised his influence in favour of the Stewarts."(191)

Initially a large force of mainly MacDonalds, Camerons, MacLeans and also including the Grants of Glenmoriston, were ordered to invade Argyllshire to prevent the Campbells from joining the Government forces gathering in Central Scotland. On route they attacked Inverlochy Castle but, due to their lack of artillery, they failed to take it. They then marched into Argyllshire and raided many of the farms and townships. They eventually reached Inverary, which was defended by a large contingent of Campbells. They refused to surrender, and the Jacobite force, not wanting to lose a large number of men on an assault of a well defended position, decided not to attack but instead raided all the surrounding area before retiring and marching north again to meet up with the main Jacobite army.

Then on 1 October 1715 Alexander Grant of Grant was ordered to bring his regiment into the 'field' to support the army of Argyll on the Government side. This he did but he remained in Speyside to try and hold the north for the Government and to keep a watch on Inverness which had been captured by the Jacobites.

Back at the main Campaign, the **Battle of Sheriffmuir** was fought on 13 November 1715. The Earl of Mar, initially based in Perth, marched his army south, intent on taking Stirling for the Jacobite cause. However, by this time the Government had brought together its own army, under John Campbell, Duke of Argyll, to counter the Jacobite force.

The Jacobite army was nearly double the size of the Government force but Argyll was an experienced soldier who had fought in Europe during the War of the Spanish Succession, fighting in the battles of Ramillies (1706) and Malplaquet (1709). In addition, most of his troops were also experienced, professional soldiers and were better equipped and trained than the Jacobite force.

MAP 16. The Battle of Sheriffmuir 1715.

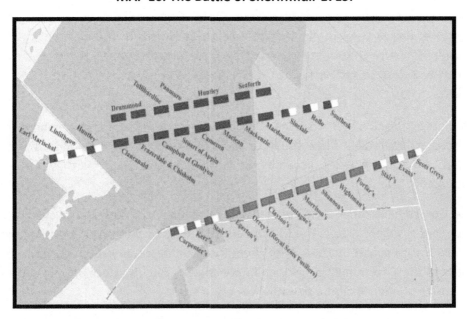

Copyright: Neil Ritchie/OpenStreetMap Contributors.

On the morning of the battle the Jacobite force arrived at the battle site first and took up position on the high ground above Sheriffmuir. The MacDonalds were given the right wing with the Grants of Glenmoriston. The Jacobite left flank was protected by a bog and Mar positioned his cavalry on the right flank to protect it from being outflanked by the Government cavalry.

The MacDonalds and Grants of Glenmoriston then attacked the Government left flank before they were fully deployed and after a brief fight, broke them. They were accompanied by the Jacobite cavalry who pursued the Government forces as they fled. Had the Jacobite cavalry and the chasing MacDonalds and Grants turned and attacked the exposed left flank of the remaining Government infantry they would have, undoubtedly, won the battle. The Master of Sinclair, who fought in the Jacobite army, described it as follows:

"The Order to attack being given, the two thousand Highlandmen, who were then drawn up in very good order, ran towards then enemy in a disorderly manner, always firing some dropping shots, which drew upon them a general salvo from the enemy ..... No sooner did that begin than the Highlanders threw themselves flat upon their bellies; and, when it slackened, they started to their feet. Most threw away their fuzies, and drawing their swords, pierced them everywhere with an incredible vigour and rapidity. In four minutes time from receiving the order to attack, not only all in our view and before us turned their backs, but the five squadrons on their left, commanded by General Whitham, went to the right about, and never looked back until they had got near Dunblane, almost two miles from us."(192)

The Jacobite centre then attacked the Government army's right flank where they were met with volley after volley of musket fire from the experienced British troops. After taking heavy casualties the Jacobite assault failed and they retreated back up the hill.

The Government force then pursued the retreating Jacobites and pushed them back towards Allen Water. The MacDonalds, Grants and the rest of the rebel army were close to defeat but luckily for them the Jacobite cavalry returned from their chase of the Government cavalry and Argyll had to call his attack off and set up a defensive position against a potential cavalry attack.

This allowed the Jacobites to regroup and they made one final attack with both infantry and cavalry. However, by this time the Jacobites were exhausted and their attack was only half-hearted. It failed and with the coming of night the battle came to an end and both forces withdrew; Mar to Ardoch and Argyll to Dunblane.

The Government force lost the most men with around seven hundred casualties in total. The Jacobites had lost around two hundred and fifty dead or wounded. Both sides claimed victory, neither had been defeated, but it was Argyll who had completed his objective: stopping the Jacobite advance south.

During the battle the Laird of Glenmoriston saved the life of the now aged Alister Dubh MacDonald of Glengarry. "Alister, now an old man, wore trews (tartan trousers) tied round the waist with a belt or thong, which unhappily gave way in the heat of a personal encounter with an English trooper. Impeded, as the old hero was, with his fallen trews, he would have been vanquished but for the timely aid of his valorous friend, the Chief of Glenmoriston."(193)

After Sheriffmuir Alexander Grant, Laird of Grant, sent his Grant clansmen to Inverness, commanded by his brother, George Grant, as Alexander himself was still at Stirling with Argyll, getting orders after the battle. He wrote to his brother urging him to be zealous in his actions for the Protestant Cause. The town was being held by Clan Mackenzie, under Sir John Mackenzie of Coul. The Grants assisted Simon Fraser, 11th Lord Lovat to besiege the town, supported by Clan Rose and Clan Forbes. The strength of the Government force was put at Frasers 800, Grants 800, Forbes 200, Roses 300 and Munro's 400. They were against 300 Mackenzies and 300 MacDonalds. The Jacobites knew they were totally outnumbered and MacKenzie of Coul escaped with 300 men using boats from Inverness Pier but they had to leave all their goods behind. The Frasers and Grants then marched into Inverness and took control of the town for the Hanoverian Forces.

By the end of December the Duke of Argyll had been joined by General Cardigan with a large number of Dutch troops. With English reinforcements this brought is army up to 10,000 men. With these new recruits he resolved to attack the remaining Jacobites stationed at Perth, despite it being the middle of winter. Alexander Grant accompanied the British Army north until they reached Aberdeen. Grant then proceeded north with his men to search for rebels and disarm them. On his way north he received the surrender of some of the principal Jacobites.

The modern Scottish archaeologist and TV commentator Neil Oliver states that in hindsight the Jacobite failure of the rising of 1715 seems astonishing in that the Jacobite leader, the Earl of Mar, could easily have moved past the Duke of Argyll to link up with the English Jacobites and Catholics in the North of England, had he had the merest sense of how to fight a campaign rather than lead a parade.

On 23 December, the Old Pretender, who had been exiled in France, landed at Peterhead, his cause largely lost. He met with Mar at Perth, but was unable to rouse his disheartened army. Argyll, reinforced and reinvigorated, soon marched north, while the Jacobite army fled to the town of Montrose and the Old Pretender returned to France. The Jacobite army then moved to Ruthven and dispersed.

Alexander Grant and the main body of Grants took a full part in the mopping up operations. On 28 February 1716 Grant placed a garrison of Grants in Brahan Castle, the seat of the Mackenzie Earls of Seaforth. He also took possession of Erchless and Borlum Castles, the former the seat of the Chisholms and the later of Brigadier Mackintosh. They then received the surrender of many of the Gordons and Abercrombies. Then throughout 1716 the Grant regiment remained in arms and were stationed in Fort William and other places.

Brigadier Alexander Grant was furious at his clansmen who had 'betrayed him' and joined the rebellion and sent word to the Government that those who were prisoners should get no favour, including William Grant of Corrimony. He also asked that John Grant of Divach, who he thought 'a dangerous fellow', should not be allowed bail but kept a prisoner.

Glengarry eventually surrendered but Iain a Chragain Grant held out, refused to lay down his arms and hid out in the mountains north of Glenmoriston. Because of this his house at Invermoriston was burned to the ground by Government soldiers.

After the end of the rebellion, Ian-a-Chragain was declared a rebel and his Glenmoriston estates were forfeited and remained Crown property until 1732, when they were sold by auction and purchased by Sir Ludovick Colquhoun(Grant) of Luss, afterwards Sir Ludovick Grant of Grant, for £1,200. Through his good offices the lands were eventually returned to John Grant of Glenmoriston, son and heir of Ian-a-Chragain.

The Laird of Glenmoriston hid out in a cave on the rock overhanging the river Moriston, near the falls of Eas-Iararaidh, until the General Amnesty of 1717 made it safe for him to again appear in public. Despite being forfeited the tenants of his Glenmoriston estates remained loyal to him and continued to pay him their rents and not the Government.

By 1720 still no rents had been paid to the Government and they appointed two brothers, William and Robert Ross, as factors for the forfeited estates of Seaforth, Chisholm and Glenmoriston in October 1720 to bring them into Government control. Their demands for payment of rent were treated with contempt by the people of Glenmoriston and they eventually collected a company of British soldiers and marched to Glenmoriston. Still the tenants refused to turn up and pay their dues.

Eventually the Ross brothers, with their soldiers, left Glenmoriston on their way to Strathglass and Kintail. Patrick Grant, 2nd son of Glenmoriston and the factor of Kintail, Donald Murchison, set an ambush in Glen Affaric. When the Ross brothers approached the Grants and Mackenzies attacked and scattered the troops along with the brothers. William Ross was wounded and his son Walter was killed. They retreated back to Inverness having collected no rents.

Nothing was done against the ambushers and Patrick Grant lived to re-acquire the Glenmoriston estate, which he enjoyed till his death, at a great age, in 1786.

Ian-a-Chragain was married twice. His second wife was one of the 11 daughters of the celebrated Ewan Cameron of Locheil. She lived to the great old age of 80. "At the time of her death she left behind her no fewer than two hundred descendants "(194), from 10 sons and 5 daughters.

In 1717 Alexander Grant retired from the army and went home to his estates looking for peace and quiet. Unfortunately his wife Anne died unexpectantly and in grief, Alexander went to stay with his father-in-law for some time in Tidworth, Wiltshire. On his way home, he became ill and died at Leith. He was buried in Holyrood Chapel. Having had no children, he was succeeded by his eldest surviving brother James Grant.

Sir James Grant of Grant, Chief of Clan Grant from 1719 until 1747. He was born in July 1679. Having no idea that he would ever become Chief of Clan Grant, he married Anne Colquhoun, heiress of Colquhoun of Luss. He was originally known as James Grant of Pluscardine because he inherited that estate through Janet Brodie of Leithen, his mother. On his marriage he assumed the name of Colquhoun, and in 1706 the Luss estates of Clan Colquhoun were inherited by him and his wife. Queen Anne Grant a new patent to the baronetcy, allowing it to pass to the heirs male through Sir Humphrey Colquhoun's daughter, Anne.

In 1715 he took part with his father-in-law in the **Loch Lomond Expedition** against Clan MacGregor. Sir Humphrey Colquhoun died in 1718 and the baronetcy passed to James, as Sir James Colquhoun of Luss. He only held this title and lands for one year. Then his elder brother, Alexander, died in 1719 without an heir and the Grant lands and Chiefship of the Clan passed to James. He immediately resumed the Grant surname and passed the Colquhoun baronetcy to his second son, James.

Moving back up to Strathspey, James Grant became MP for Inverness from 1722 until his death in 1747 and due to this lived much of his time in London. He did, however, succeed in improving his Scottish estates and promoted forestry, planting many non-native trees such as cypress, cedar, laburnum, elm, beech and willow.

James Grant of Grant.

In the 1710's James, like so many others, was nearly ruined by the 'South Sea Bubble' fiasco and suffered significant financial loss. The South Sea Company was a British Company formed in 1711 as a public-private partnership to consolidate and reduce the cost of the national debt. It was granted a monopoly to supply African slaves to the islands of the Southern Seas (Pacific) and South America. But at the time Britain was involved in the war of the Spanish Succession and Spain and Portugal controlled most of South America. There was therefore no prospect for trade to take place and the company never realised any profit from this monopoly. The Company's stock price collapsed in 1720 which ruined thousands of investors.

In 1725, six Independent Highland Companies were formed to support the Government and one of these came from Clan Grant, This companies eventually were formed into the 'Black Watch'.

James's eldest son, Ludovick Grant purchased the Glenmoriston estate in December 1730. He then conveyed the estate, not to Iain a' Chragain, who was still under attainder, but to his eldest son, John Grant. Iain a' Chragain survived until 30 November 1736.

CHAPTER 12. 1745: A DIVIDED CLAN AGAIN.

In March 1744 war was declared between France and Great Britain. The chances of a successful Jacobite rising, supported by the French, now increased considerably. Many of the Jacobite leaning Clan Chiefs sent messages of support to Prince Charles, the eldest son of the 'Old Pretender', but urged him not to come unless he was attended by a large French army and a chest of coins. "In response Charles apparently said, 'that he would try every method to procure troops, but should that fail he would, nevertheless pay us a visit."(195)

On the 23 July 1745, Prince Charles Edward Stewart, landed on the island of Eriskay, a MacDonald of Clanranald island, between Barra (to the south) and South Uist (to the north) intent on leading the rebellion he thought would restore his father to the British throne. The majority of Highland Chiefs were totally dismayed by his landing with only 7 men, famously known as the 'seven men of Moidart'. From here he wrote to all the Clan Chiefs asking them for support. But the Clan Chiefs had anticipated Charles landing with thousands of French troops, weapons and gold to 'persuade' the Jacobite sympathisers to rebel. Many of the leaders refused to join the rebellion, advising him to go back to France and return when he had the soldiers and the money to succeed. A few, however, like Cameron of Lochiel took the plunge and brought out their Clan in support of the rebellion.

James Chief of Grant was actually at Castle Grant when he heard the news of Bonnie Prince Charlie landing. He quickly left his son and heir, Ludovick in charge of the estates and the Clan and returned to London to help co-ordinate the opposition against the invasion. He advised his son to remain passive unless the Clan was called out together. He feared that the Grant lands would be ravaged by both the Jacobites and the Government forces hunting for food and provisions. Soon after he arrived in London he received a letter from the Prince, as did all the Clan Chiefs. It was delivered to Castle Grant and forwarded by post to his London address. He did not reply to the letter and, indeed, handed it unopened to the Secretary of State for Scotland, the Marquis of Tweeddale. The letter read:

"You cannot be ignorant of my being arrived in this country, and my having set up the Royal Standard, and my firm resolution to stand by those who will stand by me. I refer you to my printed declaration for the rest. On such an occasion, I cannot but expect the concurrence of all those who have the true interest of their country at heart. And I have heard such a character of you as makes me hope to see you among the most forward. By answering these expectations, you *will entitle yourself to that favour and friendship of which I shall be ever ready to give you profit."*(196)

Meanwhile while this was happening Ludovick Grant was busy gathering all the warriors of Clan Grant. "He was able to give King George the support of the whole clan except the Glenmoriston's, who opted out for the Prince."(197) One of his main problems was that, although he could bring nearly a thousand men to the Government cause, because of the Disarming Act of 1725, most of the clans weapons had been given up, except from old swords, battle axes and dirks. "Sir James was strongly opposed to the Government scheme of the Independent Companies, as he considered the best way of utilising the services of the clans loyal to the Government was to summon the whole clan under its Chief, after the usual Highland custom, and engage them in active service... such views were not acceptable to the Government, who much preferred sending the Highlanders in drafts or companies instead of in clans or battalions."(198) It was not until 12 February 1746 that Sir James Grant's offer of his whole clan was accepted by the Government.

The problem was that the Government of King George had little confidence in the loyalty even of those clans who had openly declared for the Hanoverian King. This included the Grants. Ludovick Grant himself, although he said all the right things to the Government was trying to stay as much on the fence as he could just in case the Jacobite Cause was victorious. He continued to urge his clansmen at Glenmoriston and Urquhart to remain at home and not join the Jacobite Army.

On 19 August 1745 Prince Charles journeyed by boat up Loch Shiel to Glenfinnan. "For drama and beauty, however, a better spot could not have been chosen for so auspicious an event. The imposing mountains rising up on three sides of the loch dwarfed the men as they clambered on to the shore. But the scale of mountains, accompanied by the eerie silence, simply emphasised the fact that no one else was there. It was now a matter of waiting to see if anyone would arrive."(199)

Glenfinnan was MacDonald land, belonging to Alexander MacDonald of Glenaladale. He was also one of the first to volunteer and was one of the last to give up the cause. The first Clan leader to appear at Glenfinnan and join was young Clanranald with three hundred clansmen. His grandfather had died at Sheriffmuir in 1715 fighting for the Jacobite cause. Soon after three hundred Camerons under Lochiel and three hundred MacDonalds under Alexander MacDonald of Keppoch also arrived. Then Alexander MacDonald of Glencoe soon arrived with 120 MacDonalds and they joined the Keppoch Regiment.

The Prince then raised the standard of his father and the '45 Rebellion had begun. It was simple white square on a red background. By the end of the day the Prince had over 1,400 men at his command, a good start.

The Glenfinnan Monument.

Copyright: WyrdLight.com

In the following days other clans began to come in, including the MacDonalds of Glengarry, Grants of Glenmoriston, under Patrick Grant and the Stewarts of Appin. The MacDonalds of Glengarry constituted one of the largest regiments with around 500 men. It also incorporated a smaller regiment led by Coll MacDonell of Barrisdale, which effectively became the second battalion of the Glengarry Regiment. The Grants of Glenmoriston again joined the ranks of the Glengarry regiment.

There is some uncertainty and confusion in the various histories as to whether the aging 8th Laird of Glenmoriston, Patrick Grant, took personal part in the Jacobite campaign. It is likely that, although he followed the Prince to Edinburgh with his men, he then, due to age, left his men in command of his son and returned home to Glenmoriston. One account states that Patrick Grant, "having made a hasty march to join Charles at the head of his clan, rushed into the Princes presence at Holyrood with unceremonious haste, without having attended to his toilet. The

Prince received him kindly, but not without a hint that a previous interview with the barber might not have been wholly unnecessary. 'it is not beardless boys' answered the displeased chief, 'who are to do your Royal Highnesses turn'. The Chevalier took the rebuke in good part."(200)

The Glen Urquhart Grants were also supportive of the Jacobite cause, mainly in the form of the 'Three Alexanders of Urquhart', Alexander Grant of Corrimony, Alexander Grant of Shewglie and Alexander MacKay of Achmonie. Of these Shewglie was the oldest and the wisest. It was he who in his youth killed Gille Dubh in revenge for the slaughter of his father. "Ludovick Grant described him as 'a man very remarkable for Highland cunning."(201) He had strong Jacobite connections. His father was James Grant who had fought for King James at Killiecrankie, and was slain at Corrimony. His first wife was a daughter of 'The Chisholm'; his second, a daughter of Iain a Chragain, and grand-daughter of Sir Ewan of Lochiel. One of his daughters was married to Cameron of Clunes, another staunch Jacobite. As soon as the Prince had landed in Scotland James Grant sent him a message of greeting and allegiance. Eventually Ludovick Grant persuaded James Grant of Shewglie to stay at home but two of his sons, Robert and Alexander, joined the Prince with many of their tenants, including Alexander Grant of Easter Inchbrine and Balbeg and his brother James Grant. Alexander would eventually flee to India, where he became Chairman of the East India Company.

Initially the Government and Ludovick Grant only believed a small number of hotheads would join the Prince from the Grants of Urquhart and Glenmoriston but they were woefully incorrect. Whether through loyalty to King James or whether they were coerced, a significant number of men from the two Glens joined the Jacobite Army at some point. In all about 250 men Grants marched south and joined the Jacobite army as it reached Edinburgh.

In terms of old Patrick Grant of Glenmoriston, given the losses his father and grand-father had suffered in their support of the Jacobite cause, it may well have been his prudence which refrained him from taking part in person. He did, however, wish it every success. And it wasn't just the Glenmoriston Grants, "some of the Chief of Grants own men defied their Chief and joined the Jacobites. A number of the sons of William Grant from Glen Cearneach at the foot of the Monadhlaith mountains joined the MacDonald regiment and fought at Culloden. There were at least 3 brothers, Alexander, Daniel and William (the youngest only 13). They survived and were hidden by Patrick Grant, Lord Elchies who afterwards gave them a little croft on the Haugh of Elchies."(202)

General Cope marched north with his Government army of between 3,000 and 4,000 men but he ignored Ludovick's offer of assistance. It may be that the Government did not wholly trust the Grants not to support the Jacobite cause and therefore did not want them rallied as a Clan of over 1,000 warriors. In addition, at this time General Cope did not think he needed the help of the loyal clans, being of the opinion that his professional British soldiers could easily defeat the small number of rebels who had joined Bonnie Prince Charles. Had the Government "at once sought the aid of the loyal clans, or summoned them to arms, accustomed as they were to Highland warfare, the insurgents might have been overawed and the rebellion nipped in the bud."(203) However, many of his men were inexperienced and had never fought a battle before.

At this time Ludovick Grant had other problems. The Grant lands were thought to be under threat from Jacobite clans adjacent them, such as the Duke of Perth at Athole, the Mackintoshes and the MacPhersons. At this time, therefore, he was quite content to retain his clansmen in Strathspey. It was also thought that the Jacobites could march south straight through Strathspey.

General Cope had very bad intelligence, and in September 1745 marched his army all the way to Inverness to find that the Jacobite army had bypassed him and was advancing on Edinburgh. In Inverness, General Cope concluded that the only way to reach Edinburgh first was by sea and he and his troops were loaded onto ships at Aberdeen. They sailed down the east coast and disembarked at Dunbar, south of Edinburgh, on 17 September 1745 but once again he was too late: Bonnie Prince Charlie entered Edinburgh the same day, although Edinburgh Castle remained in Government hands.

The Prince at the Battle of Prestonpans September 1745.

232

General Cope was confident that he could defeat a poorly armed Jacobite army of less than 2,000 men. On hearing of the Government army landing at Dunbar, Prince Charles ordered his force to move east out of Edinburgh on the afternoon of 20 September 1745, to meet the enemy in battle. Prince Charles wanted to attack immediately but George Murray, Duke of Athol, the Commander of the Jacobite Army, was convinced that only an attack against the open left flank of Cope's army stood any chance of victory. Then a local man, Robert Anderson, came forward and agreed to lead the Jacobite's through the marshy ground.

At 4am the entire Jacobite force began to move three abreast along the Riggonhead defile, east of the British position. General Cope was an experienced officer and to prevent being taken by surprise, he posted 200 dragoons [cavalry] and 300 infantry as sentries. These men were able to raise the alarm as the Jacobites approached. This gave Cope time to turn his army round to face the east, where the Jacobites were advancing from. The Highlanders, having successfully crossed the boggy ground, got quickly into their positions and immediately charged before all the Government troops could get into their positions.

The Grants marched in the regiment of the Glengarry MacDonalds on the right wing of the Jacobite army. "Shortly after six o'clock in the morning the Highlanders charged out of the mist, and with the government artillery only able to fire off one round they were quickly in amongst the bewildered and increasingly panic-stricken government soldiers. As Cope's line staggered under the volleys of musket fire, the men had no time to regroup before the highlanders drew their broad swords and charged into the broken ranks, hacking and stabbing. Lochiel Camerons piled into the government left flank, followed by Clan Donald, and the combination of speed and aggression proved too much for infantrymen unused to this kind of combat."(204)

On seeing the charge Cope's inexperienced artillerymen panicked and fled, leaving only the officers to fire the guns. The two dragoon regiments on the flanks also panicked and rode off, leaving their commander, Colonel Gardiner, mortally wounded on the battlefield. This exposed the infantry in the centre which was now attacked on three sides. The Government forces were over run in less than 15 minutes and they fled in a panic. Many of them were trapped by the walls of the park to their rear and were caught and cut down by the advancing Highlanders. British losses amounted to between 300 to 500 killed or wounded and 600 taken prisoner. The Jacobite losses were around 40 dead and 80 wounded. There are no records of any of Clan Grant warriors either killed or wounded in this engagement.

General Cope managed to escape and retreated south reaching Berwick with only 450 men. The Jacobite's captured all the British artillery and ammunition, together with the Army's pay chest with £2,500 inside it.

MAP 17. THE BATTLE OF PRESTONPANS 1745.

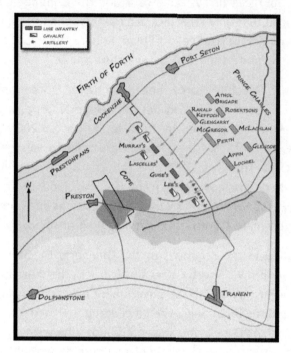

On 22 September 1745 the victorious Jacobite army re-entered Edinburgh with pipers playing and drums beating. With them were the spoils of war: the prisoners, the captured guns and the captured colours [flags]. However, Prince Charles forbade victory celebrations, keen to show that he had only reluctantly killed his father's subjects.

The Prince was keen to quickly advance into England and 'liberate' it for his father. However, the Highland Chiefs were more cautious and wanted to wait until the expected French invasion in Southern England led by Charles' brother, Henry, had taken place.

After this many of the Highlanders started to drift away from the Army, heading home with their spoils of war for the winter. Eventually the army was down to around 1,400 men. "After the battle the bulk of the Glenmoriston men, returned to their homes, but about a hundred, along with twenty men of Urquhart, followed the Prince into England."(205) These men would take part in the Battles of Clifton, Falkirk and Culloden.

Meanwhile in England, after the defeat at Prestonpans the British Government and monarchy were now taking the rebellion very seriously. Experienced regiments who were fighting in Flanders (Belgium) were brought back and King George had the royal yacht moored up the Thames at the Tower of London, where he packed all his personal belongings, just in case he had to flee quickly. Three separate British armies were formed to protect England against the Jacobite invasion and a new verse was added to the National Anthem:

'God grant that Marshal Wade

May by Thy mighty-aid

Victory bring;

May he sedition hush,

And, like a torrent, rush

Rebellious Scots to crush.

God save the King'.

After Prestonpans, Prince Charles sent young Glengarry north to get those clans who had still not 'come out' for the Jacobite Cause, to now support it. The three Alexanders of Urquhart now wanted to know if the Laird of Grant would now call Clan Grant to officially join the rebellion. They sent MacKay of Achmonie to Castle Grant but the wary young Laird was still sitting on the fence and he did not know what side would win. Officially he remained on the side of the Government. He reiterated that the men of Urquhart who had not already joined the rebellion, to remain peaceably at home. Any who disobeyed him would get no help from in the future. He then ordered all the tenants and people of Urquhart to come to Speyside where they would be protected in the heartland of Clan Grant.

The Baillie of Urquhart did so on 8 October 1745 but only about 60 or 70 tenants agreed to go, most wanting to remain and protect their property and cattle. They reached as far as Drumbuie where they were confronted by Glengarry, accompanied by Grant of Shewglie, Corrimony and Achmonie. Glengarry and Shewglie ordered them to return home and advised that the Jacobites would not raid their lands.

Lord Loudoun then reached Inverness with his regiment on 11 October 1746. After this Ludovick knew the Rebellion was likely to fail and he jumped off the fence and wholeheartedly joined the Government side. He also knew that thousands of Government troops were being brought back from the War on the Continent to defeat the Jacobites. But the three Alexanders of Urquhart did the opposite and Alexander Grant of Corrimony wrote to Ludovick on 14 October advising that they were going to join the Jacobite cause and take as many of his Urquhart tenants who he could persuade to go. Around 50 or 60 Grants and other men of Urquhart marched to Perth to join the Jacobites.

Strathspey was exposed to attack by the Jacobite clans who were all around the Grant lands. "Nevertheless Ludovick had the hills and passes patrolled, and guides ready to assist the government troops.

When Ludovick heard of Alexander Grant of Corrimony's decision to join the rebellion he became concerned that this pressure would 'persuade' more of his clansmen at Urquhart, so he mustered 600 men and marched to assist them, but as he approached Inverness on route, he was advised by James Grant of Dell, that the rebels had marched away north, and that his Glen Urquhart men had remained at home (apart from the 60 with Grant of Corrimony). He then returned home to Speyside and disbanded most of his men. At the time the Government Commander, Lord Loudoun, did not know who Ludovick Grant was marching in support of: the Government or the Jacobites.

Meanwhile, on the 31 October 1745, the Jacobite army eventually left Edinburgh and headed south to invade England and crossed the River Esk into England on 8 November 1745. The Jacobite army was only 5,000 strong compared to 30,000 in the combined British armies. The Jacobite leaders were counting on the English public rallying to the Stuart cause and a French invasion on the south coast. Neither of these events happened.

On 15 November the City of Carlisle surrendered and 5 days later the Jacobite army again marched further south. Against them General Wade was marching slowly from Newcastle with 9,000 men. The Duke of Cumberland was camped in Staffordshire with 10,000 men and another army of over 10,000 men was mustering at Finchley to protect London. Despite being outnumbered 6 to 1, the Jacobite army continued its march south.

While all this was happening up in England, Ludovick Grant was eventually ordered by the Earl of Loudoun and Lord Forbes to raise a 'Fencible' company for the

Government. By November 1745, Ludovick sent his company to join Loudoun in Inverness, under the command of his uncle, Major George Grant. Loudoun wrote to Ludovick praising him for his men's clothing, arms and general appearance. Loudoun put Major Grant in command of the Castle of Inverness (later to become Fort George). The Chief of Grant was annoyed that he had only been asked to raise one company while others, like the MacLeods, had been asked to raise four. However, he was soon pressed to raise a second company of 100 men and officers. His Lairds were particularly put out that the Grants had only been asked to raise significantly less men than the MacLeods. They were for not raising any more men and letting the Government fight without the Grants. However, the Laird of Gant persuaded them to remain on the Government side. Grant of Rothiemurchas arrived in Inverness on 3 November 1745 and was immediately told to join the Grant garrison at the Castle of Inverness.

Meanwhile a large part of Loudoun's Army marched from Inverness down Loch Ness to Fort Augustus to relieve the district from Jacobites. At the same time, Lord Findlater asked Ludovick for assistance as his estate was being harassed by the enemy. Ludovick quickly raised around 600 Grants and marched to Mulben, 4 miles from the town of Keith. The rebels only had about 300 men and they quickly withdrew to Fochabers, under the Command of Lord Lewis Gordon. 100 Grants were then sent off to Boat of Bridge, to guard this crossing of the River Spey against the rebels.

Then on 15 December 1745 Ludovick marched his men to Fochabers. "The rebels retired, but word was received that a small party was at Cullen House. A Grant party was despatched to Cullen, and Ludovick went to billet in Keith. It is of interest to note that there are grooves in the stonework of a little old bridge over the Cullen Burn below Cullen House, now known as 'Charlie's Bridge', which it is said were made by the rebels sharpening their swords on the balustrade."(206)

Then 4 Companies of MacLeods men linked up with the Grants at Cullen. Ludovick then moved up to Strathbogie and the rebels retired to Aberdeen. At Strathbogie Ludovick posted notices saying that any rebels surrendering and giving up their arms would be treated well and those who did not would be treated as traitors. There is no record of any rebels surrendering. "Here he received a letter from Lord Loudoun tacitly rebuking him for making this expedition, and intimating that it was impossible to take Mr Grants clan into the Government pay. Much against his will Ludovick was thus compelled to return to Castle Grant, leaving, however, a party of sixty men to protect the district. The folly of the Government was demonstrated when Lord Lewis Gordon, taking advantage of the withdrawal of the Grants, surprised and defeated MacLeod on 23rd December at the **Battle of Inverurie**. It was a relatively small battle with 12 MacLeods killed and 50 taken prisoner. The detachment of Grants left behind covered MacLeods retreat."(207) They secured the Spey Crossing at Boat of Bridge again and the remnants of the MacLeods escaped back to Inverness.

MAP 18. MAIN BATTLES OF THE 1745 REBELLION.

MAIN BATTLES OF THE 1745 REBELLION

Ludovick thought he might be attacked in his own lands by the Rebels from Perth, Aberdeen or Strathbogie. Loudoun remained inactive in Inverness and he would not give the Grants any weapons. Ludovick wrote to Loudoun in early January 1746 asking for arms and men to support him in defending his lands from the approach of the rebels from the South. He further added that if he was given sufficient arms he could take up the offensive himself and take back much of the North East for the Government. Loudoun replied that he awaited instructions from 'higher authority' and that he was afraid of the rebels getting possession of the fords but he offered the Grants nothing.

Back to the rebellion in the South. So far, very few Englishmen had joined their cause. The Jacobite army eventually reached Manchester, where they had high hopes of recruiting large numbers to their cause. Although the Prince was cheered as he entered the city, he was greatly disappointed by the number of recruits. He had expected 1,500 to join but only got 250.

After this recruitment failure many of the Jacobite leaders wanted to return to Scotland. However, the Prince had received a letter from his brother, assuring him that the planned French invasion would commence on 20 December 1745. With this news the Jacobite army continued its march South and on 4 December 1745 reached the City of Derby, 150 miles from London.

However, by this time many of the Jacobite leaders believed the promised French invasion would never happen. They called a Council of War, where the Commander Murray, Earl of Athol, passionately argued for a retreat to Scotland, where the main Jacobite strength lay. Eventually, Prince Charles had to accept his argument and angrily agreed to turn the army around. On the 6 December 1745 the army began its retreat North, everyone dejected and sullen as they marched.

It was chased all the way back by the army of the Duke of Cumberland. By now, however, even Scotland was not a safe haven for the Jacobites. The Government supporting Lords, who had been so shocked and out manoeuvred by the Jacobites at the beginning of the rebellion, had now got their act together and strong forces had been assembled from the Campbells, Munros and men of Southwest Scotland who all remained loyal to the Government. This was in addition to the 1,000 men of Clan Grant under Ludovick and the forces of MacLeod of Dunvegan, MacDonald of Sleat and the Campbell forces of Lord Loudon who were all based in or around Inverness.

On the Jacobite retreat the remaining rebel Grants fought in the **Battle of Clifton**, which is said to be the last battle fought on English soil. Clifton is located south of Penrith and was on the route of the march back to Scotland for the Jacobite army. On the 18 December 1745 Lord George Murray's rear-guard got news that the Duke of Cumberland, ahead of his main force, was fast approaching with 4,000 cavalry to attack the rear of the Jacobite Army. Murray hastily formed his rear-guard troops at the village of Clifton, in a bid to halt them. The MacDonalds of Glengarry with their 120 Grants were part of this force. In all the Jacobite force numbered about 1,000.

"The opening rounds were sparked in the early light when the men of the Glengarry regiment and John Roy Stuart's Edinburgh Regiment noticed horsemen on the summit of Thrimby Hill, about halfway between Shap and Penrith, as they accompanied the wagon train out of Shap village. They could also hear 'a prodigious number of trumpets and kettledrums, suggesting the presence of a large government force. Without further ado the Glengarry men threw off their plaids and rushed up the hillside, where a short and sharp fight took place with some three hundred troops of Bland's and the Georgia Rangers before the government force promptly broke off the engagement, leaving behind a substantial assortment of trumpets and drums. One government soldier was taken prisoner but he did not survive, having been cut down by the Glengarry men."(208)

In the skirmish only 12 Jacobite's had been killed (one Grant) but the Government forces lost about 100 killed or wounded. A skeleton, wearing tartan, was found at Stanhope, near Clifton, in the 1920's and is believed to have been one of the Jacobite casualties. The fight was not a large engagement but it did have the effect of halting the Duke of Cumberland's advance and the main Jacobite army was able to retreat largely unmolested.

On re-entering Scotland, the Jacobite army marched through the Lowlands and Central Scotland experiencing rejection from town after town. No-one wanted to support an army in retreat. They soon decided to head north to their highland strongholds to hopefully gather more recruits.

After the Jacobite army's retreat to Glasgow a second Jacobite force began to gather in Perth. The Earl of Cromartie, his son John MacKenzie, Lord MacLeod, and their clansmen, were joined by other reinforcements such as MacDonald of Barrisdale, young Glengarry, and Simon Fraser, Master of Lovat. This new force amounted to around 4,000 men.

With these reinforcements the Prince had the option of taking his now expanded army to march to Edinburgh and recapture the capital city, "which would have the effect of forcing a battle with the British army, something the Prince was not keen to do just yet. He still hoped that a return to England was imminent, as soon as there was a report of his brother landing in the south-east."(209) He therefore decided to besiege and re-capture Stirling Castle and marched there, where he was joined by the new recruits from Perth in early January 1746. All these new recruits helped swell the ranks of the Jacobite Army from the 4,000, which had invaded England, to 8,000.

John Mackenzie's, the son of Lord Fortrose, account of the rebellion shows great maturity for an 18 year old,"...... *some people are of the opinion that the Court of France never intended an invasion in favour of the Stuart family, but that their only design, with all the noise they then made, was to alarm the Court at London, so as to make them withdraw the British troops from the Austrian Netherlands, by which means they hoped to meet with less opposition in the measures they were then pursuing on the continent for humbling the house of Austria"*.(210)

While besieging Stirling the Jacobite's got news that a large British army was marching to meet them. At hearing this, plans were drawn up to fight a battle in and around Stirling. However, as these plans were being drawn up, a Council of Clan Chiefs was held secretly from the Prince on 29 January 1746. The Chiefs who attended were very concerned about the number of desertions in all the regiments and clans, by men who had been fighting and marching for months, and now, on the edge of the Highlands, just wanted to go home. The desertion rate was getting higher each day.

They concluded that the Jacobite army was not in a fit condition to fight the professional British Army which was now marching north and that the siege of Stirling Castle was futile and would take weeks, if not months, to be successful. They wrote a petition to Prince Charles, recommending that the army should 'retire' north to the Highlands and spend the winter and recoup their strength and numbers. By spring 1746, they ventured, an army of ten thousand Highlanders would be ready to follow the Prince wherever he wished to go.

However, before the Prince could consider the petition (which he would have likely rejected) the British General, John Huske, advanced on Stirling with about four thousand men. His overall commander, General Hawley, was to follow with an additional three thousand troops. General Huske reached Falkirk, only a few miles from Bannockburn, on 15 January 1746 and camped his force there. The Jacobites rallied all their men who could be spared from the siege and marched south to meet them. This was to lead to the last Jacobite triumph in battle and witnessed the last successful 'Highland Charge'.

On the 17 January 1746 the two armies faced each other at the **Battle of Falkirk Muir**. The two armies were roughly similar in size, about 4,000 men. The weather was terrible, a mix between rain, hail and snow. This worked in favour of the Jacobites as the horses of the Government Dragoons churned up the ground to slow the infantry and rain soaked the powder of many of the Government troop's muskets. Later, when battle commenced, one in four of their muskets failed to fire.

On the Government side the dragoons (cavalry) took the left flank, opposite a bog, and then 6 infantry battalions deployed to their right. The remaining 5 battalions formed a second line. Behind them stood the Campbell Argyll Militia. The Government reserve force was the Glasgow Militia, not thought experienced enough to get near the front line.

Facing them was the Jacobite front line consisting entirely of Highland regiments. The Jacobite right wing consisted of the MacDonalds (including the small contingent of rebel Grants), MacLeods of Raasay and the Athol Brigade. The small Jacobite cavalry was in the rear.

The battle did not start until 4pm and it must have been nearly dark. The Government Dragoons attacked the MacDonalds and Grants, thinking that a cavalry charge would spread havoc in their ranks. It did not, the Highlanders waited until they were within yards of them before they let off a single volley of musket and pistol fire. The Dragoons were cut down in droves and those who survived fled in disarray. In their attempt to flee they cut through their own infantry and chaos ensued.

MAP 19. BATTLE OF FALKIRK. JANUARY 1746.

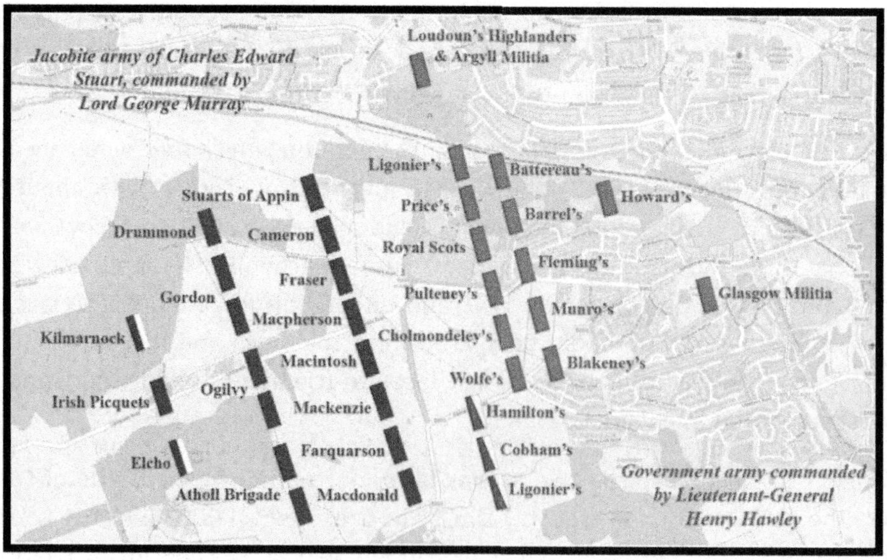

Copyright: Neil Ritchie/OpenstreetMap Contributions.

At this the entire front line of the Jacobite's charged, the MacDonalds and Grants first of all, and the bewildered Government troops turned and fled at the site of the Highlanders descending on them with pistol, claymore and targe. The clansmen then continued to chase the fleeing troops, instead of regrouping and attacking the remaining Government force from the flank. If the MacDonalds and Grants had been disciplined it could have been an even more decisive victory.

The Stewarts of Appin, who held the left flank of the Jacobite line, had the hardest time. There was a ravine between them and their enemy which slowed their charge, allowing the enemy to fire more into their ranks before they too broke and fled. It looked like a rout but the British infantry on the right wing held fast, "by our front rank's kneeling, and the centre and rear ranks firing continually upon them."(211)

But with the collapse of the British left wing the battle was over and the rout began. The Jacobites chased the Government troops and this was where most of the killing occurred. Their Highland charge was a total success. The Jacobites lost fifty dead and eighty wounded. Most of these dead came from the Frasers, Stewarts and Camerons. Robert Grant, son of the Laird of Shewglie was one of the casualties, killed by a musket ball through the heart. A further three Grants may have been killed and up to twenty others were wounded. The Government force lost around three hundred men dead, wounded or missing. Many of the British officers were killed in the battle, including Sir Robert Munro of Munro and his brother Duncan Munro, who was an army doctor. The Earl of Cromartie ordered that at least twenty of the slain officers be buried in Falkirk Churchyard and he and all the other Jacobite Chief's attended their funeral. This was the last victory for the Jacobite army. General Hawley escaped with the remnants of his army back to Linlithgow.

Immediately after the battle, instead of consolidating their position, many of the Jacobite leaders fell out and Prince Charles himself fell ill and retired to Bannockburn. The Duke of Cumberland soon arrived in Edinburgh with fresh, experienced troops. Eventually the Jacobite commanders agreed that their position in Central Scotland was undefendable and they agreed to retire north to the vastness of the Highlands where they thought they would be safe for the rest of the winter.

Although the Jacobite army had won the battle, many of the Scottish leaders were furious that they had not completely destroyed the Government forces pitted against them. They blamed the Prince's 'foreign advisors', mainly the Irishmen. "Lord MacLeod stated after the battle, he found Charles 'in a little hut on the top of the hill. Where he was sitting by the fireside' in the company of Sir Thomas Sheridan and Colonel O'Sullivan. He also observes, *'had our army been disciplin'd or', more damningly 'had we been commanded by experienced generals, I am fully convinc'd that we would have cut the King's army to pieces."*(212)

The victory was further marred by the accidental shooting of Angus Og MacDonell of Glengarry by a Clanranald MacDonald. He was the overall commander of the rebel Grants, who now lost both their commander and their Clan commander, Robert Grant. This was a severe blow to the morale of not just the Glengarry Regiment but also those of Keppoch and Clanranald. "A private soldier of the Clanranald regiment had obtained a musket as part of his spoil upon the field of battle. Finding it loaded he was engaged at his lodgings in extracting the shot; the door was open, and nearly opposite there was a group of officers standing in the street. The man extracted the ball, and then fired off the piece, to clear it in the most expeditious manner of the powder; but unfortunately it had been double loaded, and the remaining ball pierced the body of young Glengarry, who was one of the group of bystanders. He afterwards died in the arms of his clansmen, begging with his last breath that the man, of whose innocence he was satisfied, might not suffer; but nothing could restrain the indignation of his friends, who immediately seized the man, and demanded life for life."(213)

Ranald MacDonald of Clanranald was in a difficult position, as he knew that he could not protect his clansmen without starting a feud with his Glengarry kinsmen. He reluctantly handed the man over and the unfortunate man was put in front of a firing squad and shot. The poor man's own father took part in the firing squad, and put a shot into his heart, in his desire to make the death of his son as instantaneous as possible. The execution led to many of the Clanranald clansmen deserting the Jacobite army. Angus MacDonell of Glengarry was buried at Falkirk Church. After this the Jacobite army continued their retreat north.

Back in the North, after the Battle of Falkirk, General Loudoun wrote to Ludovick Grant advising that the rebels were marching north, and asked him to send out scouts to report on their movements and hold his clan ready for action".(214) The Grants were still short of weapons as was Loudoun in his base at Inverness. The information at the time suggested a large part of the Jacobite Army would march through Strathspey and ravage the land of the Grants. Ludovick continually sent letters advising that his men were ready and well armed, hoping that the rebels would obtain this information and then bypass his lands. This strategy was largely successful and the lands of the Grants were relatively untouched by the Jacobites. In reality Ludovick was continually asking for more arms and ammunition.

Meanwhile, the main Jacobite Army had reached Inverness and chased the Government defenders from the city. The Government troops retreated to the Black Isle. In February 1746 the Jacobites besieged Inverness Castle (Fort George), which was commanded by Major George Grant. With him were the Independent Company of Grants, one company of MacLeods and 80 regular soldiers to defend Fort George. They only withstood the siege for two days before surrendering on 25 February 1746. Some of the Grants who surrendered then agreed to join the Jacobite Army. After the battle of Culloden, the Duke of Cumberland wrote that "he had also arrested Major Grant, the Governor of Fort George, while enquiries were made as to how the fort was allowed to surrender, 'and as I fear He will not have any good ones to give, I shall order a Court Martial for his trial'. He was found guilty of dereliction of his duty and dismissed from the army. A new Fort George was constructed on a promontory jutting out into the Moray Firth, 8 miles from Culloden, and is still in operation today.

After this the Urquhart men in the rebel army were allowed home on leave for a few days and when they got their they told of their great experiences in England, of their bravery at Clifton and Falkirk, notwithstanding the loss of their leader at Falkirk, Robert Grant, son of Shewglie and the accidental death of Angus of Glengarry after the battle. Some of those who had fought at Prestonpans but returned home afterwards decided to return to the Jacobite army again, and fought with the Glengarry regiment. They took part in the pursuit of Lord Loudoun and the Lord President Forbes into Ross and Sutherland. They returned to fight, and many of them to die, on the Moor of Culloden. These men were commanded by the elderly Alexander Grant of Shewglie, with his remaining sons Patrick and Alexander, and by Grant of Corrimony and Mackay of Achmonie.

Meanwhile on the Government side, on 16 March Ludovick Grant and his clansmen assaulted and took Forbes Castle with only 140 men. The Jacobites sent out a large force to retake it but as the Castle was strong and they had no artillery the siege was quickly abandoned and the Grants remained in control of the fortress.

The Jacobites did capture Castle Grant but they knew they were not in a position to defend it and soon departed, leaving the Castle largely intact.

The Duke of Cumberland then took command of the Government forces in Scotland. As he and his army advanced north, the Jacobite Commanders sent out word to recall all the Highlanders, many of whom had gone home.

"He [Cumberland] asked Ludovick to raise his clan, and was informed 600 men could be raised in addition to those already under arms, if an adequate supply of weapons could be given. Ludovick gathered his clan at Castle Grant to be ready for action against a reported force of Jacobites who were supposedly marching on Strathspey. The Duke was at Perth on 24 February and was marching to Aberdeen, so Ludovick with his wife and family and 150 men marched towards Aberdeen, as Castle Grant was deemed indefensible. He awaited the Dukes orders at Inverurie, where he remained for some days, owing to heavy snow and then took possession of Castle Forbes. Meanwhile, Castle Grant had surrendered to Lord George Murray and Lord Nairn, who soon vacated it."(215) The Grants then marched onto Cullen where they joined the Duke of Cumberland's army and then proceeded to Elgin with the Government Army. Meanwhile the Jacobites captured Grant of Rothiemurchas and Grant of Dellachapple. They tried to persuade these men to join the Jacobite cause. Although they were unsuccessful they did get these two lairds to sign letters of neutrality.

Colonel James Grant was the Chief Engineer in the Jacobite army. He was mysteriously absent at the siege of Stirling which was a total disaster. He accompanied the attacking party which besieged Fort Augustus on 3 March 1746. "After some well-aimed shelling, which set fire to the powder magazine and eventually blew a breach in the outer wall, Major Wentworth surrendered on 5th[March]".(216)

The Jacobites then went on to besiege Fort William. "Colonel Grant began raising the batteries on 20 March and proceeded to pound the fort for over a week, during which he was injured. The Comte de Mirabel took over and succeeded no better .... than he had done at Stirling."(217) The siege was finally lifted when Bonnie Prince Charlie hurriedly tried to recall his forces which was spread all over the highlands, when it became clear that the Duke of Cumberland's army was advancing on Inverness, the Jacobite headquarters.

On Cumberland's orders Ludovick Grant attempted to recapture Castle Grant but when he reached Ballindalloch he was confronted by a strong force of Jacobites and had to return to Strathbogie, where he remained until 10 April when he re-joined the Dukes Army at Cullen. Ludovick and his men were then sent out on

Scouting missions and to look for Jacobite stragglers and did not take part in the Battle of Culloden on 16 April 1746.

The only Highlanders that Cumberland used at the Battle of Culloden were the Campbells, hated by most of the Jacobite Clans. It is fairly certain that the Duke did not trust either the loyal Grants or other Highland Clans to fight against their kinsmen and decided to defeat the rebels with only his professional troops.

The Jacobites waited at Inverness for the approach of the Duke of Cumberland's professional army marching up the east coast of Scotland. Initially the two armies were roughly evenly matched in terms of numbers with the Government force numbering around 8,000 and the Jacobites 7000. But not long after taking Inverness almost 1500 of the Jacobites marched north to harass the force of Lord Forbes and other Government supporting clans in Ross-shire.

Cumberland's army consisted of 16 infantry divisions, four of which were Scottish and one Irish. Many of them were experienced veterans of the Continental War. They were also better equipped, better supplied and better fed than the Jacobites who, by the middle of April 1746, were almost starving from lack of provisions. The Government force also had more and larger cannon than the Jacobite force.

On 14 April, Cumberland's Army had occupied the town of Nairn, only 16 miles from Inverness. The Jacobite leadership decided to try and surprise the Government forces by a night attack and on the evening of 15 April a large part of the army started on a night march to Nairn. The Grants in the Glengarry Regiment accompanied the night march to Nairn, all but Shewglie, who on account of his great age, returned to Inverness.

The objective of the march was to fall upon the Duke of Cumberland's Army in the dead of night, surprise them and rout the entire force. By this time, however, most troops had not been fed for days and, tired and exhausted, they could not reach Nairn before dawn. The eventually turned around and headed back to towards Inverness. They returned even more exhausted and hungry.

The Duke of Cumberland's army rose early on the 16 April 1746, well rested and well fed and began its march to Culloden Moor where the Jacobite army was positioned. It was a cold, wet and windy day. As they approached Culloden Moor the alarm was sounded and the tired, wet and hungry Jacobite's were summoned to their battles formations. The remaining Jacobite's were beset with division.

The majority of the rebel Scottish Lords wanted to retire and wait for their reinforcements before giving battle. The Prince's Irish and French advisors wanted to give battle and the Prince finally came out on their side. Battle it would be.

The Highlanders were even divided amongst themselves. The MacDonalds were upset that they had been allocated on the left, rather than the right which they thought was their ancient prerogative. The Prince had granted the right flank to Lord George Murray and his Atholmen. After a bitter argument the MacDonalds grudgingly accepted the left flank. "According to the commander of Glengarry's [regiment], when Charles gave the right to Lord George, 'Clanranald, Keppoch and I .... begg'd he would allow us our former right, but he entreated us for his sake we would not dispute it, as he had already been agreed to give it to Lord George and his Atholmen; and I heard H.R.H. say that he resented it much, and should never do the like again if he had occasion for it'."(218)

The total Jacobite force on that day amounted to around 5000 men. The Government forces arrived about midday and formed up in three lines with the dragoons (cavalry) put in the flanks. They had approximately 8000 men. Then they brought up their considerable cannon. The two armies faced each other about three hundred yards apart. It was clear to most of the Jacobite officers that Culloden Moor, with its bogs and exposed terrain, was no place to take on the disciplined modern forces of the professional British Army.

The Boggy Ground of Culloden Moor.

Eileen Sinclair 2020

"The MacDonald's, in strong resentment for having been placed on the left instead of the right of Charles Edward, refused to charge when ordered by their commander. Keppoch, uttering the touching exclamation, *'My God! That I should live to be deserted by my own children!, then charged,* "(219) On hearing this the MacDonalds immediately charged, Alexander of Keppoch at the lead, with a pistol in one hand and a drawn sword in the other. "He had got but a little way, from his regiment, when a musket shot brought him to the ground, and a clansmen of more than ordinary devotedness [later identified as his cousin, John Mackenzie], who followed him, and with tears and prayers conjured him not to throw his life away, raised him, with the cheering assurance that his wound was not mortal, and that he might still quit the field with life. Keppoch desired his faithful follower to take care of himself, and again rushing forward, received another shot, and fell to rise no more."(220)

Even with their Chief dead, his clan would not desert him. A young Keppoch warrior had been mortally wounded close to where Alexander lay. His father found him and proceeded to carry him from the field of battle. They passed the body of their Chief, and the dying young man implored his father to let him die here and save the body of their Chief from the 'insults of Cumberland's soldiers'. The father obeyed his son's last request and he carried Keppoch off the field. He took him to a hut some distance from the battlefield, where other wounded and dying men were taking refuge. The hut was soon surrounded by Government soldiers and set on fire on the orders of Cumberland himself. Everyone in it was burned alive, including the body of Keppoch.

Meanwhile, prior to the charge of Keppoch the two forces faced each other and the Government force opened up with their cannon. The inadequate Jacobite artillery could do very little in response. The cannon fire tore through the Jacobite ranks killing hundreds.

Prince Charles expected Cumberland to charge but he just continued to bombard the Highlanders. Eventually Prince Charles, unable to bare the carnage which was being inflicted on his troops ordered his army to charge. As the Highlanders charged the government artillery changed to 'canister' shells, designed specifically to rip through lines of charging men.

During the battle the left wing of the Jacobite Army, where the majority of Clan Donald and the Grants of Glenmoriston and Urquhart were located, charged three times but each time the charge quickly dissipated as the warriors were soon up to their knees in boggy marsh. Jacobite casualties here were mainly from musket fire from the Government troops positioned directly across the bog from them. It was this musket fire which had killed Keppoch. Being on the left "... condemned them to a 600 yard run over rough ground and totally exposed them to enemy fire. Furthermore a number of Clanranalds had left in protest at the execution of one of their number who had accidentally killed Glengarry at Falkirk."(221)

MAP 20. BATTLE OF CULLODEN MOOR. APRIL 1746.

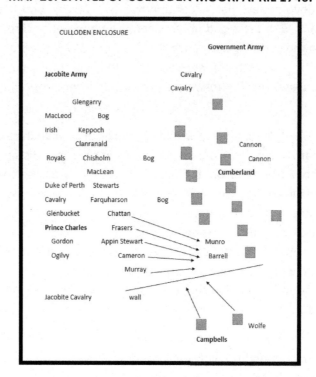

It was during these charges that 30 Grants were killed by the musket fire from the Government troops. Any who were wounded and could not be taken from the battlefield were bayonetted by the victorious Cumberland troops.

By contrast, the right flank of the Jacobite army advanced towards the Government troops on the only solid ground within the whole battlefield. The Athol Brigade, Locheil and the Appin Stewarts were able to charge towards the British line. However, the Centre, comprising mainly of Clan Mackintosh and Lovat Frasers, hampered by the boggy ground, began to swerve to the right.

All these men got entangled in a single mass as they converged on the Government forces. Canister was fired into them and hundreds again were killed before they reached the enemy. Then just as the Highlanders were close to the Government troops, they let off a volley of musket fire from point blank range, causing carnage in the Jacobite ranks.

Despite this, hundreds of Jacobites slammed into the Government ranks, but they could only break through the first ranks and the troops of the second and third ranks held their ground and the last 'Highland Charge' faltered. By the time reinforcements were brought up the Jacobites were in full retreat, unable to breach the solid ranks of the experienced Government troops. The battle was lost.

Once the MacDonalds and the Grants, still trying to advance over the boggy ground under fire, saw the Atholmen, Camerons and Appin Stewarts fall back, and with most of their leaders killed or wounded, they followed suit.

As the rout began the Frasers, Chisholms and Grants fled towards Inverness, heading for the north of Loch Ness. They were pursued by the Duke of Kingston's Light Horse, who slaughtered as they went, including some of the innocent townspeople who had come to watch the battle.

James Grant, cousin of Shewglie, made his way terribly wounded, to his aunt's house at Cradlehall, where he died in a few hours. He was buried in the Cradlehall garden. His brother, Alexander Grant, had been wounded in the head, but managed to escape. He also saved Somerled Dubh MacDonald by severing a troopers arm which was raised to strike him. During his and MacDonald's escape, as they were fording the Ness, William MacMillan was about to be struck down by a trooper, when Grant stole behind him and with one stroke of his sword brought horse and rider into the water. As the trooper floundered in the water, Grant's next strike took off the troopers head.

Alexander Grant of Corriemony, suffered two severe wounds but was carried off safely from the battleground. He then found shelter in the Cave of Morall. Patrick Grant, Shewglie's son, found refuge in the woods of Lochletter, his brother Alexander fled into exile to India, where he became Chairman of the East India Company.

Before the battle, it had been agreed to retire south to Ruthven Barracks, Kingussie if they were defeated. Many were able to do this but many, such as the Urquhart Grants were cut off from doing this by the Government cavalry. As detailed above they were forced to retire towards Inverness. Many were killed, even fighting in the streets of the Highland capital.

Being separated from the main retreating Jacobite army made them an easy target for Government Dragoons, led by Major-General Humphrey Bland. The order from the Duke of Cumberland was to give 'No Quarter' to the rebels and large numbers of fleeing Jacobites were killed. Indeed, many of those who surrendered were instantly executed.

Jacobite losses are estimated to be between 1,500 men and 2,000 men killed or wounded, many of them in the pursuit after the battle. The Government losses were reported as only 50 killed and 250 wounded, but this is likely to be a gross under reporting. Despite the defeat the Jacobites could still muster around five thousand men and could have continued the rebellion. However, by now Bonny Prince Charlie was exhausted and spent and he ordered the army to disband and disperse.

Two days previous to this some of the Glenmoriston men got the call to return to Inverness too late and never made it in time for the battle. On their way to join the Jacobite Army they met their fleeing comrades on the Moor of Caipleach and hearing the dreadful news, turned about and headed home.

On hearing of the Government victory Ludovick Grant was keen to show his loyalty to the winning side and immediately mobilised his clansmen to head towards Inverness and help mop up the fleeing rebels. On their way to Inverness, "they captured Lord Balmerino [one of the Jacobite leaders] and others. They then searched for Jacobites and arms in Strathnairn and the Mackintosh country, and afterwards in the country north of Inverness, the Aird and the Fraser country. A number of people who had been forced into rebellion were persuaded to surrender at discretion, and were marched under a strong guard to Moy.

The Laird of Grant then marched into Glenmoriston on the 4th May and he ordered those men who had taken part in the rebellion to surrender on the promise that they would then be treated leniently and their lands would be untouched. If they refused he was prepared to burn Glenmoriston to ground.   Sixty-eight Glenmoriston men (most of them Grants) surrendered at Balmacaan, as did sixteen men of Urquhart (also mainly Grants). Ludovick took them personally to Inverness and delivered them into the hands of the Duke of Cumberland, saying "that his Royal Highness might dispose of them as he should think fit. Not one word did he utter by way of intercession."(222)

A Gaelic poem laments his actions:

'O young Laird of Grant,

Great be thy evil reward –

May the cry of the fatherless children

Drive thee from the Heaven of Christ!'.

It is this action which potentially besmudges the reputation of Ludovick, as the Glenmoriston Grants felt betrayed by their Chief who they said had sworn to speak up for them but failed to do so. A harsh sentence was meted out to most of them. Grant of Shewglie, his James and the Minister of Urquhart, the Reverend John Grant, who had petitioned the Duke of Newcastle, were eventually released from their prison ship at Tilbury. The remainder were convicted without trial and shipped off as slaves to Barbados. Their treatment was so bad that by 1749 only 18 of them were left alive, and only 8 ever returned home to Scotland, three of them Grants. Others, such as Ludovick's descendant, Lord Strathspey have an alternative version of events and he wrote that "he passionately interceded on behalf of those Grants from Glenmoriston and Urquhart who had been taken with the rebels. Unfortunately, his intervention was unsuccessful."(223)

The Lairds of Glenmoriston and Corriemony both initially set out to surrender but took warning and turned back. "When Shewglie got into his saddle to accompany Ludovick to Inverness, his mare turned three times 'tuaitheal' - that is, against the sun. His old hen-wife … marked the evil omen and entreated him not to go. He went and never returned. He did, however, persuade his son not to surrender till he saw how he fared and he was spared."(224)

The remaining men and women of Urquhart and Glenmoriston were in grief and despair at the imprisonment of their menfolk "and cursed Ludovick in language which can hardly be uttered."(225) Initially Ludovick Grant was unaware of the offence he had committed in the eyes of is people. In his defence he viewed the behaviour of the rebels as a direct threat to his leadership of the Clan. Not only had they disobeyed his direct orders, their actions had also made the Government suspicious of the loyalty of the whole of Clan Grant.

He wrote to his father soon after the surrender, "…I think old Shewglie is now in a way of repenting all his villainous rebellious schemes, since he was a man in the 1715 and ever since. I have done all I could to get hold of Corrimonie and Achmonie, but have not yet succeeded."(226). However, when he reached London to visit his father he found that he was condemned by many for his dishonourable capture of his own kinsmen. Shewglie and the other 'gentlemen' captives petitioned the Duke of Newcastle. Ludovick then soon changed his stance and eventually pled the case of his imprisoned clansmen. He then wrote to the Duke of Newcastle pleading their case and that he had persuaded them to surrender to save themselves and their farms and hoped they would be treated with clemency.

Shewglie and the Minister were released from prison but only on the condition they remained in London. Shewglie died there, on 29 July 1746, of natural causes brought on by his rough treatment while he was a prisoner. His son was eventually released and permitted to return home.

Despite Patrick Grant of Glenmoriston not being officially 'Out' in the 45' his lands and tenants were treated very badly by the soldiers of the Duke of Cumberland. The worst outrages were committed by Scottish troops mainly from the Lowlands. One of the most infamous was Major Lockhart, who soon after Culloden entered Glenmoriston and committed many acts of inexcusable barbarity, even on innocent highlanders. Riding past two old men and one of their sons working in a field he had all three shot dead. He then demanded that Grant of Dundreggan bring him all his cattle immediately. When, after a short time, he was not convinced that the Grant Laird was assembling his stock quick enough, he had him stripped naked and taken to the nearby gallows. He had the three men he had executed strung up on the gallows and would have hung Grant of Dundreggan but for the intervention of Captain Grant of Lord Loudoun's Regiment. However, his men took all the rings from the fingers of his wife and threatened to cut off the fingers of anywhere the rings could only be removed with difficulty. The British troops then burned their house to the ground after they had looted it and taken all its possessions of any value.

"Lockhart is referred to in the following lines [originally in Gaelic] by a woman he had robbed:

' All my cattle are in England;

they have not left a beast with me on the field;

they have deprived me of the substance of my dower –

and Major Lockhart is the cow-keeper!' "(227)

Soon after this, "the houses of Divach and Clunemore were burnt. An officer by the name of Ogilvie was sent to destroy Corrimony House, but he spared it on account of Corriemony's wife, Jane Ogilvie."(228) Ogilvie was an officer in Kingston's Horse Regiment.

The district of Glenmoriston suffered even more than Urquhart. The Earl of Loudoun, who had escaped to Skye with the Chief of MacLeod when the Jacobites had marched on Inverness, marched back to Inverness after Culloden. "In passing through Glenmoriston the Earl and his companions lodged for a night in Invermoriston House. Next day, according to the testimony of an eye witness, Patrick Grant, tenant of Craskie, they 'burnt it to the ground, destroying at the same time all the ploughs, harrows, and other such like utensils they could find'."(229)

An eye witness later described how much of the furnishings from Invermoriston House were saved from the flames:-

"Among Sir Alexander MacDonald's following there happened to be two MacDonalds who were nephew to the old Lady Glenmoriston, who they pitied much in her then distress, and honestly told her it was not in their power to do her any other service than to take her furniture out of the house and to put it into a hut, which they accordingly did, and then they were obliged to witness the burning of their aunts house to ashes."(230)

The Government troops then did the same all over the Glen. The MacLeods were the main culprits, led by the Chief of MacLeod. Supposedly the Earl of Loudoun was against it but MacLeod thought it would get them into good favour with the Duke of Cumberland.

More was to follow, "maids and matrons were seized and violated under circumstances of gross brutality: The terror-stricken people fled to the mountains, where many of them succumbed to hunger and exposure."(231)

This was not the end of the brutality. In May 1746 the Duke of Cumberland stationed himself at Fort Augustus and all through the summer of 1746 his troops lost their humanity undertaking murder, plundering, rape and burning of land and homes all over Glenmoriston, which was so close to Fort Augustus. Colonel Cornwallis, marching through Glenmoriston with a body of soldiers, observed two men tending their land. He shouted at them to come over to him, but the men, knowing only Gaelic, did not understand him and turned their faces away and continued their work. Cornwallis immediately ordered them shot.

"The following order was issued by the Duke [of Cumberland] on 8th July:- 'There is no meal to be sold to any persons but soldiers, their wives are not allow'd to buy it – if any soldier's wife, or any other persons belonging to the Army, is known to sell or give any meal to any Highlander, or any person of the country, they shall be first whip'd severely for disobeying this order, and then put upon meal and water in the Provost for a fourthnight."(232)

One of the most tragic events in the Glen was the death of Roderick Mackenzie, who had served as one of the Prince's Life Guards during the rebellion. Roderick Mackenzie was about the same age and had a similar appearance to Charles. After splitting up from the Prince, young Roderick fled into the vastness of the Highlands and hid out in Glenmoriston. Thousands of Government troops were scouring the country in search of the Prince. The Government had placed a high price of the Prince's head and all the troops were eager to be the ones to find and capture or kill him. At some point Roderick was cornered by a party of government troops but instead of surrendering, he chose to fight and drew his sword to defend himself. After fending them off for a while he was eventually shot by one of the soldiers and mortally wounded. As he lay dying he exclaimed to the men, '*You have killed your Prince, you have killed your Prince.*' The soldiers were overjoyed at their good fortune. After he died they cut off Roderick's head and took it quickly to Fort Augustus, where the Duke of Cumberland was residing and he was also convinced that it was the head of his cousin, Prince Charles. He immediately sent it to London. This took days and the deception took a long time to be discovered, during which time the hunt for the Prince was called off.

Partly because of these outrages, some men of Glenmoriston refused to surrender and pledged an oath to each other to fight to the death. "These were Patrick Grant of Craskie, John MacDonell, Alexander MacDonald, Alexander, Donald and Hugh Chisholm {all brothers] and Charles MacGregor."(233). These men became known as the **Seven Men of Glenmoriston**. Alexander MacDonald had initially been a soldier in one of the Governments Independent Companies but had deserted to join the Jacobites. Some of the others may also have initially been on the Government side, but all had eventually served in the Jacobite Army. They knew that if they were captured they would be hung as deserters.

During the summer of 1746 they hid out in the mountains and harassed the Government soldiers whenever they could. They "bound themselves by a solemn oath never to surrender themselves or their arms to the English, but to stand by each other to the last drop of their blood."(234) Their main hiding place was Uamh Ruaraidh ne Seilg (the cave of Roderick the Hunter) in Corrie Sgainge. They were so successful that soon no Government troops would enter Glenmoriston without large numbers. In one ambush they shot two soldiers dead and the others fled, leaving their horses for the fugitives to steal. On this occasion they also took a large quantity of whisky and food on which they feasted for five days.

Soon after this incident the Seven Men encountered Robert Grant of Speyside, a known Government scout, at a place called Feith Rob (Robert's Bog) and they shot him through the heart knowing that he would disclose where they were to the Government troops at Fort Augustus. "They cut off his head and fixed it to a tree near the high road at Blairie, where the skull remained well into the next century."(235) Another spy, An Speech Ruadh, or the Red Strathspey man, was also shot by them. They buried him in the hills.

They then heard that cattle belonging to Patrick Grant's uncle had been taken by a party of soldiers who were driving them towards the west coast, by General Wades Road through Glenmoriston. Near the Hill of Lundie, by Loch Cluanie, they prepared to meet the troops. When they arrived they shouted at the British soldiers from their well-prepared positions to give up the cattle. The officer in charge refused and called on them to surrender. They refused and advised they would fight to the death and that a large band of Jacobites was hurrying to meet up with them to kill all the British troops. On hearing this the soldiers drove the cattle onwards and a running battle took place. Eventually a couple of the soldiers were wounded and many of them fled and the officer in charge was required to give up the cattle and one horse in order to escape capture.

Around the same time Bonnie Prince Charlie was being hunted from island to island. With the help of Flora MacDonald and others, he eventually escaped to the mainland and then in July 1746, he came to Glenmoriston to hide with them. At once they constituted themselves into his bodyguard and promised to defend him with their lives. They then took the Prince into the wilds of Coiredho, to a cave now known as 'Uaimh – Phrionns' in remembrance of Charles hiding out there. While hiding out there the Prince called on them to take the following oath: "That all the curses the Scriptures pronounced might fall upon them and their posterity, if they were not faithful to him in greatest dangers, or disclose to man, woman, or child that he was in their keeping, till once he was out of all danger."(236)

Patrick Grant, one of the 7 Men of Glenmoriston

So well did they keep their oath that not one of them spoke of his being with them until over a year after his departure and him reaching safety in France. The Prince called them his first Privy Council since Culloden and he promised he would not forget them and when he came into his own, i.e. when his father became King, they would be greatly rewarded. For three days he rested in the Cave and Patrick Grant went secretly to Fort Augustus and stole food for him, including ginger bread. They then moved to another cave, not wanting to remain in one place for too long. They remained here for four days. The Prince "ate and drank with them as one of themselves, and forbade them to take off their bonnets in his presence."(237)

The Prince stayed with them until 20 August 1746 and after this travelled north west and made his escape by ship to France. Patrick Grant escorted him on this next part of his journey. Hugh Chisholm, who lived until 1812, refused to shake any man by the right hand, advising that his hand had been honoured by the grateful Prince on his parting.

The bulk of the Government troops left Fort Augustus on 12 July 1746 and a month later, Lord Loudoun marched southward, leaving only a small garrison behind. Thereafter, with the exception of the 'blanket raid' in October, the people of

Glenmoriston and Urquhart were left in relative peace. Patrick Grant of Glenmoriston was, however, excluded from the Act of Indemnity but his life was spared. Grant of Corrimony was also allowed to go unpunished for fighting for the Jacobite cause.

Because of the burning of their homes and fields and the stealing of all their cattle, the winter of 1746/47 saw great hardship for the Grants of both Glenmoriston and Urquhart and many died of cold or starvation during this time. Cumberland positively encouraged this by ordering his troops to neither assist the population or even to sell them any food.

Ludovick Grant got little reward from the Government for his services and received no compensation for his outlays or for the raids on his lands by both Jacobite and Government troops. "Early in July his estate of Urquhart was overrun by Kingston's Light Horse, who burnt the house and carried away the horses, cattle, and household effects of the tenants. In October a levy of one hundred blankets was made on Urquhart for the King's troops, and a similar demand of one hundred and fifty blankets was made on the people of Strathspey the following January."(238)

After this all the Militia Fencible Companies, including the Grants, were disbanded and returned home. Ludovick then went to London to resume his MP duties and tried to obtain from the Government compensation for the great expenses that he had incurred. Both he and his father, Sir James Grant, were very short of funds as no rents had been collected during the troubles.

James Grant died in London in 1747, when he was seized by 'gout in the stomach' and was survived by at least 4 sons and 5 daughters. Ludovick then became Clan Chief. His second son, James, became Baron of Luss and took the name Colquhoun. His third son was Francis Grant, born in 1717 who became a Lieutenant General in the British Army and served with distinction. He also bought the estate of Dunphail in Elginshire and was MP for Elgin. He died in 1781. His fourth son, Charles, was born in 1723 and became a Captain in the Royal Navy. Of James Grants daughters:

- Jean born 1705, married William Duff, and later became Baron Braco of Kilbryde, Viscount MacDuff and Earl Fife.
- Ann, 'born in 1711 who married Sir Henry Innes.
- Penuel, born 1719 and married Captain Alexander Grant of Ballindalloch.

Patrick Grant of Craskie (one of the 7 men of Glenmoriston) appears never to have got over the loss of his cattle and destruction of his property in 1746. In 1751 he arrived in Edinburgh in a state of poverty, on his way to the continent to visit the Prince. As Gaelic was his only language, he was persuaded not to proceed any further. In Edinburgh he was taken in by the Minister Robert Forbes who wrote down his tales of the 7 Men of Glenmoriston and published them in 'Lyon in Mourning'. Forbes also had Patrick's portrait taken (see above).

In 1759 Patrick, like so many other Highland warriors, joined the British Army and served for some years in North America. In 1763 he returned to Glenmoriston with a 'Chelsea Pension' and there passed away the remaining days of his life in peace.

Ludovick Grant of Grant, Chief of Clan Grant from 1747 to 1773. He was born in January 1707 and lived to the age of sixty-six. He was the second son of Sir James Grant but became heir when his older brother, Humphrey died. As the second son of James Grant he inherited the titles of Luss initially and like his father took the name Colquhoun.

Sir Ludovick Grant of Grant.

As we have seen he led Clan Grant for the Government against the Jacobite's in the 1745 Rebellion. He married Marion Dalrymple of North Berwick, daughter of the President of the Court of Session, Hew Dalrymple. There must have been a great love between the couple as their marriage was initially opposed by both families but they were eventually persuaded, by the intervention of Patrick Grant, later Lord Elchies. When Patrick Grant's son, the next Lord Elchies, decided to sell Easter Elchies, Sir Ludovick was anxious to purchase it in order to ensure that it remained in the Grant family. "In a letter to his law-agent he wrote that he wished to preserve all the lands lying between the two Craigellachies in the name of Grant. These two rocky eminencies are conspicuous objects in Strathspey. The upper of western Craigellachie forms the dividing boundary between Badenoch and Strathspey, and was the rendezvous for the Grant Clan in time of war. The lower Craigellachie stands at the confluence of the Fiddich with the Spey, and forms the point of contact of the four parishes of Aberlour, Knockando, Rothes and Boharm. The upper Craigellachie is generally supposed to have furnished the crest of the Grant family, which is a mountain in flames. When the chief wished the clan to assemble, fires were kindled on both Craigellachies, hence the name, 'Rock of Alarm'."(239)

Although he was disappointed when the estate was sold to the Earl of Findlater, Easter Elchies eventually reverted back to the Grants on the succession of Sir Ludovick's grandson to the title and estates of Seafield and Findlater in 1811.

Marion died in 1727 just as he was qualifying as an advocate of the Scottish Court. In 1735 he married as his second wife, Margaret Ogilvie, the eldest daughter of the 5th Earl of Findlater and Seafield. The Findlater title could only pass in the male line, but the Seafield title could pass through the female line, and this was why the Earldom of Seafield and its estate came to the Grants and their surname became Ogilvie-Grant of Grant. They also inherited both Boyne Castle and Findlater Castle, on a rocky promontory at Cullen.

His adherence to the Government cause had nearly ruined the wealth of the Chiefs of Grant and he wrote after the 45' rebellion, "the plain consequence is, that the family of Grant has been ruined by the Revolution [the Glorious Revolution] principles, and the present royal family during the rebellions of 1715 and 1745."(240)

On his accession, Ludovick gave up his law practice and applied himself to the management of the Grant estates, although he remained M.P. for Morayshire until 1761. He died at Castle Grant on 18 March 1773 and was buried at Duthil. His heir was his only son, James, born in May 1738. He and his wife also had 7 daughters. By his 1st marriage to Marion Dalrymple they had:

- Anne Grant, born in 1720, who died unmarried at age 20.
- Another child was died in infancy.

With Lady Margaret Ogilvie they had:

- James Grant, his successor who was born in 1738.
- Marion Grant, who died unmarried in 1807.
- Penuel Grant, born in 1750 in London. She married Henry Mackenzie of the Exchequer in Scotland, author of 'Man of Feeling' and other popular works.
- Margaret, who died unmarried.
- Helen, born in 1754 who married Sir Alexander Penrose-Cumming Gordon of Altyre and Gordonstoun, 1st Baronet.
- Anna-Hope Grant, born in 1756 who married the Reverend Robert Darly Waddilove, Dean of Rippon.
- May Grant, who died unmarried in 1784; and
- Elizabeth Grant, another who died unmarried in 1804.

Ludovick Grant died at Castle Grant on 18 March 1773.

CHAPTER 13. THE END OF CLANSHIP.

The end of the 1745 Jacobite Rebellion was also the beginning of the end for Clanship. The government forces continued their reprisals against those who had fought for the Jacobite cause and also those who had not. As we have seen the Grants of Glenmoriston and Urquhart suffered terrible retribution from the British Government. The Grants of Speyside, being largely with their Chief on the winning side, suffered less from the extremes of persecution but the Highland way of life was to be dismantled and because of this many of them would also suffer.

Indeed "although a fraction of the clans had taken part …….. in the rebellion, all felt the results of its defeat. Bayonet and noose, the prescription of arms, of tartan and kilt, the abolition of the hereditary jurisdictions of the chiefs, the sequestration of their estates, began the destruction of the clan system."(241)

Many of the Jacobite prisoners were shipped across the Atlantic in prison ships to Virginia, Barbados and Jamacia, where like the Grant Jacobite prisoners, most of them died in the plantations. But this was only a very small part of the highland exodus after the rebellion and for the next 150 years hundreds of thousands of highlanders and their families departed for the America's, the West indies and then Australia and New Zealand. The Battle of Culloden was a major turning point, not just because so many felt that they had to seek their fortunes overseas but even more because the Chiefs now knew they could never win wealth or position by domestic violence and theft. The Chiefs now had to find other means of improving the viability of their over-populated estates. They did so, largely by removing their people from the land. The attitude of the Chiefs before Culloden was summed up by Chief Alexander MacDonald of Keppoch; when asked what his rent-roll was he answered, 500 men.

Emigration had begun long before the introduction of the 'Great Cheviot' sheep to the Highlands in 1791. 20,000 Highlanders left for the colonies between 1763 and 1775. In one year alone during this time, 54 emigrant ships sailed from the west coast of the Highlands. Some of these were the families of soldiers who had fought in the America's and some had chosen to settle there. Most, however, were people who wanted to escape the increasing rents which were being put up by their Chiefs and other landowners.

In addition to all the emigration either voluntarily or forced, another way out of the poverty of the highlands came to the fore at this time; professional soldiering. The expanding British Empire needed more and more soldiers and the highland warriors, now redundant, provided the perfect recruits. During the 50 years after Culloden, the Chiefs raised 22 Regiments for the British Army. Hundreds of Grants signed up to fight for the British Empire all over the globe and although many died, others found and fortune. Many of the men fighting in the America's or on the Indian Continent decided to stay after the fighting was over, and either married into the indigenous population or brought their clanswomen over to them. Some of these soldiers and sailors of the Empire are illustrated in Chapter 15.

After the victory over Napoleonic France in 1815 the highlanders continued to serve in the wars of the ever expanding British Empire. However, the clearances continued and even became more devastating, for the coastal communities at least, when the Kelp industry collapsed after the Napoleonic Wars and then to top it all the Potato Famine of 1846 decimated the principal food supply of the remaining highland community.

The Chief and Lairds of Grant, particularly in Speyside, generally looked after their people and there were few large scale evictions. The good soil and pastures of the Spey Valley kept it more arable than the rest of the highlands and, therefore, it was less beneficial to replace people with sheep estates. Some were replaced and went abroad but most who chose to stay were rehoused and re-employed in new towns like Granton-on-Spey and the Chiefs introduced new industries like fishing or whisky production.

Sir James Grant of Grant, Chief of Clan Grant from 1773 until 1811. Born in 1738 he lived until the age of 73. Commonly known as 'The Good Sir James', he married Jane Duff of Halton, only daughter and heiress of Alexander Duff and his wife Lady Ann, eldest daughter of the 1st Earl of Fife. Prior to this he went to Cambridge University and then did the 'Grand Tour'. He managed the Clan estates well and stopped Clan Grant suffering from some of the severe measures of the Highland Clearances. A verse of the time goes as follows:

'Good Sir James

Kept his Castle in the North

Hard by the thundering Spey,

And a thousand vassals dwells around,

All of his lineage they.'

He established the town of Grantown-on-Spey in 1765, which provided good housing, linen and wool factories, a town hall, jail, a school, hospital and church for his vassals who were forced to move off the land to allow agricultural improvements. During one of her Highland Tours with the Prince Consort, Queen Victoria stayed the night in the old inn of Grantown-on-Spey. Her presence was kept a secret and she left the next day.

James Grant was also MP for Moray and Banff. However, strapped for cash, he gave up his seat in Parliament in order to avoid the expense of living in London. He also decided to sell off all the outlying Grant lands, retaining only the Grant territories in Speyside. Between 1774 and 1785 he sold, Moy, Mulben, Westfield, Dunphail and Achmades, which had a total value then of £52,500.

By his good financial management and sound land management practices he turned the finances of the family around gradually. This did not stop him continuing to try and get compensation from the Government for the loses and expense of the 45' Rebellion but all his attempts fell on deaf ears.

"Encouraged by his success at Grantown, James then decided to create another town at Urquhart in 1769, so he established Lewistown (Drumnadrochit), just at the back of the castle."(242) He did all this despite having huge debts from the turmoil of the 45' Rebellion. Despite this "James was an exceptionally patriotic man and a devil for punishment, because in 1793 during the Napoleonic Wars, we find him offering a regiment of Grant Fencibles (which offer was accepted by a Royal Warrant) for service in Great Britain."(243) He raised 500 Grants for the Fencibles and they were stationed at Aberdeen, Glasgow and Dumfries but eventually disbanded in 1799. So many men turned out that he had to send 70 men back home. The one stipulation of this regiment was that it was not to be sent out of Great Britain.

A poem was written when the regiment was stationed in Paisley:

"There came the Grants into this town,

They were all stout and gallant men,

Their Commanders were all of high renown

As ever came to Paisley town.

With a Fa, la, la, etc."(244)

The Regiment was involved in one notable incident while they were stationed in Dumfries. "The Dumfries Sheriff asked the Fencibles to apprehend a group of 'Irish Tinkers', who were holed up in a house about a mile and a half from the town….. On the party's approaching the house and requiring admittance, the tinkers fired on them, and wounded Sergeant Beaton very severely in the head and groin; John Grant, a grenadier, in both legs; and one Fraser of the Light Company in the arm: the two last were very much hurt, the tinkers arms being loaded with rugged slugs and small bullets. The party pushed on into the house, and, though they had suffered so severely, abstained from bayoneting them (the tinkers) when they called for mercy. One man, and two woman in men's clothes, were brought in prisoners. Two men, in the darkness of the night, made their escape; one of them was apprehended and brought in next morning, and a party went out upon information to apprehend the other."(245)

John Grant died from his wounds. The leader of the tinkers, John O'Neill, was brought to Edinburgh, tried, convicted and condemned to hang, but this was later commuted to life banishment to Australia.

Then there was a mutiny. A group of soldiers got drunk and into a fight and were arrested and placed in confinement. It looked like they were going to be flogged but the Highlanders were indignant about this and a party of men defied their officers and freed the men. Sir James Grant marched the whole regiment to Musselburgh where five men were tried and found guilty of mutiny. Two were executed at Gullane Links on 16 July 1795, in the presence of the whole regiment.

In 1794 he also raised the 97th Strathspey Regiment which had 1500 men, predominantly Grants and other vassals. This regiment served as Marines in the Channel Fleet to protect against a French invasion. They were then drafted into other regiments and two companies joined the 'Black Watch' and were sent for service in the West Indies.

In 1795 James Grant was appointed as General Cashier for the Excise in Scotland (amusing given the amount of illicit whisky still located in Grant lands at the time). This was intended as his compensation for the losses of his family during the 45' Rebellion.

The poet Robert Burns visited James at Castle Grant in 1787 as part of his tour of the highlands and was very impressed by the reforms the Chief was undertaking in his estates without the need for full scale clearance of his people, unlike many other Clan Chiefs who wantonly sold out their clansmen for profit. Lady Grant died in 1805 and James Grant on 18 February 1811 at Castle Grant. The couple had seven sons and seven daughters, but many died in infancy. Notable among these were:

- Lady Anne Margaret Grant, who was born in July 1764 and who died unmarried at Grant Lodge, Elgin on 23 November 1827. Famous as the main heroine in 'The Raid of Elgin'. She was reportedly a lady of great beauty and cheerful disposition and the Grants of Strathspey were devoted to her.
- Lewis Alexander Grant, who was born in 1767 and succeeded his father in 1811 and in the same year succeeded his cousin as heir general to the title and estates of the 4th Earl of Seafield.
- James Thomas Grant, who was born in August 1776 and who went to India where he became a magistrate at Furruckabad, Uttar Pradesh and in 1801 was appointed Registrar of the Provincial Court of Benares. He died in India, unmarried in 1804.
- Frances William, who was born in March 1778. In 1840 he succeeded his eldest brother in the Grant and Seafield Estates and became the 6th Earl of Seafield.

"His death was considered as a calamity to Strathspey, and his funeral, the largest ever seen in that country, was attended by miles of mourners, all testifying their devoted attachment to the chief whom they loved so dearly."(246)

Sir Lewis Alexander Grant of Grant, Chief of Clan Grant from 1811 until 1840. In the same year his cousin, James, 7th Earl of Findlater and 4th Earl of Seafield died without an heir and Lewis also became **5th Earl of Seafield, Viscount Reidhaven, Lord Ogilvie of Deskford and Cullen.** After this he took the name Ogilvie Grant. Initially he was MP for Elgin but became ill and retired from public duty and was cared for by his sisters. The management of the estates was taken over by his brother Colonel Francis William Grant and he was confirmed as his immediate heir.

It was during this time that the last Great Clan Raid known as the **'Raid on Elgin'** took place in 1820. At the time Colonel Francis William Grant was travelling in Italy. Lady Anne Grant and her sisters Margaret and Penuel Grant were residing at Grant Lodge, Elgin, looking after their invalid brother Lewis. At the time there was an election and feelings were running high. With Colonel Francis abroad, the Grant opponent, Lord Fife, bribed most of the voters of Elgin to support his candidate against that of the Grant candidate. For this reason the townspeople of Elgin generally supported the opponent of the Laird of Grant and "… during the heat of the election the Grant ladies dared scarcely appear in the streets of the town, without being annoyed by the rabble."(247) In fact Grant Lodge was besieged by the townspeople and no-one could get in or out. To prevent them from voting, those members of the Town Council who were favourable to the Grants were kidnapped, ferried across the Moray Firth and beached on the Sutherland shore and threatened not to come back until after the vote had taken place.

Lady Anne organised for one of her grooms to escape with a message to young Patrick Grant, son of Major Grant of Auchterblair, telling him of their predicament and asking for his help, even though he himself was only 15 years old (where his father was is not known). A similar note was also written and delivered by the groom to Captain Grant of Congash, the factor for Strathspey. The two men acted immediately.

Lady Anne Grant.

"The fiery cross was sent around, and in the course of a few hours some five or six hundred men were on the march from Strathspey to Elgin …….. Arriving at Elgin, they marched through the town to Grant Lodge, which they found besieged by the townspeople, who, alarmed by the numbers and resolute bearing of the Highlanders, instantly fled. Lady Anne gave the men a hearty welcome. The Provost of Elgin, in fear and trembling that the town would be sacked, is said to have contrived to get access to Grant Lodge by a back door entrance to induce the Highlanders to spare the town and return to Strathspey ..... Lady Anne consented to send them home after food was provided for them. They then started for Strathspey."(248)

Lady Anne sent orders to Forres and every inn on the road home to give the Grant clansmen everything that they wanted. At Forres many of them got drunk and ended up dancing until the morning. They then returned to their march home to Strathspey. This is said to have been the last full raid by a Highland Clan. It clearly shows that, despite the Clan system having been dismantled, the Grants still supported their Chief and his descendants. The Grant candidate was duly elected to Parliament.

The young Patrick Grant who took part in this raid became afterwards Field Marshal Sir Patrick Grant (see Chapter 15) and the famous soldier called this his first campaign.

DIAGRAM 5. THE CHIEFS OF CLAN GRANT.

Name	Chief Number	Title	From	Until
Colonel Sir Frances William Ogilvie-Grant	25	7th of Grant, 6th Earl of Seafield.	1840	1853
Sir John Charles Ogilvie-Grant	26	8th of Grant, 7th Earl of Strathspey, 1st Baron Strathspey	1853	1881
Sir Ian Charles Ogilvie-Grant	27	9th of Grant, 8th Earl of Seafield, 2nd Baron Strathspey	1881	1884
Sir James Ogilvie-Grant	28	10th of Grant, 9th Earl of Seafield, 1st Baron Strathspey (2nd Creation)	1884	1888
Sir Francis William Ogilvie-Grant	29	11th of Grant, 10th Earl of Seafield, 2nd Baron Strathspey (2nd Creation)	1888	1888
Captain Sir James Ogilvie-Grant	30	12th of Grant, 11th Earl of Seafield, 3rd Baron Strathspey (2nd Creation)	1888	1915
Sir Trevor Ogilvie-Grant	31	13th of Grant, 4th Baron Strathspey (2nd Creation)	1915	1948
Sir Donald Patrick Trevor Grant	32	14th of Grant, 5th Baron Strathspey (2nd Creation)	1948	1992
Sir James Patrick Trevor Grant	33	15th of Grant, 6th Baron Strathspey (2nd Creation)	1992	--------

The raid became famous throughout the whole of Great Britain. When King George IV visited Scotland in 1822, he attended a ball at Holyrood house, Edinburgh. While there he asked one of the Lords attending him to point out the lady on whose account so many highlanders had marched on Elgin two years before. Lady Anne was pointed out and the King exclaimed, "Well, truly she is an object fit to raise the chivalry of a clan."(249)

Lewis Grant was responsible for the rebuilding of the village of Cullen. The old historic village of Cullen was subject to extensive flooding when it rained heavily. Lewis had plans drawn up and moved the town half a mile away from its original position. It also provided him with more privacy from his main residence at Cullen House. The new village was built between 1820 and 1822 from a plan by George MacWilliam and is famous for Cullen Skink, a traditional soup made from smoked haddock, milk, potato and onion.

Lewis never married and when he died on 26 October 1840, aged 74 and he was succeeded by his brother **Colonel Sir Francis William Grant of Grant, 6th Earl of Seafield, Viscount Reidhaven and Lord Ogilvie of Deskford and Cullen, Chief of Clan Grant** from 1840 until 1853. He married, firstly, Ann Dunn and after she died, Louisa Emma Maunsell. He was the 4th son of Sir James Grant by his wife Jane Duff, but owing to the death of his two elder brothers, he became next in line to his eldest brother.

Born in 1778, he was commissioned into the Grant Fencibles as a Lieutenant in 1793 aged 15, and the following year was made a Major in the Fraser of Lovat Fencibles. In 1799 he was promoted to Lieutenant-Colonel in the 3rd Argyllshire Fencibles when he then became known as Colonel Grant. In 1800 he was sent to Gibraltar with his regiment but returned home the following year when peace was concluded.

In 1802 he became an M.P. which position he retained until 1840. He was also Lord Lieutenant of Invernesshire as well as looking after the estates and tenants of his brother. After his succession he took his seat in the House of Lords and in all, sat in Parliament for a record 50 years. He was particularly noted for tree planting on the Grant estates. He undertook improvements to Cullen House, Cullen and Portsoy Harbours.

A story is told of a sailing match which once took place on the Thames, between a Strathspey woodman with his currach and a number of the Thames boatmen. The contest was occasioned by the following circumstances. The Laird of Grant, being in

London on a visit, was one day looking, with an English friend, at the shipping on the Thames, when the latter made some remark in disparagement of the Laird's native river, and its ability to produce a similar spectacle. This elicited the rejoinder, from the Laird, that he had a subject on the Spey who could outstrip, in his boat of bullocks hide, the fleetest of the boats on the Thames. The Englishmen ridiculed the idea, and the result was that a wager of considerable amount was laid on the matter. The Laird appealed to his woodmen, and a youth of eighteen years soon appeared in London with his currach to vindicate the honour of his chief. On the day appointed he took his place amongst a numerous host of completions, and, without the slightest difficulty, easily succeeded in distancing them all. The Laird won his wager, and established the fame of his native stream and the inhabitants of Strathspey.

Colonel Frances William Grant of Grant.

He died in 1853 aged 76 at Cullen House and was buried at Duthil. He had six sons and a daughter by his first wife, Mary Anne Dunn, although two of his sons pre-deceased him. He was succeeded by his third son, John Charles and his fourth son, James, succeeded his brother. His only daughter, Jane, married Major General Forester Walker, who was of the same family as the third wife of his son James Grant. His 2nd wife was Louisa Emma Maunsell, with whom he had no issue.

Sir John Charles Ogilvie Grant of Grant, Chief of Clan Grant and 7th Earl of Seafield from 1853 until 1881. Born in 1814, he joined the Royal Navy as a midshipman at the age of 14. He married Caroline Stuart and left the navy in 1840 when he became Viscount Reidhaven. In 1858 he also became **Baron Strathspey of Strathspey.** He continued the work of his forebears in promoting the re-afforestation of his estates and treated his tenants well. He lived predominantly at Cullen House, Castle Grant or Balmacaan. He then fell out with his brothers over money and inheritance and disentailed the estates so as they did not have to inherit in the male-line. He continued his father's work in improving the estates, building new houses, roads and reclaiming waste land. He was also a strong supporter of the Highland Railway.

In 1850 he married Caroline Stuart, youngest daughter of the 11th Lord Blantyre. He died at Cullen House and was buried at Duthil, the last 'proper chief' who looked after the interests of his clansmen and tenants. Their only son, **John Charles**, was born in 1851 but died at Claridge's Hotel in London in 1854 after an operation. He was buried at Duthil.

John Charles Grant 7th Earl of Seafield & son Ian.

272

Ian Ogilvy Grant of Grant, Chief of Clan Grant and 8th Earl of Seafield, Viscount Reidhaven and Lord Ogilvie of Deskford succeeded his brother in 1881. He was unmarried and had no children and left his mother as heir of his estates. His tiles went to his uncle, James Ogilvy Grant.

The Dowager Countess of Seafield from 1881 until 1911 inherited the estates including those of Grant, amounting to over 300,000 acres. She was a recluse and was the last Grant to be buried at Duthil.

Sir James Ogilvie Grant of Grant, Chief of Clan Grant, 9th Earl of Seafield, Viscount Reidhaven and Lord Ogilvie of Deskford was Chief of Clan Grant for a short period of time from 1884 until 1888. He inherited the titles but not the estates. He was the 4th son of the 6th Earl of Seafield.

The Arms of James Grant Ogilvie, Earl of Seafield.

ARMS OF OGILVIE GRANT, EARL OF SEAFIELD.

Sir Francis William Ogilvie Grant of Grant and 10th Earl of Seafield, was Chief of Clan Grant in 1888 for less than a year. He emigrated to New Zealand and became a sheep farmer but soon lost this and all his capital. He and his family moved to Oamaru and became an estate agent. This also did not go well and at one point he ended up as a labourer and his wife Nina a domestic servant. He was still a labourer

273

in 1884 when he became Viscount Reidhaven and then succeeded as the 10th Earl of Seafield in 1888 when the Dowager Countess sent him a large remittance in her will.

He did not get to enjoy his title of inheritance as he died the same year in December 1888. His wife Nina survived him until 1933 when she died in Hove, Sussex. They had one daughter and a number of sons, including James and Trevor.

Captain Sir James Ogilvie Grant of Grant, 11th Earl of Seafield was Chief of Clan Grant from 1888 until 1915. He was born in Oamaru, New Zealand and succeeded to the Earldom at the age of 12. Schooled in New Zealand he studied agriculture and forestry. He married Anna Nina and they had one child, a daughter, Nina. The couple were well travelled but at the outbreak of World War I James was commissioned into the Cameron Highlanders in 1914. "The battalion went to France in 1915 and fought in the Battle of Loos where they suffered great losses and James became a company commander, mainly because all the other officers were dead or wounded... The whole battalion was down to only 101 men (all ranks), instead of the 800 – 1000 men it started with. Then the Battle of Ypres commenced, and James was in command of the battalion, being about the only trained officer left. One morning he went into the very shallow trenches, full of water, and with a low parapet. He was as brave as a lion. The enemy were on the famous Hill 60. He was visible to the enemy, and was shot in the head by a sniper; he died some hours later, in a field hospital behind the lines. He was buried at the British cemetery at Poperinghe, called Boschepe."(250) His daughter **Nina Ogilvie Grant became Countess of Seafield** and his brother inherited the **Chief of Grant title and became Lord Strathspey, Chief of the Clan.**

Sir Trevor Ogilvie Grant of Grant became Chief of Clan Grant. He was also born in New Zealand in 1879. He had no real connection with the Scottish Grants. He was succeeded by **Sir Patrick Grant of Grant** in 1948 who dropped the Ogilvie name and held no Seafield titles. He was the 5th Chief in succession who owned no Grant lands at all. The current Clan Chief is **Sir James Patrick Trevor Grant,** 6th Lord Strathspey and hereditary Chief of Clan Grant.

Cullen House is one of the finest in the whole of the highlands. It has the story of the 'Mad Earl' who was an Ogilvie and not a Grant. He was the 6th Earl of Findlater and 3rd of Seafield who succeeded in 1714. "He used to suffer bouts of madness, and when he felt one of these attacks coming on he used to lock himself in the library and throw the keys down to his factor, who had instructions to unlock the door when he considered the attack had passed. One day the factor was rather premature in releasing his master, who is said to have fallen on him and killed him. Soon after, when the Earl was restored to his right mind he naturally felt terribly contrite and killed himself. The little room where this suicide is supposed to have occurred was empty except for a bluish stain on the bare boards which could not be removed. The Earl haunted that part of the house, pacing up and down."(251)This was until the Countess had his ghost exorcised.

Cullen House.

Copyright: Anne Burgess.

Grant Lodge, Elgin was the 'lowland' home of the Chiefs of Grant and the Earls of Seafield. The Lodge was built by 'The Good Sir James Grant' in the 1760's from a design by Robert Adam.

Speyside Scots Whisky. Speyside is famous for its whisky and much of it is made by the Grants, including Grants Stand Fast, Strathspey, Glen Grant, Grants Royal, Glenfarclas and Long John. However, the most famous is 'Glenfiddich'. All are made at Grantown-on-Spey. "Whisky has been distilled in Scotland for centuries, but the first written record of distilling occurs in the year 1494. The Gaelic word for 'water of life' was 'uisagebeatha' which rather difficult word was concertinaed into 'uisage' and the 'usky', and finally 'whisky'. For centuries it was used as a medicine in Scotland".(252)

Speyside had a very large number of cottage or glen side distilleries for hundreds of years until they were shut down by the excise officers. Today there are around 40 distilleries around Speyside. Many of the illicit stills were operated by the MacGregors who were given sanctuary by the Grants, much of it on land leased from the Grants. Sale of whisky grew rapidly after the Act of Union. In 1707 the official production of whisky was only 50,000 gallons per annum but 50 years later in 1758 this had risen to over 434,000 gallons, a nine-fold increase. This, however, was only a small fraction of what was actually being produced as most whisky continued to be distilled in 'illicit duty free stills'.

"On Speyside it is stated that in 1820 there was over 200 illicit stills but not one legal still".(40) The Government then clamped down on it and virtually eradicated all these illicit stills by 1840. "An illuminating few words were written by Lady Elizabeth Grant of Rothiemurchas in 1813 (when she was 16) about the forestry workers of those days. *When the men met in the morning they were supposed to have breakfasted at home, and had perhaps had their private dram, it being cold work in a dark wintry dawn, to start over the moor for a walk of some miles to end standing up to their knees in water; yet on collecting, whisky was always handed round; a lad with a small cask – a quarter anker- on his back, and a horn cup in his hand that held a gill, appeared three times a day among them. They all took their 'morning' raw, undiluted and without accompaniment so they did the gill at parting when the work was done; but the noontime dram was part of a meal. There was a twenty minutes' rest from labour, and a Bannock and a bit of cheese taken out of every pocket to be eaten leisurely with the whisky. When we were there the horn cup was offered first to us, and each of us took a cup to the health of our friends around us, who all stoop up. Sometimes a floaters wife or bairn would come with a messenger; such messenger was always offered whisky. Aunt May, had a story that one day a woman with a child in her arms, and another bit thing at her knee came up among them, the horn cup was duly* handed to her, she took a 'grey guid drops' herself, and then gave a little to each of the babies. 'My goodness child', said my mother to the wee thing that was trotting by the mothers side, 'doesn't it bite you?', 'Ay, but I like the bite', replied the creature."(253)

In 1745, three Grant brothers who fought for the Jacobites fled to Banffshire where they were hidden by relatives. The great-grandson of one of these men herded cattle at the age of seven, was apprenticed to a shoemaker, worked in a limeworks, then became a book keeper at the local whisky distillery where he worked for 20 years and eventually became manager.

In 1886 he quit his job and with his own savings opened his own distillery. The Glenfiddich Distillery began production on Christmas Day, 1887. The sole employees were William Grant and his nine children. Grant pioneered single malt whisky. Until the Glenfiddich Distillery opened, proprietary whisky was blended.

William Grant built the famous Glenfiddich Distillery by hand with the aid of his sons and daughters. It began production on Christmas Day 1887. They eventually built a 2nd Distillery at Balvenie.

CHAPTER 14. CADET BRANCHES OF CLAN GRANT.

The Grants of Arndilly descend from William Grant (1625 – 1683) who was the 3rd son of the Grants of Monymusk. The Arndilly Grants established themselves in the 17th century. Their seat was Arndilly House, located north of Cragellachie, near Aberlour. William Grant 1st of Arndilly died in June 1720.

Arndilly House.

He was succeeded by his eldest son, Walter Grant of Arndilly who died in June 1720. Next in line was Thomas Grant, 3rd Laird of Arndilly. In 1740 he was appointed a Commissioner of the Highlands of Scotland. He died on 25 November 1758. The 4th Laird was Colonel Alexander Grant. He died in Jamacia in August 1779. Many of the family died in Jamacia, including his brother Alexander Grant and his two sons, David and James.

In 1779 the estate was inherited by Mary Eleanor Grant, daughter of Colonel Alexander Grant, and she became 5th of Arndilly. She married David McDowall, who took the name Grant. This couple built Arndilly House. She died in August 1832. Their eldest son, William McDowall Grant, inherited but when he died in 1849, the estate passed to his brother, Hay McDowall Grant, 7th of Arndilly (1806 – 1870). Marjory Alexandrina McDowal Grant was the last of the family to hold Arndilly. She was the eldest daughter of William McDowall Grant.

The Grants of Ballindalloch estate centres on where the River Avon enters the River Spey with its main old castle of Ballindalloch. The Grants of Ballindalloch were traditionally the Clan Captains for the Chiefs of Clan Grant. Patrick, twin brother of John Grant, 2nd Laird of Freuchie was the ancestor of this Grant family. By 1520 Patrick was a prominent member of the family. His wife is not known but they had at least 4 sons and 2 daughters. He was succeeded by John Grant who was killed in September 1559 in a quarrel with the Grants of Carron.

In 1613, Patrick Grant of Ballindalloch, with the Laird of Freuchie, was pardoned for hiding and aiding Clan MacGregor. He had previously been fined £5,000 Scots. In 1645 Montrose burned the three houses of the Laird of Ballindalloch. By the time of John Roy Grant, 7th of Ballindalloch the estates were in significant debt. His creditors took the lands which were subsequently purchased by Colonel William Grant, younger of Rothiemurchas.

Ballindalloch Castle was known as the 'Pearl of the North', it is located at Ballindalloch, Banffshire and is the family homes of the Macpherson-Grants since 1546 when the first tower was built. There is a lintel in one of the castle's bedrooms with the date 1546. "It is said that the intention was to build at a better site [on the high ground to the east of the castle] but when building commenced whatever was built in the day was thrown down at night. Eventually the laird, annoyed by the problem, heard a mysterious voice saying 'Build in the cow haughs, and you will meet with no interruptions'. He did so, and there was no further problem with the building."(254)

The castle was burned by the army of Montrose in 1644 but was soon restored again in 1645. By 1682 the estate was in financial ruin and the new Laird had to promise to settle the estates debts in order to gain possession of his inheritance. Perhaps hoping for debt relief, John Grant of Ballindalloch was one of those Grants who supported the Jacobites in 1689. By 1690 and the defeat of the Jacobites his plan backfired as the Castle and estate was garrisoned by Grants loyal to the Chief and the Government against him. Soon afterwards he was forfeited and then in 1711 Ballindalloch passed to William Grant of Rothiemurchas, who was able to clear the debts and was also a staunch supporter of the Hanoverian King George I. The estate passed to his nephew, George Macpherson in 1806, who adopted the name Macpherson-Grant.

In 1770 an extension was added by General James Grant, of the American War of Independence, whose ghost is still said to haunt the castle. Another extension was added in 1850 by architect Thomas Mackenzie who transformed it from a Castle to a House. Today the castle houses an important collection of 17th century Spanish paintings and the grounds contain a 20th century rock garden and a 17th century Dovecote. The dining room of the Castle has a 'Green Lady' who haunts it. There are not many Scottish Castles, however, who do not have a green lady ghost.

Ballindalloch Castle.

It is still occupied by the Macpherson-Grant family and open to tourists in the summer months and Ballindalloch Scotch Whisky distillery is located on the estate.

Grants of Carron were cadets of the Grants of Glenmoriston. The first was John Roy Grant of Carron who obtained a charter from the Bishop of Moray for the lands of Carron in 1541. He was the illegitimate son of John Grant of Glenmoriston. He was involved in the murder of John Grant of Ballindalloch on 11 September 1559 which sparked the long feud between the two families. He died on 28 February 1598.

Patrick Grant of Carron was charged with 'molesting' the lands of Alexander Lord Elphinstone of Kildrummy and was declared a rebel and put him to the 'horn'. His son was killed in 1628 by John Grant of Ballindalloch.

Colonel John Grant of Carron, was killed in the assault on Fort Lazaro at Cartagena, in the West Indies in April 1741. This was part of the 'War of Jenkin's Ear' between Great Britain and Spain. The war was fought predominantly in the Caribbean when the British tried to capture key Spanish ports in the region. One was Cartegena de Indias in present day Columbia.

In March 1741 the British opted for a combined naval and land attack on Cartegena. After a series of unsuccessful assaults the British were forced to retreat with up to 11,500 killed, although many of them died from disease. Colonel John Grant was killed leading one of the assaults. He left two daughters and the eldest, Elizabeth Grant, married Captain Lewis Grant of Anchterhlar. They were succeeded by Captain James Grant of Carron who as an 18 year old Lieutenant fought at the Battle of Fontenoy in 1745 for the British.

Grants of Corriemony, in the Parish of Urquhart and Glenmoriston who were the descendants of John Grant, son of John Grant, 2nd Laird of Freuchie who inherited the estate around 1509. Alexander Grant of Corriemony fought for the Jacobites in the 45' and was wounded at the battle of Culloden. He then hid in a cave at Corriemony Waterfalls. His son, James Grant of Corriemony, Advocate of Edinburgh, sold the estate.

Grants of Dalvey owned Polmaily House which is now a hotel. They are descended from the first Grants of Ballindalloch. Sir James Grant was 1st Baronet of Dalvey, Elgin in 1695. Sir Alexander Grant, 5th Baronet (1705-1772) was a Scottish slave trader and plantation owner, who co-owned Bunce Island in Sierra Leone. 10,000 Africans were shipped from this island to the North American Colonies of South Carolina and Georgia as slaves.

Bunce Island, Sierra Leone.

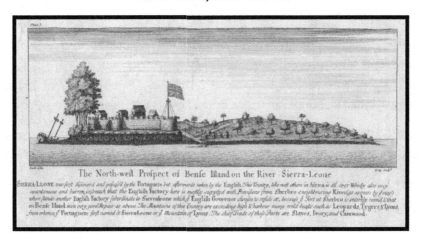

281

They operated the island under Grant, Oswald and Company from 1748. "in 1773 Henry Smeatham, an English botanist visited the island and recorded how 6 members of the Company played golf on the island, attended by African caddies, draped in loincloths of a tartan design made from wool that had been woven in one of the partners' industrial ventures, a factory near Glasgow."(255)

Polmaily House, Drumnadrochit.

Grants of East Elchies in the Parish of Knockando. The 1st Grant of Easter Elchies was Duncan Grant, son of James Grant, 3rd Laird of Freuchie. He was granted the estate of Easter Elchies in January 1543. In 1569 he received a pardon for taking part in the rebellion of the Earl of Huntly. He died in October 1580. But his line did not continue after his son and the lands passed to the Freuchie line of Patrick Oig Grant.

His descendant Patrick Grant became Lord Elchies. He was a Scottish Judge and Lord of Session. He was raised to Lord Elchies in March 1737. He is buried in Greyfrairs Kirkyard in Edinburgh in the area known as the Covenanters Prison.

Grants of Gartenbeg. The most famous member of this branch was Rear Admiral John Grant C.B and D.S.O.

Grants of Glenmoriston. Glenmoriston is a small village around 7 miles north of Fort Augustus. The progenitor of this branch was Iain Mor, son of John Mor, illegitimate son of John Grant, 2nd of Freuchie, who received a charter for the lands of Glenmoriston and part of Glenurquhart. Their main seat was Invermoriston House which was burned to the ground in 1931 and a new house was built in 1958.

John Mor "…. received, at Stirling, 8th December, 1509-10, a Crown charter to himself and his heirs male of the lands of Glenmoriston in the lordship of Urquhart and County of Inverness, which lands were then erected into a barony in his favour, to be called the Barony of Glenmoriston."(256) After this they expanded their lands to include the lands of Wester Elchies and Kincardine in Strathspey and the lands of Culcabock, Knockintinnel and the Haugh.

The Glenmoriston's, separated by Loch Ness and several mountains from Strathspey, were, therefore, outside the immediate influence and easy command of the Chiefs of the Clan. Thus they have, over the centuries, tended to act as a clan on their own. They were, in fact, pretty powerful, as it is known that in the Jacobite Rebellion they fielded 300 fighting men."(257) After the defeat at Culloden, Patrick Grant of Glenmoriston hid Bonnie Prince up in Glenmoriston for a number of days "…. [His descendants] are still in possession of the cooking pot he used, and of miniature painting of the Prince and Patrick Grant."(258)

They had an almost continual feud with their neighbours the MacDonalds/ MacDonnells of Glengarry. Although, saying this, they also fought alongside them during the Jacobite Rebellions of the 18th century.

There is an interesting local tale of Patrick Grant, 9th Laird of Glenmoriston who succeeded to the Lairdship in 1786. He was renowned for possessing great strength. "Riding home late at night along the Fort Augustus road, he found the gate of the bridge that spans the river closed., and having failed to rouse the sleeping toll-keeper, he laid hold of it, and by mere force wrenched it off its hinges, and threw it over the parapet into the river, to the bewilderment of the keeper, who next morning found it unaccountably gone. It was an iron gate and firmly tied."(259)

Invermoriston House is the hereditary home of the Lairds of Glenmoriston. It is currently the home of James Ewan Grant, the present Laird of Glenmoriston. The first House was burnt down by the Government after the Jacobite Rising of 1715. John Grant lost his home and also his estates which were forfeited, although he eventually managed to buy back the land and the estates.

The House was burned again by the Hanoverian troops after the defeat of the 1745 Rebellion. Invermoriston House was rebuilt again but was once more destroyed by accident in 1930. The present House is a modern one, and smaller than the one it replaced.

The Grants of Kilgraston in Perthshire are lineally descended from the 9th Laird of Grant. John Grant, Chief Justice of Jamaica from 1783 to 1790, purchased the estates of Kilgraston and Pitcaithly in Strathearn. He died in 1793 without children and was succeeded by his brother, Francis Grant.

A son of this branch, Major-General Sir James Hope Grant, 5th son of Francis Grant of Kilgraston entered the army in 1826. He was a Major in the war with China under Lord Saultoun, and received a medal for his services and then campaigned in India. At the battle of Sabraon in 1846 he commanded the 9th Lancers, for which he received another medal. He also commanded the regiment in the Punjab Campaign and fought in the Battle of Chillianwala and the Battle of Gujerat.

In 1854 he was promoted to Colonel and took an active part in the suppression of the Indian Mutiny in 1857-8. He was then made a Knight Commander of the Bath. He eventually became a Major-General. In 1860 he was in command of the British forces in China.

The Grants of Kinchurdy in Strathspey. The ancestor of this branch of the family was Mungo Grant, 9th son of Sir John Grant, 6th of Freuchie, called Kinchurdy, but sometimes of Duthil and Gellovie. He obtained these lands around 1650. In 1670 he was 'warned' because of his intention of sending two of his sons to France to be educated by a 'Father Grant', a Catholic Priest.

Robert Grant of Lurg. 1769.

The Grants of Lurg, in the Parish of Abernethy. The first of this family was Robert Grant of Lurg, younger son of Duncan Grant, Younger of Freuchie. In 1613 Robert Grant was fined for helping the MacGregor outlaws in 1613. He died in 1634. His grandson, another Robert Lurg, known as 'Old Stachan', was the subject of the following portrait.

The Grants of Monymusk. Their ancestral home is Monymusk House, in Aberdeenshire, in which they still live. The 1st Monymusk Grant was Archibald Grant of Ballintomb, youngest son of James Grant, 3rd of Freuchie (1528-1553). The Estate was purchased in 1713 by Sir Francis Grant, 1st Baronet of Monymusk and Lord Cullen. His son, also Archibald Grant, was a famous agricultural reformer and introduced the turnip to Scotland and planted millions of trees in his lifetime.

Muckrath Castle.

The Grants of Rothiemurchas were founded by Patrick Grant who built and lived at Muckrath Castle. He received these lands from his father, John Grant, 4th of Freuchie and then moved to the new estate. He received the estate of Murcherach in 1570 and then Rothiemurchas in 1580. "a large armorial stone bearing the date 1598, with the initials PG for Patrick Grant, and J.G. for Jean Gordon, his wife, with two shield of arms, surmounted by the motto, 'In God is al my traist' still exists at the Doune of Rothiemurchas, where it is built into a wall behind the mansion. The stone is said to have been brought from Muckrath when Patrick Grant changed his residence to Rothiemurchas."(260)

The Grants of Shewglie. Alexander Roy Grant was the 1st of Shewglie. He was the son of John Grant, 2nd of Corrimony. He obtained the lands of Shewglie in 1609. During the 1745 Jacobite rebellion there were 6 Grants of Shewglie as junior officers in the Glengarry Regiment. These were Alexander and Patrick Grant of Shewglie and their cousins Alexander Grant of Inchbrere (known as the Swordsman) and his brothers James and Archibald. Their father, Captain Robert Grant of Milton also accompanied them.

The Grants of Tullochgorm are reputed to be the oldest cadet branch of Clan Grant, known as the Sliochd Phadnck. Patrich Grant was the 1st of Tullochgorm and he obtained the estate in April 1530. The family were great supporters of the outlawed MacGregor Clan and Patrick 3rd Larid and John 4th Laird were both fined by the Government for hiding and assisting the proscribed clan.

The Grants of Wester Elchies in the Parish of Knockando. James Grant was the 1st Grant of Wester Elchies. He had a dispute with his kinsmen, Duncan Grant of Easter Elchies over the land border in the moors between the two estates. This was settled through arbitration by the Laird of Freuchie rather than going through the law courts. James died in February 1591 and was succeeded by his son Lachlan Grant. The estate eventually went to John Grant of Carron and then to James Grant of Freuchie.

Septs of Clan Grant include:

McJochie, McConnachie, McFinlay, McRobie, McWilliam, More, Bain, Bowie, Lauson, Roy, Allan, Allan, Bissett, Duie, Gilroy, MacAllan, MacGilroy, MacKerron, MacKiaran, Pratt, Sultie.

CHAPTER 15. FAMOUS GRANTS AFTER THE END OF THE CLAN SYSTEM.

James Grant, Laird of Ballindalloch (1720-1806), purchased a commission in the Royal Scots on 24 October 1744. He then fought with them at the Battle of Fontenoy during the War of the Austrian Succession. By 1757 he was a Major in the 77th Regiment of Foot (Montgomerie's Highlanders) fighting in the French and Indian War in the Americas.

Ludovick Grant of Creichie, Aberdeenshire who is believed to be the ancestor of up to half the Cherokee Nation in North America. Ludovick fought for the Jacobite Cause in the 1715 Rebellion where he was part of the Scots army sent south to raise the English and was captured at the Battle of Preston and sentenced to hang as a traitor and rebel. Eventually his sentence was commuted and he was sent to Carolina as an indentured servant for 7 years. After his time was served he stayed in the American Colonies and began working as a trader to the Cherokee Nation and he was soon accepted into that tribe.

He met and began a relationship with a Cherokee, Eughioote, and with her he had a daughter. Although this was his only Cherokee child she went on to have so many children that Ludovick is the direct descendant of between one third and a half of all Cherokees today.

But it also appears that Ludovick left a wife behind in Scotland, named Margaret Redwood, whom he had married in 1710. In 1736 she began divorce proceedings against him. Ludovick deid in America.

Commodore Alexander Grant, was the younger son of Patrick, 8th Laird of Glenmoriston. He joined the British Navy and sailed for America in May 1758, landing at Halifax. He then served in the expedition against Fort Duquesne. He was promoted to Lieutenant in 1759 and served under General Amherst in the expedition against Ticonderoga and Crown Point where he commanded a sloop of sixteen guns on Lake Chaplain.

In 1764 he was appointed Commodore of the King's vessels on Lake Erie. "In 1776 he obtained a grant of 500 acres in Charlotte County, between Crown Point and Ticonderoga. In 1805 he administered the Government of [Upper] Canada during the absence of the Lieutenant Governor."(261) He was a member of the Executive and Legislative Council of Upper Canada.

He died in May 1813 at the age of 81 at Gossport, near Detriot.

General Sir John Colquhoun Grant (1772 – Dec 1835) joined the 36 Foot Regiment in 1793 as an Ensign before then joining the 25th Light Dragoons Cavalry Regiment. He served at the Siege of Seringapatam which was the final confrontation of the 4th Anglo-Mysore War between the British East India Company and the Kingdom of Mysore.

After this he re-joined the infantry and went to South Africa where he fought against the Batavian Army at the Battle of Blaauwberg, where he was wounded. The British Commander, Sir David Baird, wrote about Grant in dispatches after the victory:

"Your lordship will perceive the name Lt-Col Grant among the wounded; but the heroic spirit of this officer was not subdued by the misfortune, and he continued to lead his men to glory as long as an enemy was opposed to the 72nd Regiment."(262) He re-joined the Cavalry again in 1808 and took part in Sir John Moore's expedition to the Peninsular (Portugal and Spain), being wounded at Sahagun fighting the French. He returned to Spain in January 1813 and led a cavalry brigade at the Battle of Morales.

General Wellington was not impressed with the performance of Grant's Hussar Brigade at the Battle of Vitoria and Grant was eventually replaced in command. However, with friends in high places he quickly returned and fought through to the end of the Peninsular War. At the **Battle of Waterloo**, 18 June 1815, Grant commanded the 5th Cavalry Brigade, which was positioned in the centre of the allied position.

During the battle he had five horses shot under him. Afterwards Grant was promoted to Lieutenant-General in 1830 and became an MP for Queenborough on the Isle of Sheppey, Kent. He was also Groom of the Bedchamber to Prince Ernest Augustus, Duke of Cumberland, later King of Hanover.

He was said to be the strongest man in the British Army and was given the nickname, 'The Black Grant'. He died in 1835.

Field Marshall Sir Patrick Grant (11 Sept 1804 – 28 March 1895) was the son of Major John Grant. He joined the Bengali Native Infantry as an ensign in 1820 and by 1832 was promoted to Brigade Major in 1834. He then fought in the **Battle of Maharujpore** in December 1834 during the Gwalior Campaign. He then took part in the **Battle of Mudki** in December 1845, where he was twice wounded, the **Battle of**

Fevozeshah and the **Battle of Soloraon** in February 1846 during the First Anglo-Sikh War.

He then fought in the Second Anglo-Sikh War, when he took part in the **Battles of Chillianwala and Gujerat** in 1849. He then took part in the expedition against the Pathan tribes in Kohat in 1850. By 1854 he was promoted to Major General and then became Commander-in-Chief of the Madras Army.

The Battle of Gujrat 1849.

When General Anson died of Cholera in May 1857, Grant, as senior commander in India was temporarily promoted to Commander-in-Chief India in May 1857 and took command of operations against the Sepoy Mutineers which led to the relief of Cawnpore and Luchnow. On the arrival of Sir Colin Campbell in India as Commander-in-Chief, Grant again returned to command the Madras Army.

He became Governor of Malta in 1867 and was promoted to full General in 1870. He retired in 1877 with the rank of Field Marshal. He died in London in March 1895.

President Ulysses S. Grant is probably the most famous Grant. Hiram Ulysses Grant was born on 27 April 1822 in Point Pleasant, Ohio, USA to Jesse Grant and Hannah Simpson Grant. Soon after they moved to Georgetown, Ohio where his father ran a tannery.

Grant entered the US Military Academy at West Point in 1839. His forms were incorrectly filled out and his middle name, Ulysses, was put down as his first name.

Grant accepted the error and from that moment his official name was Ulysses S. Grant. He graduated from West Point in 1843 where he was known as a good horseman but an undistinguished student, graduating in the middle of his class and failing to get the cavalry posting he wanted.

He joined the 4th US Infantry as a Second Lieutenant. In 1844 he met Julia Dent, a sister of one of his West Point classmates, and they married soon after. They had four children, Frederick Dent Grant, Ulysses S. Grant jnr, Nellie Grant and Jesse Grant. She was the daughter of a Missouri slave owner.

He then fought in the Mexican-American War (1846-1848). It was a great victory for the United States with Mexico losing nearly 1/3rd of its territory, including nearly all of present day California, Utah, Nevada, Arizona and New Mexico. Although he did not believe in the validity of this war, he fought bravely as a regimental quartermaster, riding through enemy fire to bring ammunition to his men.

In his early career he spent much of his time assigned to remote army posts on the West Coast. In 1854 he resigned from the army to spend more time with his family. He had a number of unsuccessful jobs but eventually became a clerk in his father's leather store in Galena, Illinois, working under his elder brother.

When the American Civil War began in April 1861, Grant re-enlisted as a Colonel of the 21st Illinois Volunteers. He was only given this post and command because he was the only West Point graduate available.

Later Abraham Lincoln made Grant a Brigadier-General. His first victory came in February 1862, when his troops captured Fort Donaldson in Tennessee. Then in July 1863 Grant's forces captured Vicksburg, Mississippi, a Confederate stronghold. He was now earning a reputation as a tenacious and determined leader and was appointed a Lieutenant-General by President Lincoln on March 10, 1864, and given command of all US Armies. He went to "Washington to receive the specially created rank of lieutenant general, last held by George Washington. He held command of all the armies of the United States, 533,000 armed men, and he had something in many ways more potent – the confidence of a President with a long history of dissatisfaction with his generals."(263)

He then led a number of campaigns which ultimately won the war for the Union Army, although initially his command of the whole army started off badly. When Grant's army was caught by surprise at Shiloh with fearful losses, the newspapers called for his removal, Lincoln withstood them: 'I can't spare this man', he said, 'He fights'. On 9 April 1865 Confederate General Robert Lee surrendered to Grant at Appomattox Court House in Virginia, effectively ending the Civil War.

General Ulysses S. Grant.

After the war Ulysses Grant became a national hero and he was appointed the first 4 star General by President Andrew Johnston and then he was brought into the President's administration.

In 1868 Grant was nominated as the Republican candidate for the Presidency of the United States. He won the election and at the age of 46, he became the youngest president-elect in US history up to that time. As 18th President he worked hard on the reconstruction of the South as it's States were brought back into the Union. He tried to foster peace and reconciliation between the North and South and even pardoned former Confederate leaders while also trying to protect the civil rights of freed slaves.

He enacted legislation giving black men the right to vote and signed legislation aimed at limiting white terrorist groups such as the Klu Klux Klan. He was also responsible for the establishing the US Weather Bureau and the creation of Yellowstone National Park, America's first National Park.

Despite accusations of corruption he won the 1872 Presidential election but he then lost the election in 1876. In 1884 Grant was bankrupted when his son's partner swindled the Company's investors. To provide for his family the former President decided to write his memoirs. In 1884 he was also diagnosed with throat cancer.

Grant died at the age of 63 on 23 July 1885 in Mount McGregor, New York. His memoirs were published the same year by his friend, Mark Twain, and became a major financial success. More than a 1m people watched his funeral procession in New York City.

Thousands of people from all over the world donated a total of $600,000 for the construction of Grant's tomb in New York City. Known as Grants National Memorial, it is America's largest mausoleum and was dedicated on 27 April 1897, the 75th Anniversary of his birth.

Grant National Memorial, New York City.

Lieutenant-Colonel James Augustus Grant was a Scottish explorer of east equatorial Africa. He was born 11 April 1827 at Nairn where his father was a parish minister. In 1846 he joined the Indian Army and saw active service in the Sikh War

(1848-49) and then served throughout the Indian Mutiny of 1857 and was wounded at the siege and evacuation of Lucknow.

He returned to Great Britain in 1858 and in 1860 took part in the John Hanning Specke expedition to East Africa which found the source of the River Nile at Lake Victoria. In 1864 he published a journal of the expedition, entitled, 'A Walk across Africa'. In the same year he was awarded the Patrons Medal by the Royal Geographical Society, and in 1866 he was given the 'Companionship of the Bath' in recognition of his services to the expedition.

In 1868 he then served in the intelligence section of the Abyssinian Expedition (now Ethiopia). At the end of this war he retired from the army with the rank of Lieutenant-Colonel. Grant married Margaret Thomson Laurie. Their two sons also became involved in Africa, James Augustus Grant junior as a surveyor and explorer, and Alister Grant who was killed in 1900 in the Second Anglo-Boer War.

Lieutenant-Colonel James Grant died in 1892.

Sketch of James Augustus Grant.

Peter Grant (1824 – 1868) was born in Ireland and joined the British Army. Grant was 33 years old and a private in the 93rd Regiment of Foot (later the Argyll and Sutherland Highlanders) during the Indian Mutiny. He was awarded the V.C. for the following action which took place on 16 November 1857 at Secundra Bagh,

Lucknow, India. For great personal gallantry, on the 18th November 1857, at the Secundra Bagh, in killing five of the enemy with one of their own swords, who were attempting to follow Lieutenant-Colonel Ewart, when that officer was carrying away a colour [enemy regimental flag] which he had captured. Elected by the private soldiers of the Regiment.

He died from an accidental drowning in the River Tay in Dundee, Scotland in January 1868.

Dr. Gabriel Grant (Sept 1826 – Nov 1909) was an American doctor and Union Army Officer who was awarded the Medal of Honor for his actions at the American Civil War Battle of Fair Oaks (or Battle of Seven Pines) in May/June 1862. This battle was the culmination of an offensive up the Virginia Pennisula by Union Major-General George B. McClellan, in which the Army of the Potomac reached the outskirts of Richmond, the Confederate Capital.

Gabriel Grant served as a surgeon in the 2nd Infantry Regiment of the New Jersey Volunteers. His Medal of Honor citation reads:

'Removed severely wounded officers and soldiers from the field while under a heavy fire from the enemy, exposing himself beyond the call of duty, thus furnishing an example of distinguished gallantry'.

In this action he was himself wounded. Gabriel died in Manhatton, New York in November 1909, aged 83. One of his sons was the 'infamous' **Madison Grant**, who in the early part of the 20th century was an American lawyer, zoologist, anthropologist and writer known for his works as a conservatist, eugenicist, and advocate of scientific racism. Grant was noted for his advocacy of Nordicism, a form of racism which views the 'Nordic' race as superior.

Major General Lewis Addison Grant (1828 – 1918) was a teacher and lawyer who joined the Union Army during the American Civil War. In September 1861 he joined the army as a Major in the 5th Vermont Infantry and was soon promoted to Colonel in September 1862. He was wounded at the Battle of Fredericksburg and then assumed command of the famed Vermont Brigade and led it during the 1863 Gettysburg Campaign. The First Vermont Brigade was an infantry Brigade in the Union Army of the Potomac and it suffered the highest casualty count of any brigade in the history of the United States Army, with some 1,172 killed in action.

During his military career he fought in most of the major battles of Civil War. He was awarded the Medal of Honor for his personal gallantry and intrepidity in commanding his brigade and leading it in the assault at Salam Church, Virginia in May 1863, where he was wounded.

Grant was then appointed Brevet Major General in October 1864 for gallantry and courage in the face of the enemy. He was honourably discharged from the Army in August 1865. After the war he moved to Illinois, Iowa and finally Minnesota. He was Assistant U.S. Secretary of War during the administration of President Benjamin Harrison. He died in Minneapolis, Minnesota in March 1918.

Robert Grant (1837-Nov 1874) was born in England and joined the army straight from school. He was 20 years old and a Corporal (afterwards promoted to Sergeant) in the 1st Battalion, 5th Regiment of Foot (later the Northumberland Fusiliers) during the Indian Mutiny. On 12 October 1860 at Alurnbagh he proceeded under heavy fire to save the life of Private E. Devenay, whose leg had been blown off. He reached him under heavy fire and carried him safe into camp. For this he was awarded the V.C. After leaving the army he joined the London Police. He died of Consumption (Tuberculosis) in 1874.

General Sir Henry Fane Grant (1848 – 1919) was the son of General Sir Patrick Grant and served in the Queens Own Hussars and took part in the Nile Expedition in 1884. He then became Assistant Adjutant-General in Bengal, India in 1891. He then went on to be became General Community Officer of the 5th Division in 1903 and Governor of Malta in 1907 before he retired in 1909.

In retirement he became Lieutenant of the Tower of London. He was killed in a shooting accident while out rabbit hunting in Scotland. He is buried at Duthil Church, Speyside.

Colonel Charles Grant (Oct 1861 - Nov 1932), was born in Bourtie, Aberdeenshire, Scotland. He attended the Royal Military College, Sandhurst and was then commissioned into the Suffolk Regiment in May 1882. By the age of 29 he was a Lieutenant and fought in the Anglo-Manipur war where he won his V.C. in 1891, during the revolt in the Eastern Indian State of Manipur. Some British nationals were murdered and some imprisoned. Lieutenant Grant was stationed at the border post of Tamu, some 55 miles from Manipur. On hearing of the revolt he immediately marched his detachment of 80 Punjabi and Gurka soldiers to the relief of the British survivors.

He captured the village of Thoubai but the next day the Manipuris prepared to attack the village with a large force. Before they attacked Grant and forty of his men charged the enemy before they could form up properly. For the next 9 days he repulsed all attacks and inflicted heavy casualties on the enemy. The whole Manpuris army was kept at bay, with Grant only losing one man killed and 4 wounded, including himself.

Lieutenant Charles Grant VC, 1st April 1891.

Grant eventually withdrew to meet up with a large British force which was advancing towards Manipur. He then took part in this campaign to relieve the city of Imphal (Kangla), the Manipur capital, where he was again wounded. The British took the city on 26 April, bringing an end to the war. For his bravery he was awarded the Victoria Cross.

Charles Grant later achieved the rank of Colonel and was given command of the 89th and 92nd Punjabis Battalions. He retired in 1911 and settled in England but re-joined the army during World War One serving as a 'drafting officer'. He then lived in Sidmoth, Devon where he died in 1932 aged 71.

General Sir Charles John Cecil Grant (Aug 1877 – Nov 1950) was a senior British Army Officer who saw active service in the 2nd Boer War in South Africa from 1899 to 1902, then World War One and finally World War Two.

He joined the Coldstream Guards as a 2nd Lieutenant in February 1897 and was soon promoted to Lieutenant in May 1898. He served in the 2nd Boer War where he was part of Kimberley's Relief Force and was then wounded at the **Battle of Belmont** in November 1899.

At this battle the British, under Lord Methven, assaulted a strong Boer position on Belmont Kopje. The British won but suffered significant casualties. During World War One he served with the British Expeditionary Force in France from 1914. During the war he was awarded the Distinguished Service Order, was seven times Mentioned in Dispatches and was again wounded.

After the war he became Commanding officer of the Coldstream Guards in 1919 and between the Wars held a variety of senior commands. In 1937 he was appointed Commander in Chief of Scottish Command and Governor of Edinburgh Castle. He retired in 1942 but then served as deputy-lieutenant of Shropshire until the end of the World War II. He is buried in the family grave at Balmacaan, Glen Urquhart.

John Duncan Grant (Dec 1877 – February 1967) was born in Northern India but educated in England and then he attended the Royal Military College, Sandhurst. After graduating he joined the 8th Gurkha Rifles as a Lieutenant, which was part of the British expedition to Tibet in 1903-04. This was effectively a temporary British invasion of Tibet.

Fortress of Gyantse Djong, Tibet.

On 6 July 1904 John Grant was involved in the storming of Gyantse Djong, where he commanded the storming company which had to advance up a bare, almost

precipitous rock-face with little cover, under heavy fire from the defenders on the walls and towers of the fortress. He and his men had to advance one at a time, whilst being showered by rocks and stones. Lieutenant Grant attempted to scale the walls but he and another soldier were wounded and hurled back down the slope. Despite their wounds they tried again to reach the breach and this time they were successful, allowing the fortress to be taken. For this action John Grant was awarded the Victoria Cross.

He was eventually promoted to Major. During World War One he served in the Persian Gulf 1915-16, France and Belgium in 1917 and Mesopotamia (Iran and Iraq) in 1918. In 1919, after then end of the War he, now a Lieutenant Colonel, was put in command of the 13th Rajputs in the Waziristan Campaign (1919 – 1920), where he was awarded the Distinguished Service Medal (DSO) for his bravery. From 1926 - 1928 he was Assistant Adjutant General of the Army of India and Deputy Director of the Auxiliary and Territorial force in India 1928-1929. He retired in 1929 with the rank of colonel and he died in Turnbridge Wells aged 89.

Sergeant John Grant (1889- Nov 1970) was a soldier in the New Zealand Military Force during World War One. Originally a builder he enlisted in the New Zealand army in 1915 and was sent to the Middle East where he joined the Wellington Regiment. It was sent to the Western Front in March 1916, where it saw active service during 1916 and 1917, including the **Battle of Flevs-Courcelette** where the regiment lost 25% of its men. It then took part in the **Battle of Broodseinde.**

In early 1918 John Grant was promoted to Sergeant. From August to early September 1918 his regiment was engaged in the **Second Battle of Bapaume**, which had the objective to capture the town of Bapaume in Northern France. During this battle his Battalion came under heavy fire from a number of German machine-gun posts which threatened their advance. Despite this, Grant's platoon pressed on and Grant, followed by another soldier, broke ahead and entered one of the machine-gun posts, killing some of the gun crew and capturing the rest. He then attacked another machine-gun post and did the same thing again, allowing the advance to continue. For this action he was awarded the V.C.

He ended the war as a second-lieutenant and after the was retired to civilian life. However, he found it difficult to hold down a regular job, probably suffering from the effects of post-traumatic stress disorder. He did, however, get elected as a Councillor for his home town of Hawera, married and had two children. He died in 1970 aged 81.

Rear-Admiral John Grant (1908 -1996) joined the Royal Navy on the HMS Queen Elizabeth in 1926 and specialised in anti-submarine warfare. During World War II he served in the Atlantic, Artic and Mediterranean. In 1941 he commanded the destroyer HMS Beverley before being posted to the anti-submarine warfare training school HMS Osprey in a training role in 1942. He ended the war as Assistant Staff Officer at Headquarters: Western Approaches.

After the war he commanded the destroyer HMS Opportune, the destroyer HMS Fame and the destroyer HMS Crispin. He then went on to command the cruiser HMS Cleopatra in 1952 and then became Commander of HMS Vernon in 1955. He was promoted to Rear Admiral in 1959 and retired in 1960. He died in 1996.

Dr Isobel Grant founder of the Highland Folk Museum which tells the story of ordinary Highlanders from 1700 to the middle of the 20th century. Born in Edinburgh in July 1887 she grew up with a love of the Highlands, especially Strathspey and its links to Clan Grant. She was from the family of the Grants of Tullochgorm and the grand-daughter of Field Marshall Sir Patrick Grant.

Doctor Isobel Grant.

Isobel became an author, writing such words as 'The Social and Economic Development of Scotland before 1603 (1930) and the Lordship of the Isles (1935) amongst many others. In 1930 she organised and curated the Highland Exhibition in Inverness Town Hall and then another exhibition in Edinburgh Usher Hall in 1932.

In 1943 she bought Pitman Lodge, a large Georgian House, together with 3 acres of land near the train station at Kingussie, about 12 miles east of Laggan and in June 1944 the Highland Folk Museum opened to the public incorporating an Inverness-shire cottage, a Lewis Blackhouse and Highland But and Ben. In the 1980's the site was moved to larger premises at Newtonmore.

Isobel died in September 1983 and is buried in Dalrossie, Speyside.

Cary Grant, (Jan 1904 -November 1986) the famous film actor was not actually born a Grant but took the name to enhance his acting appeal. He was born Archibald Alec Leach in Bristol and was famous for his mid-Atlantic accent, debonair demeanour, light-hearted approach to acting and sense of comic timing. He was one of Hollywood's classic leading men and was nominated twice for an Academy Award. In 1999 he was named by the American Film Institute as the 2nd greatest male star of the Golden Age of Hollywood, after Humphrey Bogart.

After taking up acting in England he soon moved to the US and established for himself in Vaudeville in the 1920's and toured the US before moving to Hollywood in early the early 1930's. He soon gained renown for his romantic screwball comedies such as the 'Awful Truth' (1937), 'Bring Up Baby' (1938), and 'The Philadelphia Story' (1940). He was then nominated for an Academy Award for Best Actor for 'Penny Serenade' (1941) and 'None but the Lonely Heart' (1944).

He then had a close working relationship with Alfred Hitchcock who cast him in 4 films, 'Suspicion' (1941), 'Notorious' (1946), 'To Catch a Thief' (1955) and 'North by North West' (1959). He is revered by critics for his unusually broad appeal as a handsome, suave actor who did not take himself too seriously and Able to maintain his dignity in comedies, not sacrificing it entirely.

He married 5 times but only had one daughter, Jennifer, in February 1906. He died of a stroke, in the company of his wife in November 1986. Cary Grant's sexuality has been the subject of speculation and rumours for many years but he never publicly confirmed any specific orientation during his lifetime. His daughter refuted that her father was a bi-sexual. He remains one of cinema's greatest actors.

Cary Grant.

Steven Grant Rodgers (Captain America) is the fictional character primarily portrait by actor Chris Evans in the Marvel Universe film franchise, based on the Marvel Comic Character of the same name, **Captain America.** Grant Rodgers is depicted as a World War II super soldier who was given a serum that provided him with superhuman abilities including enhanced durability, strength and athleticism. During his fight against Nazi secret organisation Hydra, he became frozen in the Artic for nearly 70 years until being revived in the 21st century.

Captain America.

Rodgers becomes a founding member and leader of the Avengers. Following internal conflict within the Avengers as a result of the Sokovia Accords and Thanos initiating the Blip, Rodgers leads the team on a final mission and they successfully restore trillions of lives across the universe and defeat Thanos. After returning the Infinity Stones to their original timelines, he remains in the 1940;s with his lost love Peggy Carter. They marry and Rodgers lives a full life. He then chooses Sam Wilson to be his successor, passing his shield and title of Captain America onto him. This is, of course, pure fantasy but shows that the name Grant is still taken to emulate strong and courageous individuals.

Bryan Morel Grant (25 Dec. 1909 – 5 June 1956) was an American amateur tennis champion. At 5ft 4 inches (163 cm) he was the smallest American man to win an international tennis championship. He was able to beat men much taller and more powerful than himself such as Don Budge and Ellsworth Vines. His nickname was 'Itsy Bitsy the Giant Killer'.

During World War II he served in in the Pacific Campaign as a US Army Rifleman in and around Papua New guinea. His letters home to his wife he tells how he fought out of a foxhole for several months and repulsed numerous heavy and repeated assaults. He died at the age of 76 at his home in Townsend Place.

Grant at Wimbledon 1937.

Richard E. Grant (born 5 May 1957) is an English actor and presenter, although he was actually born in Switzerland as Richard Grant Esterhuysen. He made his film debut as Withnail in the comedy film 'Withnail and I' (1987). He then starred in a number of other films including Warlock (1989), Hudson Hawk (1991), Bram Stoker's Dracula (1992), The Little Vampire (2000), Gosford Park (2001), Can You Ever Forgive Me (2018) and Star wars : The Rise of Skywalker (2019). Grant joined the cast of the Marvel Universe series, Loki, as 'Classic Loki' an older variant of Loki himself.

Richard E. Grant.

Amy Grant (born Nov 1960) is an American singer-songwriter and musician. She began her career in contemporary Christian music before crossing over to popular music in the 1980's and 1990's and has been referred to as 'The Queen of Christian Pop'. By 2009 she had sold over 30 million albums worldwide, won six Grammy Awards, 22 Gospel Music Association Dove Awards and had the first Christian album to go 'Platinum'. She was honoured with a star on the Hollywood Walk of Fame for her contribution to the entertainment industry and in 2002, she was announced as the recipient of the 'Kennedy Center Honors'.

Amy Grant.

Hugh John Mungo Grant (born 9 September 1960) is an English actor who established himself as a charming and vulnerable romantic leading man, and has since turned into a more dramatic character actor. After a number of smaller films he emerged as a star in the romantic comedy Four Weddings and a Funeral (1994) for which he won a Golden Globe and a BAFTA Award for Best Actor.

He then starred in other romantic comedies such as Notting Hill (1999), Bridget Jones Diary (2001) and it's 2004 sequel Bridge Jones: The Edge of Reason, About a Boy (2022) and Love Actually (2003). After this he began playing non-romantic types and received great acclaim for his roles in Cloud Atlas (2012), Florence Foster Jenkins (2016) and Paddington 2 (2017).

Hallmarks of his comic skills include a nonchalant touch of sarcasm and characteristic physical mannerisms. He has been outspoken about his antipathy towards the acting profession, his disdain towards the culture of celebrity and his hostility towards the media, including suing News Corporation over its phone hacking scandal.

BIBLIOGRAPHY.

(1). A History of Clan Grant. Lord Strathspey. Phillimore. 1983. Pg 81.

(2). The Highlanders of Scotland Vol.II. William F. Skene. London. 1837. Pg.254.

(3). The Highlanders of Scotland Vol.II. William F. Skene. London. 1837. Pg.254.

(4). www.clangrant.org/index/MonymuskText

(5). www.clangrant.org/index/MonymuskText

(6).The Rulers of Strathspey, A History of the Lairds of Grant and Earls of Seafield. Archibald Kennedy, Earl of Cassilis. 1911. Inverness.

(7). www.wikipedia.org/wiki/Siol_Alpin

(8). www.wikipedia.org/wiki/Siol_Alpin

(9). Scotland: The Story of a Nation. Magnus Magnusson. William Collins. 2000. Pg.33.

(10). www.wiki,pedia.org/wiki/Dunadd_Castle

(11). Scotland: The Story of a Nation. Magnus Magnusson. William Collins. 2000. Pg.35.

(12). Scotland: The Story of a Nation. Magnus Magnusson. William Collins. 2000. Pg.35.

(13). Scotland: A New History. Michael Lynch.1991. Century Lid. Pg.17.

(14). Clan Macgregor. Forbes MacGregor. Clan Gregor Society. 1977. Pg.30.

(15). Scotland: The Story of a Nation. Magnus Magnusson. William Collins. 2000. Pg.40.

(16). Anderson, Early Sources, pp 428-9; Annals of Ulster, s.a. 937.

(17). Urquhart and Glenmoriston. William MacKay. 2nd Edition. 1914. Pg.5.

(18). Urquhart and Glenmoriston. William MacKay. 2nd Edition. 1914. Pg.5.

(19). Urquhart and Glenmoriston. William MacKay. 2nd Edition. 1914. Pg.6.

(20). The Lion in the North. John Prebble. Pg.51.

(21). Documents illustrative of Scotland. Ed.Rev.J.Stevenson. vol2. Pg.211-3.

(22). Scotichronicon. Book 11. Chapter 28.

(23). Scotland. The Story of a nation. Magnus Magnusson. William Collins. 2000.

(24). Scotland. The Story of a nation. Magnus Magnusson. William Collins. 2000.

(25). Scotland. The Story of a nation. Magnus Magnusson. William Collins. 2000.

(26). William Wallace. Andrew Fisher. John Drummond Publishers. 1986. Pg 55.

(27). William Wallace. Andrew Fisher. John Drummond Publishers. 1986. Pg 80.

(28). William Wallace. Andrew Fisher. John Drummond Publishers. 1986. Pg 82.

(29). Scotland. The Story of a nation. Magnus Magnusson. William Collins. 2000.

(30). Urquhart and Glenmoriston. William MacKay. 2nd Edition. 1914. Pg.26.

(31). Robert The Bruce: King of Scots. Ronald McNair Scott. Peter Bednick Books, New York, 1989. Page 81.

(32). A History of Clan Grant. Lord Strathspey. Phillimore. 1983. Pg 4.

(33). A History of Clan Grant. Lord Strathspey. Phillimore. 1983. Pg 4.

(34). The Brus. J.Barbour. ed and tr. G.Eyre.1907. Page 184.

(35). Robert The Bruce: King of Scots. Ronald McNair Scott. Peter Bednick Books, New York, 1989. Page 81.

(36). History of the Macdonalds and lords of the isles. With genealogies of the principal families of the name. Alexander Mackenzie. A. King and Company. Aberdeen. 1881. Pg.4.

(37). 120). History of the Macdonalds and lords of the isles. With genealogies of the principal families of the name. Alexander Mackenzie. A. King and Company. Aberdeen. 1881.Pg 33.

(38). The Declaration of Arbroath. 1320.

(39). A History of Clan Grant. Lord Strathspey. Phillimore. 1983. Pg 5.

(40). The Chiefs of Grant. William Fraser. Edinburgh 1833. Pg xl.

(41). The Chiefs of Grant. William Fraser. Edinburgh 1833. Pg xliii.

(42). www.castleroy.org.uk

(43). The Black Douglas: James The Good. David R. Ross. Luath Press. 2008.

(44). The Black Douglas: James The Good. David R. Ross. Luath Press. 2008.

(45). The Black Douglas: James The Good. David R. Ross. Luath Press. 2008.

(46). History of MacKenzie. Alexander MacKenzie. Inverness 1879. Pg 52.

(47). The History of the House and Race of Douglas and Angus. By David Hume. Mortimer and MacLeod, Aberdeen 1820. Pg.97.

(48). The History of the House and Race of Douglas and Angus. By David Hume. Mortimer and MacLeod, Aberdeen 1820. Pg.98.

(49). The Chiefs of Grant. William Fraser. Edinburgh 1833. Pg xxiv.

(50). A History of Clan Grant. Lord Strathspey. Phillimore. 1983. Pg 10.

(51).The Chiefs of Grant. William Fraser. Edinburgh 1833. Pg 33.

(52). The Chiefs of Grant. William Fraser. Edinburgh 1833. Pg 50.

(53). The History of the House and Race of Douglas and Angus. By David Hume. Mortimer and MacLeod. Aberdeen.1820.Pg. 149.

(54). The History of the House and Race of Douglas and Angus. By David Hume. Mortimer and MacLeod. Aberdeen.1820.Pg. 160.

(55). A History of Clan Grant. Lord Strathspey. Phillimore. 1983. Pg 10.

(56). History of the MacDonalds and lords of the Isles. With genealogies of the principal families of the name. Alexander MacKenzie. A. King and Company. Aberdeen. 1881. Pg.63.

(57). Bonnie Dundee: For King and Conscience. Magnus Linklater and Christian Hesketh. Cannongate Press. 1989. Pg 212.

(58). The Chiefs of Grant. William Fraser. Edinburgh 1833. Pg 52.

(59). Urquhart and Glenmoriston. William MacKay. 2nd Edition. 1914. Pg.71.

(60).The Great Feud – The Campbells and the MacDonalds. Oliver Thomson. Sutton Publishing. 2005. Pg 30.

(61). History of the MacDonalds and lords of the Isles. With genealogies of the principal families of the name. Alexander MacKenzie. A. King and Company. Aberdeen. 1881. Pg.79.

(62). Scotland. The Story of a nation. Magnus Magnusson. William Collins. 2000. Pg. 253.

(63). The Lion in the North. John Prebble. Penguin Books. 1981.

(64). Scotland. The Story of a nation. Magnus Magnusson. William Collins. 2000. Pg. 253.

(65).The Rulers of Strathspey, A History of the Lairds of Grant and Earls of Seafield. Archibald Kennedy, Earl of Cassilis. 1911. Inverness. Pg.23.

(66). The Lion in the North. John Prebble. Penguin Books. 1981. Pg. 146.

(67). The Lion in the North. John Prebble. Penguin Books. 1981. Pg. 146.

(68). The Douglas Book. William Fraser Vol.II. Angus Memoirs. Edinburgh. 1885. Pg. 74.

(69). The Lion in the North. John Prebble. Penguin Books. 1981. Pg. 148.

(70). A History of Clan Grant. Lord Strathspey. Phillimore. 1983. Pg 12.

(71). The Great Feud – The Campbells and the MacDonalds. Oliver Thomson. Sutton Publishing. 2005. Pg.44.

(72). The Rulers of Strathspey, A History of the Lairds of Grant and Earls of Seafield. Archibald Kennedy, Earl of Cassilis. 1911. Inverness. Pg.27.

(73). A History of Clan Grant. Lord Strathspey. Phillimore. 1983. Pg 13.

(74).Urquhart and Glenmoriston. William MacKay. 2nd Edition. 1914. Pg.75.

(75).The Rulers of Strathspey, A History of the Lairds of Grant and Earls of Seafield. Archibald Kennedy, Earl of Cassilis. 1911. Inverness. Pg.29.

(76). The Chiefs of Grant. William Fraser. Edinburgh 1833. Pg 63.

(77). The Grants of Glenmoriston. Rev.A. Sinclair. Edinburgh.1887.Pg 6.

(78). 189). Urquhart and Glenmoriston. William MacKay. 2nd Edition. 1914. Pg.92.

(79). A History of Clan Grant. Lord Strathspey. Phillimore. 1983. Pg 14.

(80). The Rulers of Strathspey, A History of the Lairds of Grant and Earls of Seafield. Archibald Kennedy, Earl of Cassilis. 1911. Inverness. Pg.69.

(81). Urquhart and Glenmoriston. William MacKay. 2nd Edition. 1914. Appendix One.

(82). www.thecastleguy/Urquhart

83). The Rulers of Strathspey, A History of the Lairds of Grant and Earls of Seafield. Archibald Kennedy, Earl of Cassilis. 1911. Inverness. Pg.33.

84). Border Raids and Reivers. Robert Borland. Dalneatie. 1898. Pg.63.

85). The Grants of Glenmoriston. Rev.A. Sinclair. Edinburgh.1887.Pg 8.

86). Macdonalds of Clanranald. Andrew Mackenzie. Inverness. Pg.15.

87). History of the MacDonalds and lords of the Isles. With genealogies of the principal families of the name. Alexander MacKenzie. A. King and Company. Aberdeen. 1881. Pg.382.

88). Scotland: A New History. Michael Lynch.1991. Century Lid. Pg.17.

89). Macdonalds of Clanranald. Andrew Mackenzie. Inverness. Pg.14.

(90). Historical Account of the Family of Frisel or Fraser, particularly Fraser of Lovat. John Anderson. Edinburgh and T.Cadell, Strand. London. Pg.88.

(91).The Chiefs of Grant. William Fraser. Edinburgh 1833. Pg 111.

(92). Urquhart and Glenmoriston. William MacKay. 2nd Edition. 1914. Pg.100.

(93). Urquhart and Glenmoriston. William MacKay. 2nd Edition. 1914. Pg.102.

(94). A History of Clan Grant. Lord Strathspey. Phillimore. 1983. Pg 15.

(95). The Grants of Glenmoriston. Rev.A. Sinclair. Edinburgh.1887.Pg 9.

(96). The Rulers of Strathspey, A History of the Lairds of Grant and Earls of Seafield. Archibald Kennedy, Earl of Cassilis. 1911. Inverness. Pg.44.

(97). A History of Clan Grant. Lord Strathspey. Phillimore. 1983. Pg 17.

(98). The Campbells Are Coming. Glen Harold Campbell. New York 1947. Pg.109.

(99). The Rulers of Strathspey, A History of the Lairds of Grant and Earls of Seafield. Archibald Kennedy, Earl of Cassilis. 1911. Inverness. Pg.46.

(100). Scotland. The Story of a Nation. Magnus Magnusson. William Collins. 2000. Pg. 353.

(101). The Chiefs of Grant. William Fraser. Edinburgh 1833. Pg 139.

(102). Urquhart and Glenmoriston. William MacKay. 2nd Edition. 1914. Pg.103.

(103). Urquhart and Glenmoriston. William MacKay. 2nd Edition. 1914. Pg.103.

(104). The Chiefs of Grant. William Fraser. Edinburgh 1833. Pg 146.

(105). www.ballindallochcastle.co.uk

(106). The Chiefs of Grant. William Fraser. Edinburgh 1833. Pg 163.

(107). The Rulers of Strathspey, A History of the Lairds of Grant and Earls of Seafield. Archibald Kennedy, Earl of Cassilis. 1911. Inverness. Pg.69.

(108). A History of Clan Grant. Lord Strathspey. Phillimore. 1983. Pg 17.

(109). A History of Clan Grant. Lord Strathspey. Phillimore. 1983. Pg 20.

(110). The Chiefs of Grant. William Fraser. Edinburgh 1833. Pg 173.

(111). The Chiefs of Grant. William Fraser. Edinburgh 1833. Pg 174.

(112). A History of Clan Grant. Lord Strathspey. Phillimore. 1983. Pg 22.

(113). The Grants of Glenmoriston. Rev.A. Sinclair. Edinburgh.1887.Pg 12.

(114). Urquhart and Glenmoriston. William MacKay. 2nd Edition. 1914. Pg.125.

(115). A History of Clan Grant. Lord Strathspey. Phillimore. 1983. Pg 22.

(116). A History of Clan Grant. Lord Strathspey. Phillimore. 1983. Pg 22.

(117). The history of Clan Mackenzie; with genealogies of the principle families. Alexander Mackenzie. Inverness 1879. Pg.158.

(118). The history of Clan Mackenzie; with genealogies of the principle families. Alexander Mackenzie. Inverness 1879. Pg.161.

(119). www.wikiepedia.org/wiki/CharlesI_of_England

(120). A History of Clan Grant. Lord Strathspey. Phillimore. 1983. Pg 23.

(121). Urquhart and Glenmoriston. William MacKay. 2nd Edition. 1914. Pg.141.

(122). The Rulers of Strathspey, A History of the Lairds of Grant and Earls of Seafield. Archibald Kennedy, Earl of Cassilis. 1911. Inverness. Pg.175.

(123). The Chiefs of Grant. William Fraser. Edinburgh 1833. Pg 227.

(124). The Grants of Glenmoriston. Rev.A. Sinclair. Edinburgh.1887.Pg 17.

(125). The Chiefs of Grant. William Fraser. Edinburgh 1833. Pg 231.

(126). The Rulers of Strathspey, A History of the Lairds of Grant and Earls of Seafield. Archibald Kennedy, Earl of Cassilis. 1911. Inverness. Pg.93.

(127). The Rulers of Strathspey, A History of the Lairds of Grant and Earls of Seafield. Archibald Kennedy, Earl of Cassilis. 1911. Inverness. Pg.95.

(128). The Rulers of Strathspey, A History of the Lairds of Grant and Earls of Seafield. Archibald Kennedy, Earl of Cassilis. 1911. Inverness. Pg.90.

(129). The History of the Scottish Wars from the Battle of the Grampian Hills in the Year 85, to that of Culloden, ...in which are included the Conflicts of the Clans and the Feuds of the Great Families. Second Edition. 1825 page 203.

(130). Lion In The North. John Prebble. Penguin Books. 1981. Pg 254.

(131). Urquhart and Glenmoriston. William MacKay. 2nd Edition. 1914. Pg.152.

(132). The Chiefs of Grant. William Fraser. Edinburgh 1833. Pg 253.

(133). The Campbells are Coming. Glen Harald Campbell. New York. 1947. Pg. 164.

(134). The Great Feud – The Campbells and the Macdonalds. Oliver Thomson. Sutton Publishing. 2005. Pg.81.

(135). The Great Feud – The Campbells and the Macdonalds. Oliver Thomson. Sutton Publishing. 2005. Pg.82.

(136). A History of Clan Grant. Lord Strathspey. Phillimore. 1983. Pg 24.

(137). The Rulers of Strathspey, A History of the Lairds of Grant and Earls of Seafield. Archibald Kennedy, Earl of Cassilis. 1911. Inverness. Pg.99.

(138). Urquhart and Glenmoriston. William MacKay. 2nd Edition. 1914. Pg.154.

(139). The Chiefs of Grant. William Fraser. Edinburgh 1833. Pg 262.

(140). www.clan-cameron/battles/1645

(141). The Glencairn Uprising 1653-54. Helen Baxter. 2005. Dept of Linguistics, Lancaster University.

(142). www.electricscotland.com/history/cairngorm

(143). www.electricscotland.com/history/cairngorm

(144). www.electricscotland.com/history/cairngorm

(145). A History of Clan Grant. Lord Strathspey. Phillimore. 1983. Pg 25.

(146). The Rulers of Strathspey, A History of the Lairds of Grant and Earls of Seafield. Archibald Kennedy, Earl of Cassilis. 1911. Inverness. Pg.111.

(147). The Rulers of Strathspey, A History of the Lairds of Grant and Earls of Seafield. Archibald Kennedy, Earl of Cassilis. 1911. Inverness. Pg.113.

(148). Urquhart and Glenmoriston. William MacKay. 2nd Edition. 1914. Pg. 488.

(149). Urquhart and Glenmoriston. William MacKay. 2nd Edition. 1914. Pg. 488.

(150). Urquhart and Glenmoriston. William MacKay. 2nd Edition. 1914. Pg. 488.

(151). Urquhart and Glenmoriston. William MacKay. 2nd Edition. 1914. Pg.180.

(152). The Rulers of Strathspey, A History of the Lairds of Grant and Earls of Seafield. Archibald Kennedy, Earl of Cassilis. 1911. Inverness. Pg.118.

(153). The Rulers of Strathspey, A History of the Lairds of Grant and Earls of Seafield. Archibald Kennedy, Earl of Cassilis. 1911. Inverness. Pg.114.

(154). The Chiefs of Grant. William Fraser. Edinburgh 1833. Pg 299.

(155). The Rulers of Strathspey, A History of the Lairds of Grant and Earls of Seafield. Archibald Kennedy, Earl of Cassilis. 1911. Inverness. Pg.115.

(156). Bonnie Dundee: For King and Conscience. Magnus Linklater and Christian Hesketh. Cannongate Press. 1989. Pg166.

(157). Bonnie Dundee: For King and Conscience. Magnus Linklater and Christian Hesketh. Cannongate Press. 1989. Pg171.

(158). Urquhart and Glenmoriston. William MacKay. 2nd Edition. 1914. Pg.198.

(159). Bonnie Dundee. For King and Conscience. Magnus Linklater and Christian Hesketh. 1992. Canongate Press. Pg. 182.

(160). The Chiefs of Grant. William Fraser. Edinburgh 1833. Pg 313.

(161). The Chiefs of Grant. William Fraser. Edinburgh 1833. Pg 314.

(162). The Chiefs of Grant. William Fraser. Edinburgh 1833. Pg 316.

(163). A History of Clan Grant. Lord Strathspey. Phillimore. 1983. Pg 66.

(164). Bonnie Dundee. For King and Conscience. Magnus Linklater and Christian Hesketh. 1992. Canongate Press. Pg. 203.

(165). History of the Clan Mackenzie; with genealogies of the principle families. Alexander Mackenzie.Inverness.1879. Pg.267.

(166). Bonnie Dundee. For King and Conscience. Magnus Linklater and Christian Hesketh. 1992. Cannongate Press. Pg. 215.

(167). Bonnie Dundee: For King and Conscience. Magnus Linklater and Christian Hesketh. Cannongate Press. 1989. Pg 212.

(168). History of the MacDonalds and lords of the Isles. With genealogies of the principal families of the name. Alexander MacKenzie. A. King and Company. Aberdeen. 1881. Pg.420.

(169). Bonnie Dundee. For King and Conscience. Magnus Linklater and Christian Hesketh. 1992. Cannongate Press. Pg. 217.

(170). Bonnie Dundee. For King and Conscience. Magnus Linklater and Christian Hesketh. 1992. Cannongate Press. Pg. 221.

(171). The Grants of Glenmoriston. Rev.A. Sinclair. Edinburgh.1887.Pg 24.

(172). The Chiefs of Grant. William Fraser. Edinburgh 1833. Pg 317.

(173). A History of Clan Grant. Lord Strathspey. Phillimore. 1983. Pg 26.

(174). The Chiefs of Grant. William Fraser. Edinburgh 1833. Pg 318.

(175). Clan Gregor. Forbes MacGregor. The Clan Gregor Society 1977. Pg.119.

(176). Clan Gregor. Forbes MacGregor. The Clan Gregor Society 1977. Pg.119.

(177). A History of Clan Grant. Lord Strathspey. Phillimore. 1983. Pg 28.

(178). The Chiefs of Grant. William Fraser. Edinburgh 1833. Pg lxxxviii.

(179). The Chiefs of Grant. William Fraser. Edinburgh 1833. Pg xc.

(180). The Chiefs of Grant. William Fraser. Edinburgh 1833. Pg 323.

(181). The Chiefs of Grant. William Fraser. Edinburgh 1833. Pg 326.

(182). Urquhart and Glenmoriston. William MacKay. 2nd Edition. 1914. Pg.220.

(183). Urquhart and Glenmoriston. William MacKay. 2nd Edition. 1914. Pg.221.

(184). Urquhart and Glenmoriston. William MacKay. 2nd Edition. 1914. Pg.221.

(185). A History of Clan Grant. Lord Strathspey. Phillimore. 1983. Pg 28.

(186). The Chiefs of Grant. William Fraser. Edinburgh 1833. Pg 327.

(187). The Rulers of Strathspey, A History of the Lairds of Grant and Earls of Seafield. Archibald Kennedy, Earl of Cassilis. 1911. Inverness. Pg.122.

(188). A History of Clan Grant. Lord Strathspey. Phillimore. 1983. Pg 29.

(189). History of the Clan Mackenzie, with genealogies of the principal families. Alexander Mackenzie. Inverness. 1879. Pg. 219.

(190). History of the Clan Mackenzie, with genealogies of the principal families. Alexander Mackenzie. Inverness. 1879. Pg. 220.

(191). Urquhart and Glenmoriston. William MacKay. 2nd Edition. 1914. Pg.228.

(192). History of the MacDonalds and lords of the Isles. With genealogies of the principal families of the name. Alexander MacKenzie. A. King and Company. Aberdeen. 1881. Pg.228.

(193). The Grants of Glenmoriston. Rev.A. Sinclair. Edinburgh.1887.Pg 26.

(194). The Grants of Glenmoriston. Rev.A. Sinclair. Edinburgh.1887.Pg 27.

(195). Jacobites. A New History of the 45' Rebellion. Jacqueline Riding. Bloomsbury Paperbacks. 2017. Pg. 82.

(196). A History of Clan Grant. Lord Strathspey. Phillimore. 1983. Pg 30.

(197). A History of Clan Grant. Lord Strathspey. Phillimore. 1983. Pg 33.

(198). The Rulers of Strathspey, A History of the Lairds of Grant and Earls of Seafield. Archibald Kennedy, Earl of Cassilis. 1911. Inverness. Pg.132.

(199). Jacobites. A New History of the 45' Rebellion. Jacqueline Riding. Bloomsbury Paperbacks. 2016. Pg. 97.

(200). Major Alpin's Ancestors and Descendants. Aberdeen. Rev. James Aberrigh-Mackay. 1904. Pg 15.

(201). Urquhart and Glenmoriston. William MacKay. 2nd Edition. 1914. Pg.243.

(202). www.cheeryble.net/culloden

(203). The Chiefs of Grant. William Fraser. Edinburgh 1833. Pg 406.

(204). Culloden. Trevor Royale. Abacus. 2017. Pg. 27.

(205). Urquhart and Glenmoriston. William MacKay. 2nd Edition. 1914. Pg.252.

(206). A History of Clan Grant. Lord Strathspey. Phillimore. 1983. Pg 34.

(207). The Rulers of Strathspey, A History of the Lairds of Grant and Earls of Seafield. Archibald Kennedy, Earl of Cassilis. 1911. Inverness. Pg.141.

(208). Mackenzie. Inverness. 1879.

(209). Culloden. Trevor Royale. Abacus. 2017. Pg. 56.

(210). 238). Jacobites. A New History of the 45' Rebellion. Jacqueline Riding. Bloomsbury Paperbacks. 2016. Pg. 338.

(211). 1745: A Military History of the last Jacobite rising. Stuart Reid. Staplehurst Printing. 1996.

(212). Jacobites. A New History of the 45' Rebellion. Jacqueline Riding. Bloomsbury Paperbacks. 2016. Pg. 371.

(213). History of the MacDonalds and lords of the Isles. With genealogies of the principal families of the name. Alexander MacKenzie. A. King and Company. Aberdeen. 1881. Pg.353.

(214). A History of Clan Grant. Lord Strathspey. Phillimore. 1983. Pg 35.

(215). A History of Clan Grant. Lord Strathspey. Phillimore. 1983. Pg 35.

(216). Jacobites: A New History of the 45' Rebellion. Jacqueline Riding. Bloomsbury. 2016.Pg. 383.

(217). Jacobites: A New History of the 45' Rebellion. Jacqueline Riding. Bloomsbury. 2016.Pg. 383.

(218). Jacobites. A New History of the 45' Rebellion. Jacqueline Riding. Bloomsbury Paperbacks. 2016. Pg. 371.

(219). History of the Clan Mackenzie, with genealogies of the principal families. Alexander Mackenzie. Inverness. 1879. Pg. 242.

(220). History of the MacDonalds and lords of the Isles. With genealogies of the principal families of the name. Alexander MacKenzie. A. King and Company. Aberdeen. 1881. Pg.496.

(221). The Great Feud – The Campbells and the MacDonalds. Oliver Thomson. Sutton Publishing. 2005. Pg 114.

(222). Urquhart and Glenmoriston. William MacKay. 2nd Edition. 1914. Pg.285.

(223). A History of Clan Grant. Lord Strathspey. Phillimore. 1983. Pg 35.

(224). Urquhart and Glenmoriston. William MacKay. 2nd Edition. 1914. Pg.281.

(225). Urquhart and Glenmoriston. William MacKay. 2nd Edition. 1914. Pg.286.

(226). Urquhart and Glenmoriston. William MacKay. 2nd Edition. 1914. Pg.286.

(227). Urquhart and Glenmoriston. William MacKay. 2nd Edition. 1914. Pg.295.

(228). www.historyand legends/UrquhartandGlenmoriston pg 292.

(229). www.historyand legends/UrquhartandGlenmoriston pg 293.

(230). Glenmoriston: Places of Interest. William Owen.

(231). Urquhart and Glenmoriston. William MacKay. 2nd Edition. 1914. Pg.298.

(232). Urquhart and Glenmoriston. William MacKay. 2nd Edition. 1914. Pg.299.

(233). The Grants of Glenmoriston. Rev.A. Sinclair. Edinburgh.1887.Pg 31.

(234). Urquhart and Glenmoriston. William MacKay. 2nd Edition. 1914. Pg.299.

(235). www.historyand legends/UrquhartandGlenmoriston pg 304.

(236). The Grants of Glenmoriston. Rev.A. Sinclair. Edinburgh.1887.Pg 33.

(237). www.historyand legends/UrquhartandGlenmoriston pg 311.

(238). The Rulers of Strathspey, A History of the Lairds of Grant and Earls of Seafield. Archibald Kennedy, Earl of Cassilis. 1911. Inverness. Pg.143.

(239). The Chiefs of Grant. William Fraser. Edinburgh 1833. Pg xxi.

(240). The Chiefs of Grant. William Fraser. Edinburgh 1833. Pg 451.

(241). The Highland Clearances. John Prebble. Penguin Books.1963. Pg.13.

(242). A History of Clan Grant. Lord Strathspey. Phillimore. 1983. Pg 35.

(243). A History of Clan Grant. Lord Strathspey. Phillimore. 1983. Pg 38.

(244). The Chiefs of Grant. William Fraser. Edinburgh 1833. Pg 451.

(245). The Chiefs of Grant. William Fraser. Edinburgh 1833. Pg 455.

(246). The Chiefs of Grant. William Fraser. Edinburgh 1833. Pg 442.

(247). The Rulers of Strathspey, A History of the Lairds of Grant and Earls of Seafield. Archibald Kennedy, Earl of Cassilis. 1911. Inverness. Pg.152.

(248). The Rulers of Strathspey, A History of the Lairds of Grant and Earls of Seafield. Archibald Kennedy, Earl of Cassilis. 1911. Inverness. Pg.153.

(249). The Rulers of Strathspey, A History of the Lairds of Grant and Earls of Seafield. Archibald Kennedy, Earl of Cassilis. 1911. Inverness. Pg.154.

(250). A History of Clan Grant. Lord Strathspey. Phillimore. 1983. Pg 55.

(251). A History of Clan Grant. Lord Strathspey. Phillimore. 1983. Pg 78.

(252). A History of Clan Grant. Lord Strathspey. Phillimore. 1983. Pg 83.

(253). A History of Clan Grant. Lord Strathspey. Phillimore. 1983. Pg 83.

(254). A History of Clan Grant. Lord Strathspey. Phillimore. 1983. Pg 85.

(255). www.wikiepedia.org/wiki/Bunce_Island

(256). The Rulers of Strathspey, A History of the Lairds of Grant and Earls of Seafield. Archibald Kennedy, Earl of Cassilis. 1911. Inverness. Pg.193.

(257). A History of Clan Grant. Lord Strathspey. Phillimore. 1983. Pg 66.

(258). A History of Clan Grant. Lord Strathspey. Phillimore. 1983. Pg 66.

(259). The Grants of Glemmoriston. Rev.A. Sinclair. Edinburgh.1887.Pg 36.

(260). The Chiefs of Grant. William Fraser. Edinburgh 1833. Pg lxvi.

(261). Major Alpin's Ancestors and Descendants. Aberdeen. Rev. James Aberrigh-Mackay. 1904. Pg 15.

(262). www.wikiepedia/wiki/Colquhoun_Grant

(263) The Civil War. Geofrey C. Ward. Vintage Books. New York. 1990. Pg. 240.

Dear Reader, thank you for purchasing my book on Clan Grant. The information contained within can always be updated and corrected. If any of you have any comments to make or additional information, please contact me at vance.sinclair16@gmail.com. I can always use your information to add to further editions.

Thank you.

Vance Sinclair

Printed in Great Britain
by Amazon

32713807R00176